D0038301

# Sunshine Girl

## an unexpected life

# Julianna
# Margulies

# Praise for *Sunshine Girl*

"Over the course of her illustrious career on screen, Julianna Margulies has played any number of unforgettable characters but as this memoir proves, she might be most fascinating as herself. . . . Not every celebrity autobiography has a truly compelling story to tell, but this one does and tells it with style, humor, and flair."

—*Town & Country*

"[A] thought-provoking and revelatory memoir . . . Though Margulies's anecdotes may be outside readers' own realms of experience, she relates them with such intimacy and candor that readers might recognize in her a kindred spirit. . . . A deeply reflective narrative that will appeal to both Margulies's fans and anyone who enjoys a warm and well-crafted memoir."          —*Library Journal*

"Margulies . . . shares her path to stardom in this frank memoir. . . . Readers looking for salacious Hollywood tales won't find them here; instead Margulies's fans and all readers interested in TV careers will enjoy learning her origin story."          —*Booklist*

"[An] intriguing tale . . . This book is more about the strength of the storytelling than the star power of the author. What the author shares and doesn't is deliberate, all offered to advance the fascinating story she wants to tell. It's the mark of a talented storyteller. . . . Margulies's unflinching quest to explain her life makes her well-crafted memoir compelling whether you know her roles or not."

—*Kirkus Reviews*

"[*Sunshine Girl* is] full of piquant anecdotes . . . and subtle, evocative character studies. . . . The result is an entertaining and revealing portrait."          —*Publishers Weekly*

"*Sunshine Girl* is at once a tender coming-of-age story and a deeply personal look at a young woman making sense of the world against a chaotic and peripatetic childhood. You will feel inspired by the way she has lived her life: with grit, grace and gratitude."

—Katie Couric

"*Sunshine Girl* is a probing, fearless, beautifully written coming-of-age story. The word that comes to mind is "transcendent." Julianna Margulies has transcended a complicated childhood, transcended a difficult ten-year relationship, transcended her own demons, transcended fame itself to become whole and wise. I loved this book."

—Dani Shapiro, *New York Times* bestselling author of *Inheritance: A Memoir of Genealogy, Paternity, and Love*

"It should be no surprise that Julianna Margulies writes with the same insight, precision, and kindness with which she imbues the characters she portrays. This book is a revelation. Be prepared to gasp!" —Alan Cumming, *New York Times* bestselling author of *Not My Father's Son: A Memoir*

"I read this book in one day and truly loved it. Julianna Margulies's level of introspection is remarkable. Personality and destiny are largely forged from childhood and family, yet few of us are able to weave that journey into a compelling memoir that examines the harder parts of our lives with such honesty. I rooted for her at every turn, especially during her present chapter."

—Lee Woodruff, *New York Times* bestselling author of *In an Instant: A Family's Journey of Love and Healing*

# sunshine girl

DISCARD

# sunshine

AN UNEXPECTED LIFE

# girl

# JULIANNA
# MARGULIES

BALLANTINE BOOKS

*New York*

2022 Ballantine Books Trade Paperback Edition

Published in the United States by Ballantine Books, an imprint of Random House, a division of Penguin Random House LLC, New York.

BALLANTINE and the HOUSE colophon are registered trademarks of Penguin Random House LLC.

Originally published in hardcover in the United States by Ballantine Books, an imprint of Random House, a division of Penguin Random House LLC, in 2021.

Grateful acknowledgment is made to Scholastic Inc. for permission to reprint "Heavy Load" from *Zen Shorts* by Jon J Muth, copyright © 2005 by Jon J Muth. Reprinted by permission of Scholastic Inc.

LIBRARY OF CONGRESS CATALOGING-IN-PUBLICATION DATA
Names: Margulies, Julianna, author.
Title: Sunshine girl: a memoir / Julianna Margulies.
Description: First edition. | New York: Ballantine Books, [2021] |
Identifiers: LCCN 2020037123 (print) | LCCN 2020037124 (ebook) |
ISBN 9780525480341 (trade paperback) | ISBN 9780525480334 (ebook)
Subjects: LCSH: Margulies, Julianna, 1966- | Television actors and actresses—
United States—Biography.
Classification: LCC PN2287.M4829 A3 2021 (print) | LCC PN2287.M4829 (ebook) |
DDC 791.4502/8092 [B]—dc23
LC record available at https://lccn.loc.gov/2020037123
LC ebook record available at https://lccn.loc.gov/2020037124

Printed in the United States of America on acid-free paper

1st Printing

randomhousebooks.com

Designed by Debbie

70909171

TO MY PARENTS, FRANCESCA AND PAUL MARGULIES

# contents

# preface

In the opening scene of the pilot episode of *The Good Wife* the camera follows the lead character, Alicia Florrick, and her husband, Cook County State's Attorney Peter Florrick, down a hotel hallway on their way to a press conference. They are holding hands as the viewer sees them walk in slow motion through double doors to a large banquet hall, where they take their places on the stage: Peter at the podium, Alicia standing a foot behind him to his right. The press faces the stage, flashbulbs from their cameras blasting off every second like artillery from a firing squad.

Peter Florrick announces that he is resigning as state's attorney. And while he admits to adultery with prostitutes, he denies there was any mishandling of state funds; all payments came from his own pocket, his only crime was cheating on his wife and throwing his family into the spotlight in such a degrading way. As he speaks the camera zooms in on Alicia's face; she is trying to hold herself together, looking only at Peter's right shoulder. She focuses on a piece of lint dangling from the upper right arm of her husband's navy blue suit. She slowly lifts her left hand in an effort to remove the small white fleck, and just as she is about to take it, her husband grabs her hand and leads her out of the hall; the press conference is over.

They scurry down the back hallway to a waiting elevator. Alicia's eyes are glazed over, a shell-shocked look on her face, revealing to the audience that she is distant to her surroundings. When the elevator doors open the Florricks find themselves in the hotel basement. They walk into the bleak corridor that will lead them to the back exit and into their waiting car. Only a few steps out of the elevator Alicia stops, now staring at the floor. Peter says, "Alicia? Are you all right?" She looks up and, in one fell swoop of her arm, slaps him hard across the face. She tugs at her blazer, straightening it, takes a deep breath, and walks down the barren corridor alone. Slowly and with strained determination she makes her way to the exit doors only to see through the window the paparazzi lying in wait. Flashbulbs igniting the dank air, buzzards waiting to catch their prey. She takes a few steps back, away from the glaring lights, and leans on the wall praying it will hold the weight of what just happened to her life. She is motionless now, trapped between the gray-painted cinder blocks and the circling vultures. With her head resting on the blank canvas of the wall, she closes her eyes, trying with all her might to disappear. End scene.

After we wrapped, I hung up Alicia's wardrobe in my trailer and put on my own comfortable clothing. Usually, when a long day of filming is finished, there is a sense of relief, a time to wind down and relax. I learned a long time ago that you need to leave your work on the set if you want to function as a normal human being in your own life. There have been only a handful of times in my twenty-plus-year career that I haven't been able to do that. But as I headed back to my hotel after this scene, I seemed to sink deeper into an acute sadness I hadn't felt in years. There was what felt like an immense weight sitting right in the middle of my chest that I couldn't shake.

When I got back to my room I replayed the scene over and over again in my mind. Sitting upright in a chair, feet planted on the floor, looking at the generic hotel furniture, I tried to understand why I felt so desperately lonely and off-kilter. What had I tapped into that seemed so devastating to me? My own life at the time resembled the exact opposite of that of the woman I was playing. I had never put my career on the back burner for a man as Alicia had done, despite her overwhelming talent as a lawyer. My own life in marriage had just begun, my baby was barely thirteen months old. I was living in that golden light of new love, new life. I had never been happier. And yet that scene haunted me for quite some time. Even years after it aired I still felt a tremendous sense of loss just thinking about it: the character's vulnerability in that moment is colossal, her utter isolation from the world, not knowing the next steps or what lies ahead of her. Her fear of uncharted territory is too frightening to comprehend. I understood all of her feelings, but why couldn't I, the actress playing her, shake them off me at the end of the day, as I had trained myself to do on so many other occasions?

As I dug deeper to try to pull myself out of this sadness, I started to comprehend the familiarity of these feelings. They may not have resulted from a philandering husband, but they had a presence in my life from the day I was born. Even though I may not have seen them or understood them, I unknowingly felt them. When I walked down that hallway as Alicia, those feelings I had buried so deep that I was never fully aware they existed erupted with such a force I was rendered speechless. It was as if they now demanded exploration and examination.

Acting is such a curious profession. What part of ourselves do we bring to a role that makes our portrayal different from someone else's? When an actor is on a long-running television show, especially when the writing is superb, as was the case with *The Good Wife,* the character becomes a second skin; she grows as you grow, she changes as you change. Being an actress gives me the luxury of discovering myself. All the feelings that came up from playing Alicia allowed me to look back at my life and tap into my own vulnerability. My personal fear of the unknown reared its ugly head as I studied this character, its source most likely from the ever-present unpredictability of my childhood.

This book came about after I'd completed the run of *The Good Wife* and finally had a minute to reflect on my own life as an actress, mother, wife, daughter, sister, and friend. I had spent seven years in a perpetual hurry. I logged in more hours trying to figure out how Alicia would respond to any given situation than how I would. She was always on my mind. Dialogue that was written for her rattled around in my head constantly. Long court monologues that I would prepare for the next day could easily wake me up in the middle of the night. I would run to check the script to make sure I had all the words down correctly, inside and out, so I could deliver each line with conviction. I wish I could say that Alicia had a calming effect on my psyche, but she didn't. I tried my hardest to shut her out on my days off, but she was always on the surface, orbiting my inner thoughts.

The storm that found a comfortable home in my brain calmed down only after we wrapped the show. We filmed the last scene of our 156th, final episode. It had been an emotional day, saying goodbye to the cast and crew, who had become my family. Every moment of the day was spent thinking, *This is the last time I will ever walk down this hallway, wear this suit, eat lunch with these people.* I took off my painful high heels one last time and hung up Alicia's clothes in my dressing room and drove home to my sweet husband and son. I imagined I would be celebrating the long, hard, but ultimately amazing journey that had finally ended. I had envisioned treating myself to sleeping in late and eating breakfast in bed while luxuriating over the newspaper the next morning. Instead, the moment I walked in the door to our apartment I felt so weak I flopped onto the couch, unable to move. Every joint in my body ached. I kept trying to ball up my hand in a fist but found it too taxing. My skin felt sensitive to the touch, as if there was a small fire brewing underneath my flesh. Something was not right, my body was a stranger to me.

"What's wrong with me?" I asked my husband.

"Honey, you just finished seven years on a TV show, you're exhausted," he answered. Yes, I was exhausted, but this was something else, this wasn't just exhaustion.

I went to bed with a fever of 102.6. I told myself it was probably the flu and sleep was the only cure. At three in the morning I was catapulted awake by what felt like burning insects marching up my body in attack formation. They were coming fast and furious, pounding my skin with every step, like needles puncturing me. I ran to the bathroom and looked in the mirror. To my horror, small round blisters were breaking out all over my body, my face. They were in my ears, down my throat, all over my eyelids, everywhere. As I stood there looking at myself, I could see them popping up like popcorn in the microwave, invading my body with piercing pain. I had the chicken pox.

My strong, able body was finally signaling me to stop. I had been holding on for so long, unable to allow myself peace of mind or physical rest in order to do my job and also be there for my husband and son, that I had ignored the signs of sheer mental and physical exhaustion.

The chicken pox forced me to lie in bed for three weeks. I had never done that in my life. I am a doer by nature; lying in bed all day has never been on my to-do list.

But in time, when the blisters turned to scabs and the pain subsided, I began to look at this illness as a gift. The chicken pox had given me the gift of time, which I began to unwrap very slowly, savoring every moment.

This was the first time I had been alone in my home in seven years. Once my son got off to school and my husband went to work, I would walk around my apartment taking everything in; looking at my pieces of furniture more like long-lost friends rather than mere objects. I had spent so many years running out of the house in the morning with my checklist in hand, I forgot how miraculous just a hot cup of coffee could be when sipped slowly while perusing a book. I had nowhere to go, no place to be but right where I was.

What a luxury to get back into bed. As I lay there in the comfort of my own home, I began to reflect on the years I had spent in Alicia's shoes. I went back to that first scene we filmed when Alicia had slapped her husband and thought about the unshakable sadness I had absorbed in the aftermath. And finally, I began to understand why this character had affected me so deeply as feelings from my own childhood began to reemerge.

Slowly I let Alicia slip away as I pondered my own life. What had I learned? I began writing things down, unraveling the knots that had not been attended to because I was always too busy. This book was born during my recovery, when I finally had the time to sit back and ruminate on my own life. The rest came about over time, four years to be exact. I had no idea how much easier it was for me to examine the life of a character I was playing rather than my own.

# sunshine girl

# ONE
# nothing was planned

**M**y parents' marriage was pretty much over by the time I was born. My father was away on a business trip when I was due, and when my mother picked him up at the airport with her large belly protruding over her waistline, my father looked at her and said, "You're still pregnant?"

Maybe he was kidding. But to a woman nine months pregnant I can see how this could sound harsh. In any event, I waited for him to come home and entered this world three weeks late, a whopping ten pounds, four ounces. My mother likes to say, with a laugh, that she's *still* recovering.

Janice Marylin Gardner married Paul Eli Margulies in 1960 after meeting him on a blind date. A ballerina for most of her life, she was born in Brooklyn to Isabel, a pianist who had studied at the Mannes

School of Music and was considered a "wunderkind" who would be one of the great hopefuls to become a concert soloist. Her dreams were quashed when she met my grandfather and found herself pregnant with my mother at seventeen.

My mother's father, Michael Gardner, owned a beauty salon on Flatbush Avenue. He was handsome and charismatic, nursing a bubbling charm with the ladies, not unlike the character Warren Beatty played in the film *Shampoo*. He was open about his infidelities in front of my mother, telling her this was their secret. In doing so, he made her feel special, made her his accomplice, having enough trust in her to keep this secret from my grandmother. She became his ally, too young to realize that she was joining him in his deceit.

My mother tells me ballet saved her life. From the age of ten she took the long subway ride from Flatbush Avenue to the School of American Ballet in Manhattan every day, by herself. Ballet shielded her from a home fraught with tension, alcohol, and an unhappy marriage.

She became a member of the American Ballet Theatre company right after ballet school and stayed with them for two years. At the time it was called the Ballet Theatre; it eventually became ABT. As she said, "I left because I didn't feel I was strong enough on my toes to go any further than the chorus. I just wasn't good enough to be a soloist."

Instead she pursued Broadway, television, and anything that would give her a decent paycheck where she could utilize her dance background. Her first Broadway show was *First Impressions* with Polly Bergen and Hermione Gingold. She was a chorus girl and an understudy.

My mother was on *The Fred Waring Show,* the Johnny Carson show a couple of times, she toured with Sammy Davis Jr. She traveled with the General Motors Motorama show, making a living good enough to rent her own apartment in Manhattan. She was a great beauty, often compared to Ava Gardner. Slender hips, dancer's legs, deep brown, velvety eyes surrounded by dark voluminous curls.

She met Lee Guber (who later married Barbara Walters) when she was twenty-one years old. He was fifteen years her senior and nervous about the age difference, but they were together for three years. He championed her singing and dancing career with great coaches; she met Jule Styne, who saw her potential as a big Broadway star. "I didn't want it enough," my mother later told me.

At the age of twenty-three, she met my father backstage when she was in the original production of *My Fair Lady*. He was extremely handsome, smart, charming, and stylish. Proffering humor and intellectual conversation. After their first date, he walked her to the lobby of her Upper West Side apartment, hoping she would invite him up. When she bid him good night at the door my father gazed into her big brown eyes and said, "I can hope, I can think, and I can wait."

She had never met anyone like him. My father came from a good family. "He was Ivy League," she mused when reminiscing about their first date. His father, Irving Margulies, was in the leather business, mostly for upholstery. His mother, Henrietta Greenspan Margulies, was a lawyer. They lived in an impressive home in Riverdale, they were respected members of their community, they put both their sons, my father and his younger brother, Michael, through the private Horace Mann school in New York and then Dartmouth College, where my father majored in philosophy.

By the time my mother came into the picture, my father was newly divorced, having just ended a short-lived marriage, and had dropped out of Columbia Law School after one year. His explanation for dropping out: "I was always in the Philosophy Library, I had no interest in the law."

He had married a young woman named Marcia Pressman when he was just twenty years old, between his junior and senior years at Dartmouth. She lived with him in an off-campus apartment, but by the time he got to Columbia the romance had worn off, I suppose. There are many different versions of that story, none that I can say I really know for sure, except that by the time he met my mother he was already divorced at the age of twenty-four and a law school dropout.

My father had an apartment on Carmine Street in the West Village, where he imagined his life as a poet, a writer, or a philosopher. He was a dreamer, a romantic, a profound thinker. When I asked my mother her first impression of my father's apartment, she said, "Bach was playing on the record player, candlelight flickered on every surface, dinner was on the table. I think his mother sent Carlos, her cook from Riverdale, to supply the food; she used to do that when Paul announced he was a vegetarian. Carlos would show up with beef bourguignon and a note from Henrietta saying, 'You need to eat meat, I don't want you to die.'"

Quite soon in their romance my mother discovered she was pregnant with my eldest sister, Alexandra. She thought the best course of action was to move to Las Vegas; she could make a living dancing in one of the many shows there and raise the baby by herself. She hadn't even thought about getting married. Paul, on the other hand, was excited at the prospect of becoming a father. They were in love so he asked her to marry him. She was turning twenty-four and already tired of show business; getting married seemed like the right thing to do.

They married in June 1960; my mother was six months pregnant. It was a small family gathering at the Waldorf Astoria; she wore a green minidress. Two days later they were on a boat to Israel via Spain. They honeymooned in Spain and then made the journey to Israel, where my sister was born. To this day I can't get a straight answer about why they moved to Israel. I know my father had a job there, but I've never understood what it was or why it was so important for them to be there. I have letters my father wrote to his best friend, Alan Sklar (my godfather). In one he writes, *It's nice here. Uncomplicated. Maybe once a week we go to the movies. The landscape is stark, few trees on rolling hills, bright suns and blue skies. And no physical luxuries.*

What fascinates me in this paragraph is the word "uncomplicated." My father craved an uncomplicated life, a life where he could just sit back and read his books, write from time to time, teach now and then, and have a peaceful existence. Our life was anything but that. My father was one of the most complicated men I have ever known. My mother, probably the most complicated woman I will ever meet. Our life wasn't drawn from the peaceful blue skies and sun-filled landscapes he speaks of in his letters. Growing up for me was a life in chaos, sometimes beautiful, always filled with love, but much of the time insecure in structure and habitat. I spent most of my childhood trying to navigate rocky terrain and almost all of my adult life, at least up until now, searching for calm.

After a year in Israel, my parents moved back to New York City, where they lived on the Upper West Side. My mother describes this time as tranquil and ideal in every way. She was a young mother, happy to walk to the park with my big sister, Alexandra; my father had secured a decent job as a copywriter in an advertising agency. Not his ideal job, but now with a wife and a child he needed to make a good living, and even though it wasn't poetry, he still was able to write for a living. They had a boatload of friends, an active social life. They enjoyed going to the theater and to dinner parties. They were a gorgeous couple with the world at their fingertips.

Two and half years after Alexandra, my middle sister, Rachel, was born. My parents were still relatively happy at this point, until my father decided that in order to have a healthy life for the children they should move to the suburbs, to Spring Valley, New York, about a forty-five-minute train ride from Manhattan. This is where my mother says it all went wrong.

With the help of his parents they bought a four-bedroom house on Renfrew Road, in a community where every fifth house was exactly the same. Ours was one level, lifted up about five feet from the ground, with a wraparound porch and stairs leading to the front door. There was a wooded area in the backyard and a small patch of green on the front lawn. The house had a large basement where my mother installed a ballet barre, as the space was large enough for ballet lessons. She held classes there a few times a week; my eldest sister took to it naturally.

As time wore on, my mother felt more and more isolated in Spring Valley, and my father became drained from the daily commute. He would come home from work exhausted, with no energy left for her or the children. When my mother talks about this time in their lives, she always wonders out loud why she hadn't insisted on moving back to the city, where they had been happy.

"I didn't know any better," she says. "And we were so young!"

Instead of fixing the problem, they drifted apart. My father's job was demanding and required him to travel too often, and eventually my mother sought companionship and attention elsewhere. That's where I come in. Apparently I was quite a surprise. It may have been from one of my parents' "makeup sessions," or "let's see if we can make it work" moments. Nothing was planned, and before they realized it, I was on my way into the family. There was a glimmer of hope that a new baby could solve the problematic marriage. That was not the case.

# from left bank to right bank

When I was a year old, my parents legally separated and my father moved to Paris, leaving my mother and her three small children in a nice suburban home in Spring Valley. By both their accounts this was a very painful time for them.

My father, at the age of thirty-two, was hired by Mary Wells of Wells Rich Greene to be the creative director for their advertising agency in Paris. The time lines are blurred, but from dated letters my father wrote to Alan, I have been able to discern that my mother moved us all to Paris in August 1969. I had just turned three . . .

Janice found an ancient elegant apartment on the left bank filled with velvet curtains and threadbare oriental rugs and enough China and silver for forty guests of the state. It looks like it belongs to an elderly couple with dwindling wealth and indeed it does. But the kids are having a ball there, making believe they're princesses. And I enjoy having the children nearby.

The way my mother describes our move to Paris: "There was no way I was going to stay in the suburbs while he was off in Paris, why would I do that? I hated the suburbs. I refused to just linger there, for what? I needed a life, I needed to find myself!"

I am guessing through the evidence of these letters that my parents' relationship was strained. In a letter dated May 1, 1969, three months before we moved to live near him, he wrote:

I am worried that Janice is too incomplete a person to be a good enough mother for them. She is incredibly selfish and limited but she is obviously going through a great struggle and I am not without some sympathy for her. Still, I feel that ultimately I must take the children with me for she provides them no sense of endurance or moral fiber.

He never took us away from her. He couldn't. Even though my eldest sister has told me that when we lived in Paris on the Left Bank, with my father living on the Right Bank, she begged him to let us live with him; she was nine years old. My mother recently shared with me that my father *had* proposed he take us so she could be free to have the life she wanted, but the idea of losing her kids "made me want to throw up. I couldn't fathom losing my children. I became a better mother after that," she confessed.

I'm not sure how my father could have managed three little girls by himself; his workload was suffocating, requiring him to fly from one country to another, sometimes four different countries in one week. He was good at his job, but he was never home and he was struggling to find out who he was and what he really wanted out of life.

In September 1969 he wrote to Alan:

The thing is, we all proceed a lot more unconsciously, mechanically, than we would care to admit, and to do otherwise requires tremendous strength, and a constant effort not to lie to ourselves, which is something I'm trying to do with all of my might.

It's Sunday night now and I just got back from a weekend in the country with the kiddies. (Did I tell you about this beautiful farm in Normandy that I rented for a month where I take them on weekends?) I really enjoy being with them, though it is somewhat unnatural and sometimes a bit of a strain.

During this time my mother was experimenting with gorgeous Frenchmen. Jean-Jacques, Jean-Georges, Jean-Paul, Jean-Jean. She was trying to discover her own "self." She has told me that she looks back at this period in her life and sees herself as cold and selfish, but that she just couldn't help herself. Maybe having so many boyfriends gave her a sense of identity? Perhaps she saw herself through their lenses. As I read my father's letters I can imagine the delight my mother took in having us away from her for the weekend to do as she pleased, sleep with whom she wanted, and not have my eldest sister's disapproving glances, or the chance that she would tell my father. Not that that stopped my mother during the week, when we were under her watch, or rather the au pair's watch.

We always had a college student living with us in Paris. In exchange for room and board, they would look after us when our mother went out for the evening. There are many stories of my mother coming home in the early hours of the morning with different men. One time she brought home a Hare Krishna, and we woke up in the morning to find that the apartment, which had been full of threadbare oriental rugs and velvet curtains, had been ransacked, all the china and silver stolen.

Or the time she came home with a man she met at a nightclub who had a pet monkey. She sauntered into the apartment with him, opened our bedroom door, and left the monkey in our room as she invited the stranger into hers. The way I remember it (or perhaps the way it was told to me; the stories vary depending on which sister I ask) was that I woke up with a monkey staring straight into my face, his wrinkled hands holding my plump cheeks together. I screamed, which made the monkey jump up to my sister's bed; in turn she awoke and began to scream, waking my other sister, until we were all screaming and the monkey was flying around the room in an agitated state. My mother opened the door, flipped on the light, and said, "What is all this ruckus about?"

"Mom, Mom, there's a wild monkey in our room!" we cried.

"Oh Lord, it's just a monkey, calm down," she said as she closed the door and went back to her lover.

My mother swears this never happened. But how can three sisters all recount the same experience, slightly altered in each rendering but still so similar?

My father, ever the philosophy student, was always digging deeper to find the "true meaning" of his life on this earth. He was only in his early thirties but had already immersed himself in Anthroposophy, the philosophical teachings of Rudolf Steiner. The school we attended in Paris was a Steiner school. He told me that he discovered the Rudolf Steiner school on Seventy-ninth Street in New York City when my parents were looking to enroll my eldest sister in nursery school. When he went to visit the school, what struck him most was how calm the children were, so quiet in the classroom, how they sang so beautifully and were engrossed in forming beeswax figures, painting, knitting. He was moved by the environment, gentle pastel hues on the walls, soft lighting to create an almost womblike experience.

We lived in Paris for two years, my sisters and I shuttling back and forth from the Left Bank to the Right. This period of time plays in my memory like a grainy, sepia-toned movie reel. I remember being doted on by everyone. I was a naturally happy child with huge round cheeks, which the old French ladies would stop me on the street to pinch. My sisters loved me fiercely. My mother called me her "Sunshine Girl." I was joyful and easygoing. I only felt adored and loved. I assumed that everyone's parents lived in separate houses, as this was all I knew.

When my father had us on weekends, it was a fun adventure, and during the week my mother's lap was where I sat contentedly after every meal. I think I looked at the world as a safe place because I always felt loved. I am told that my first sentence was "Leave me 'lone," most likely because my sisters and my mother were always grasping to hold me. I didn't know what life was like before my parents broke up, I didn't have that compass point. And I see now how that shielded me from knowing any better, or mourning a loss at a young age. When my parents told Alexandra they were separating, her response was "Don't worry, Mommy, I'll be your husband." She was seven.

I must have had some sense of responsibility though, as my father would recount the following story to anyone who was willing to listen, and always with tremendous pride: "When Julianna was about three years old, we were in a clothing store on the Boulevard Saint-Germain, and the saleslady helping us was very friendly. Julianna took a liking to her immediately, looked up at her with a big smile, and said, *'Mon Papa est très joli, n'est-ce pas?'*" (My daddy's very pretty isn't he?).

I must have sensed that he was lonely and wanted a woman in his life. I also understood at an early age that my chubby cheeks alone could bring a smile to an unhappy face, and I think I felt a tremendous obligation to live up to my mother's name for me— Sunshine Girl.

# jesus and the van

We moved to England at the end of June 1970. My father lived in London and headed up the new Wells Rich Greene office there. My mother decided that it would be a good idea for all of us to be in the same country, and there was a Rudolf Steiner school in Sussex, about thirty miles south of London. There was also a Steiner school in London, which would have made all our lives easier, but at this point my mother was searching for a career. Like my father, she was becoming more and more interested in Steiner's work. She decided to explore what that would mean to her by attending Emerson College in Sussex, which taught Steiner's pedagogy and also had a Eurythmy program (Eurythmy is a form of dance: speech and music through movement). Having been a dancer, my mother gravitated toward Eurythmy; it seemed the best way for her to incorporate what she already knew with her newfound interest into Anthroposophy. The college was in Forest Row, the same small village as our new school.

I don't remember my father's apartment in London, but I do know that we got to see him there most weekends, and I remember Vicky being a part of our lives at this point. Vicky was my father's girlfriend. They had met on a commercial shoot when she had been hired as a stylist.

Vicky got her start working for the photographer Bert Stern. She was Bert's "it girl"; she did everything for him, booking photo shoots, styling, organizing his schedule. On the last photo shoot that Marilyn Monroe ever did, Vicky was there. Marilyn had promised Bert a nude photo session, but when she got there, she had adamantly changed her mind. Vicky was standing next to Bert, wearing a diaphanous scarf wrapped around her neck. Bert asked Vicky for her scarf and held it out to Marilyn. "Would you do it naked with this in front of you?" he asked her. Marilyn thought it was a great idea, and she posed with Vicky's scarf shadowing her naked body. No one realized that this would be the last time Marilyn would ever be in front of a camera.

Vicky is the opposite from my mother in every way. She has never been interested in "finding" herself. She loved fashion and home décor, posh restaurants and hot spots for the rich and famous. She came to America from Yugoslavia when she was two years old, with a teenage mother who didn't speak English and a much older father, Boris, who was a portrait photographer. Her family lived in an apartment above her father's photography studio in Douglaston, Queens.

She was beautiful. Tall with straight, reddish brown hair that she wore down past her shoulders, bangs cut to frame her Slavic face. She had high cheekbones and a strong nose, hazel eyes with flecks of green. Where Vicky was angular in shape, my mother was soft and voluptuous, small hipped and lithe. They could not have been more different. My mother asserted herself in every possible

situation, demanding to be heard and paid attention to. Vicky tim-
idly sat on the sidelines, nodding her head in agreement, never
wanting to cause a stir. Vicky worshipped my father. And even
though she had no interest in his philosophical pursuits, she was
happy to go along for the ride. According to my father's letters to
Alan, there were many stops and starts to their relationship; in the
end Vicky prevailed. She squeezed him fresh orange juice every
morning and had all his shirts perfectly ironed, his eggs cooked just
how he liked them, soft but not runny. She doted on him like he was
a king. My mother could never be that for him. The idea of waking
up to serve your man was not on her agenda, ever.

What I do recall so vividly is the home my mother found for us
to live in for the next three years: a fifteenth-century rented house
called Pock Hill Cottage. The aged stone and wood structure sat
right on the edge of the Ashdown Forest in Ashurst Wood, down a
long dirt road, narrow and curvy with deep ditches on both sides,
barely wide enough for one car. I remember countless times that my
mother would be trying to maneuver her large, clunky vehicle when
another car would come barreling toward us from the opposite direction. Inevitably we would end up in a ditch, unable to pull ourselves out without the help of a kind passerby. We would sit in the
car waiting for help, our bodies thrown to one side of the backseat,
trying to find our balance, wondering how late we would be for
school that day, or if we would ever make it home.

The house itself was quite beautiful and had a typical vintage
English charm. Having been built so many centuries ago, the ceilings hung low to keep in the heat, held up by dimpled, dark wood
beams that any visitor taller than a child would bump their head on.

Rachel and I were sure the house was haunted. We shared a
room in that drafty old place, and almost nightly I would run to her,
sure that I had seen a ghost hovering over my bed, staring down at
me. I remember so distinctly that feeling when someone or something is right there, looking at you, daring you to engage with them.
I would squeeze my eyes shut as tight as I could, willing whatever it

was to go away as I sprinted across the room, holding my breath, trying my best not to let my feet touch the floor, and I would dive into Rachel's bed for safety.

Rachel, always the wiser, braver one, decided that the only way we would conquer our fear was to be kind to the ghosts, to show them hospitality, to welcome them so we could live in harmony together. I don't know if she really felt this way or was just trying to assuage my anxiety, but it worked, and I soon began to view the ghosts as friends rather than the enemy.

I began kindergarten at the Michael Hall School. Having spent the two prior years in Paris, I was fluent in French but found myself among a class full of British accents. I was only four years old, but I remember making a promise to myself that I would learn to sound just like them. I caught on quickly and developed a perfect West Sussex accent. When my mother would speak to me in French, I refused to answer her in the same language and would defy her every time by answering back in English.

My mother dove wholeheartedly into her new environment. She loved Emerson College and took her studies of Eurythmy and Steiner very seriously. She soon fell in love (again), with a man named John. He was a student at Emerson and fully immersed in Steiner's ideology. The most I can remember about John is that he was tall with a head of light brown hair, a slightly receding hairline, and a large, bushy mustache, and I remember how happy my mother was around him.

When my mother was in love, life for us was calmer, she was joyful. My stability, I learned quickly, depended on my mother's happiness, and her state of mind fluctuated with each boyfriend. In Paris her relationships were fleeting, a few months here, a month or two there, nothing serious. Her taste in men varied dramatically. To this day I haven't grasped what it is that she's attracted to, although as she got older she shifted her gaze to younger men. She needed to be adored and she needed to be heard. Not all of her boyfriends were Anthroposophists, in fact I think most of them weren't. She was complicated in that regard; she wanted them to inspire her and also to be able to talk to them on a spiritual level, but they needed to be physically attractive and not too self-involved so they could attend to her needs.

She fell in and out of love quickly, the slightest off-putting gesture of any kind would send her latest paramour out the door. If she was in the midst of a bad breakup, her mood lingered like a dark cloud hanging over us. We braced ourselves for the storm to break—sometimes it would, sometimes it ebbed back. If someone she was madly in love with broke her heart, her sadness enveloped me. I don't remember a time in my life when I *wasn't* registering the temperature of other people's feelings. I made sure to do everything in my power to make things better for my mother, to sit on her lap longer after dinner, or try to make her laugh. If *she* had been the cause of a breakup, the cloud would lift pretty quickly. She was happy to be rid of him and usually on to the next shiny object, the excitement of something new sweeping the clouds away.

My mother's boyfriend John became something of a staple fixture in our home, for a while anyway, and although my mother was wrapped up in him *and* her path to "find her true self," her warm lap still provided me a place to sit every night. I always felt loved by her: "You were easy and happy," she would say. "You never cried. When you were a baby I would wake up at nine in the morning and rush into your room, afraid that I hadn't heard you crying, and there you would be, wet from head to toe, just standing in your crib with a smile on your face, so happy to see me." I wore the title of Sunshine Girl like a badge of honor.

My mother began to dress more like the students at Emerson College, wrapping her hair up in fringed headscarves, wearing Birkenstocks dyed purple in the kitchen sink. Her elegant New York–Parisian form-fitting style morphed into chic hippie attire, often the cause of tremendous embarrassment for my eldest sister. I was too little to pay much attention to how my mother dressed, but as I got older, I too shuddered at some of her outfits, especially the purple Birkenstocks. I would beg her to stay in the car if she was picking me up from school.

"Can't you just wear your hair the way normal people do, Ma? Why do you have to wrap it up in a headscarf all the time?"

As my mother flourished in her newfound identity, my eldest sister, Alexandra, assumed the role of caretaker for the family. "Mom! We need to go now! I don't want to be late for school." We were always late for school; my mother could never get it together in the morning.

"Mom, we don't have any clean clothes to wear!"

My sister showed my mother how to organize the linen closet. "This is how it's supposed to be done, Mom," she would say with disdain. My mother would tell us with a laugh that my sister was "just born that way. I was never going to be the kind of mother she wanted. I could tell the moment she looked at me when she was a baby in my arms, she already had made up her mind."

I can't imagine the responsibility my sister felt. She craved normalcy. My mother could never provide that for her. She was eccentric, whimsical, dramatic, and self-absorbed. But as a child, I found her to be warm and embracing, especially when she was happy. And if she was sad I looked at it as an opportunity to cheer her up.

I think birth order has a lot to do with how you perceive this world. Because I was the youngest, I had an easier time. When my mother was having a "blue period" after one of her breakups, where she seemed despondent and unavailable to me, my sisters would care for me. I think you get away with a lot when you are the youngest. I was always watching, taking in everyone's mood, inhaling disapproving glances. I was the baby of the family, so I had the luxury of acting like one, and I would do so in order to lighten the mood. I even used to talk like a baby. My mother called it "The Baby June

Act." She was delighted when I spoke in my baby voice and would encourage me to keep doing it, even though I was well past a baby's age. When I could sense that her mood was darkening, I would put on my Baby June voice to get a laugh out of her. My father hated my Baby June voice and came up with a signal every time I accidently slipped into it when I was with him for the weekend. He would say, "Tuna fish!" and I knew to stop. I did it so much when I was home with my mother I would forget to rein it in when I was with my father, causing me tremendous embarrassment every time I heard him say "tuna fish."

I was too young to really understand anything except the tenor of the house. The tension between my eldest sister and my mother was always palpable. Their arguments increased as my sister got older and as my mother immersed herself more deeply in Anthroposophy and spirituality. She became more and more inattentive to our daily needs; organization was always on the back burner, never in the forefront of our lives. Getting out of the house in the morning for school was more like scrambling to beat the clock, chaotic and seemingly overwhelming for her.

Yet in that disheveled space, I strangely didn't feel neglected. She didn't cross her t's or dot her i's; that wasn't her way. I never had the proper outfit to wear or neatly folded, matching socks to take out of a drawer. Those things didn't seem important to her. Love was bigger than any organized lunch box, and her way of showing it to us came in warm hugs and kisses. If my sister came into the kitchen in the morning upset because she didn't have the right skirt to match her school uniform, my mother would say, "Oh, honey, it doesn't matter, you would look beautiful in a burlap sack. No one is looking at what you're wearing when you have the face of an angel."

My father continued to be engrossed in Steiner, but he studied him from a philosophical perspective. He read Steiner's books and then tried to translate them into laymen's terms for others to appreciate. He held study groups on the subject. *Knowledge of Higher Worlds,* a book Steiner wrote, became the subject of many of his lectures later on in life. But he was able to find a balance in his daily life; he didn't abandon his responsibilities for the sake of Steiner. He showed up at work every day, on time, and he was excellent at his job. The joke in our family was that my father made a living writing television commercials and we weren't allowed to watch TV, let alone have one in the house. I had no idea how famous my father was in the advertising world until I got to college and someone asked me what my dad did for a living. When I told them he wrote the jingle "Plop, plop, fizz, fizz, oh what a relief it is," they screamed: "Oh my *God*! Your dad wrote *that*? That's the best commercial ever written!" The irony that I became successful in television was not lost on our family either. The forbidden fruit yielded a promising return in the end.

I had always known that my father was successful and looked up to in his industry, but I didn't know the extent of his success. I wasn't privy to his everyday life, never hearing him talk about work at the end of the day. He was my weekend father. Later he would become my twice-a-year father. I never knew his day-to-day life, nor he mine.

My mother seemed to lose herself completely in her quest to find a "higher meaning." Daily tasks seemed mundane to her when she could be developing her spirituality. She seemed to be floating above the ground, rather than walking firmly on it. The way she describes it: "I finally felt that I had a purpose, that I belonged somewhere."

She took her newfound beliefs to extremes, including changing her religion. Both my parents were born Jewish. In much of Steiner's work he talks about "The Christ Within Us." Our schools had a very Christian slant. Every Christmas the school put on a Christmas pageant play. I was Mary Magdalene when I was in the sixth grade. I was the Angel Gabriel my senior year in high school. Christianity played a big role in every school I went to.

As a family we celebrated Christmas and Easter, but we never went to church. Christmas for me was about seeing my father, presents under the tree, and singing carols. Easter was only about chocolate bunnies and jelly beans, maybe painting an egg. My mother's faith in Christianity deepened over time, and she would try to instill in us some kind of belief in Jesus Christ, but we weren't interested. I grew up knowing I was Jewish without any Jewish foundation to call my own, celebrating Christian holidays with no religious attachment. Once I became a teenager I made it very clear to my mother how much her proselytizing angered me. "It might work for you, Mom, but stop trying to get me to believe," I would retort every time she went on some jag about Jesus and the Christ within us. It enraged me. I grew up feeling strongly that I had no religion whatsoever. When I was asked what religion I was, my answer was always the same: "I'm Jewish, but we celebrate Christmas."

My mother told me that she always felt alienated from the Jewish faith; she didn't feel she belonged there. Her relatives were Russian immigrants, but they didn't practice Judaism. The family spoke Yiddish and ate Jewish food, but the religious part of Judaism didn't play a big role in her life. When she went to Emerson College and began studying Steiner, she felt she finally belonged somewhere. There was a real sense of community, and she wanted to be a part of that.

The man who founded Emerson College was named Francis Edmunds. My mother was enamored with him; whatever he said, she believed. His wife, Elizabeth, was her Eurythmy teacher. She put Francis Edmunds so high up on a pedestal and referred to him as though he walked on water. The negative impact for us was that my mother ventured so deeply into Anthroposophy that small practicalities of daily life floated away. It's important to note here that Anthroposophy isn't a cult, even though it may sound like one. They don't ask for money, they are a far cry from Scientology or other organized religions. Anthroposophy is a way of thinking, delving into the spirit life, understanding what Steiner was trying to say in his more than sixty books. What my mother loved about Francis Edmunds was that he had trained in Steiner's pedagogy for decades; she worshipped his ideas and drank in his knowledge. I think she viewed him as a father figure.

At the age of thirty-five, my mother converted to Christianity. A ceremony was planned for the day of her baptism. Her boyfriend John was there with a handful of her college friends and a frightening-looking priest in long, drab robes who spoke in a strange singsongy voice. Her three daughters were in front of the adults, all of us with looks of confusion on our faces, and there in our backyard at Pock Hill Cottage, surrounded by the overgrown grass and the untended garden of weeds with the occasional bluebell sticking out, my mother was baptized. She was christened Francesca, taking the name of St. Francis of Assisi and Francis Edmunds. Janice Marylin Gardner no longer existed. Francesca Margulies would be her name going forward.

By the age of five, still in England, I began to surmise that when we were living with my mother, we were poor, but when we visited my father on weekends in London, we seemed rich. I quickly figured out how to traverse between my two lives. I knew what fork to use at a five-star restaurant but also how to live in a VW camper for months on end, peeing in the woods, cooking on a makeshift fire by the side of some European roadway, not bathing for days.

When we showed up at my father's house for the weekend, we often looked like ragamuffins. Torn woolly tights; scuff-marked shoes; coats with tears in them, the lining hanging down past the hemline. My father's face would tighten, his lips purse in disbelief. Vicky would come to the rescue and take us out to posh London stores, buy us Laura Ashley dresses and velvet capes. We left his house looking like little princesses, after a weekend of theater and fancy restaurants.

I was always sad to leave my father after our weekends together. When I was in his world, life had a sparkle to it; back with my mother life felt more difficult. She was always pinching pennies, worrying about money. We never talked about money with my father. It's strange to think back on these days and recognize that we were scared to bring up the subject of money. My father had a gentle disposition, he never yelled at us or frightened us in any way. With him it was always about having a good time. I don't know why I had it in my head that money was the forbidden topic. Perhaps I could sense his shoulders rise up to his ears whenever finances were spoken of. I never wanted to upset him when I was with him; time was too precious to ruin with unwanted conversation. I tried to savor every minute I had with him.

At the same time, I knew that I wanted to live with my mother. She was easier to talk to and handed out affection in buckets. I sat on her lap after dinner every night until I was almost fourteen and couldn't fit there anymore. Her love comforted me in ways my father couldn't. I don't think I ever once sat on his lap. He was generous with his hugs, and by all standards incredibly loving. I grew up feeling torn between wanting to be with him and wanting to be with her, which is probably why I fantasized that they would get back together someday.

When I dig deep to try to understand why acting became my profession, even though I had much bigger plans for myself when, as a teenager, I was plotting out my adult life, I see now that nothing else would have made sense. What else could I do? I was always trying to be another person as a child. Whether it was changing my accent, speaking in a different language, living the high life, or just getting by. I was constantly changing who I was, or trying to become someone I thought I was supposed to be. I wanted to fit into whatever situation was thrown at me. I became very good at determining which direction I needed to follow, depending on where I was or who I was with.

I don't know how long John was in our lives, a year, perhaps longer. I do remember that I liked him. Rachel did too; she was always kinder to my mother's boyfriends than Alexandra. Sometimes when one of my mother's boyfriends called the house and she answered the phone, my eldest sister would say, "My mother doesn't love you anymore," and hang up. I was too young to do anything but accept them. I imagine for Alexandra each boyfriend represented more chaos. History had shown her that these relationships didn't end well, so maybe she was just trying to cut them off at the pass. I don't blame her for trying.

When John and my mother broke up, she was devastated. I don't know if it was so much that they broke up, or that she suddenly felt alone. After any breakup with a boyfriend there was always an adjustment period we had to go through. My mother's mood would change. She could be melancholic and weepy, or moody and angry. Sometimes her breakup would leave her needy for our affection. I do remember my mother spiraling downward after John and all of us feeling a sense of loss. We had grown accustomed to his presence. It was nice to have a man around the house, not that he lived with us, but he was there most of the time. After their breakup we tiptoed on eggshells around my mother in the morning. She would sit at the breakfast table smoking a Marlboro Red, drinking her coffee in silence, staring out at nothing in particular. She seemed fragile in these moments, which was always surprising to me, because when she was happy and in love, she was indestructible, self-assured, strong willed, and determined.

My mother's joyful disposition shone so brightly when she was happy, it was infectious. If I was alone with her I could allow her mood to dictate my own. If my eldest sister was around, I would try to gauge her reaction to my mother before I decided how I was supposed to respond. I wanted to please them both. Rachel was my safe zone. If Alexandra and my mother were fighting, Rachel and I would disappear into our room and play on our own, coming up with original plays or inventing what we thought were riveting stories. When I was alone with Rachel, she was my leader. She was creative, musical, and fun. It was much simpler for me to just follow.

During our second year at Pock Hill Cottage, somehow we managed to talk my mother into letting us have budgies. I was fascinated by these happy little birds and loved them immensely. Their colors were remarkable: radiant purples, blues, greens, reds, and yellows. We had about six of them. I called them my little gemstones, wondering how they could be real, marveling at their feathers. They lived in roomy cages in the living room by the drafty mullioned windows. I would bid them good morning every day on my way to the kitchen for breakfast and play with them when I got home from school. Rachel and I tended to them carefully. That was the rule. My mother would agree to having them only if Rachel and I took care of them; she had no interest in caring for pets of any kind.

One day we got home from school to find all the windows in the house wide open and the birdcages empty. When we asked our mother where the budgies were, she said nonchalantly, "Oh, they needed to fly, they were too cooped up in those cages. I couldn't bear it anymore, so I let them fly outside, they needed their freedom. They'll come back, don't worry."

They never came back. Instead they died, with a depressing thud as each one fell to its death on our overgrown lawn. Rachel and I trudged around the straggly garden trying to find them: small lumps of jeweled feathers everywhere. I immediately began to cry, and Rachel, in her "ever the solution seeker" mode, took me by the hand and set me on the task of finding as many little boxes as I could. I rummaged through our disorganized house, finding large matchboxes and odd little shoeboxes. We stuffed soft wool into each one, creating a bed, and ultimately had six small coffins for our departed friends. Rachel put on a cape and made crowns out of tissue paper, a red one for me and a yellow one for her. She put three of the coffins in my hands, piled up like a ritualistic offering of some kind, and she carried the other three as we marched, funeral-procession style, from the house to a soft spot under a large, leafy tree in our backyard. Rachel sang a melancholic tune as we dug holes in the ground and knelt down to gently place the birds in their graves. We covered the holes with dirt, and Rachel genuflected and made the sign of the cross as she recited a prayer wishing them a happy afterlife. We were such good Jewish kids.

Toward the end of our third year in England, my father was offered a job back in New York. We were finally going home to the States. Alexandra had a mixed accent, both American and British; Rachel's accent had a French lilt mixed with British; and I sounded like a complete Brit.

My mother had finished her three-year training at Emerson and was determined to advance in the Eurythmy teachers' training program so she could earn her degree and get a job at any Waldorf school in the world. As luck would have it, there was a Eurythmy school very close to the Green Meadow Waldorf School in Spring Valley, where my sisters had been enrolled before we left for Europe.

We were going back to our old house on Renfrew Road, which had been rented out for the five years we were away. Everyone seemed excited. I didn't remember the house, I only gleaned the excitement I was meant to feel because of my sisters'.

My father would finish his job in London by the end of July; as always, he had us for the month of August. This year he had rented a house in Portugal. My mother was tasked with finding something for us to do for the two months we had in between school and Portugal. And so right after my sixth birthday, when school was finally letting out for the summer holidays, my sisters and I arrived home to Pock Hill Cottage to find a light blue VW van with a red-and-white striped pop-out roof that my mother had just purchased secondhand. Her current boyfriend, "Jesus Christ," was standing next to her.

Her boyfriend, Peter I think his name was, truly looked like Jesus Christ, so that's what the three of us called him behind his back. He had long brown hair parted in the middle with an untrimmed mustache and scraggly beard. He wore a jean shirt unbuttoned down to his navel, with faded jeans and a brown, worn leather belt and sandals. He was Jesus.

"We're going on a trip, kids," my mother sang. "It's going to be so much fun, an adventure. We will camp out at night, or if you want to sleep inside, the pop-out has two bunk beds!" she said with a radiant smile.

Her enthusiasm didn't transfer to Alexandra. She most likely gave my mother an eye roll. I remember thinking it sounded kind of fun, although maybe a little frightening. I looked to Rachel to see what her reaction was, and as far as I could tell she seemed excited too.

Like it or not, we were going on a trip for almost two months in a VW van with Jesus Christ and my mother.

We packed up all of our belongings at Pock Hill Cottage. Rachel and I ran to say goodbye to all the things we loved. We went to our room to bid farewell to the ghosts. We ran out to the field behind our house to the Ashdown Forest and waved goodbye to the abundant bluebells that grew impossibly wild, covering the forest floor in a sweep of deep purple. We jumped up to touch the beams in the house one last time. We paid homage to our beloved dead birds by their graves under the tree.

I grabbed Rabbity-Jones and Lamby, the two stuffed animals I treasured most in the world. Alexandra had made Rabbity-Jones for me in one of her sewing classes at school out of a soft pink flannel. My mother had given me Lamby, a stuffed animal made out of wool she had found at one of our school fairs. The two creatures slept with me, one in the crook of each arm, every night. We climbed inside the van, each one of us staking our claim, mine being the very back, which accommodated me perfectly. And off we drove. The four of us, and Jesus Christ. Away from Ashurst Wood, away from our school and our friends, away from the life we had finally grown to love.

We took the hovercraft from Southampton to France. The itinerary was to drive down the coast of France through the Pyrenees

Mountains and then down the coast of Spain. At the end of our journey my mother would put us on a plane to Portugal.

Early on in the trip, my mother and Jesus decided to pick up two hitchhikers. Apparently the van wasn't crowded enough with three young girls and two hippie adults. They pulled over and invited in this odd, seemingly harmless couple who had few belongings and gamy hygiene.

Because my habitat was the very back of the van, I had a clear view of everyone in front of me. The woman was slight, with long black hair that hadn't seen a bottle of shampoo in what I imagined had been a long time. I was mesmerized by her and not without good reason. She had a twitch that would inject itself into her neck every few minutes, dispatching her head with a hard jerk to the left. I was fascinated and wondered if she was aware she was doing it, or if she was oblivious. I knew better than to ask, but it was the first time I remember really focusing on someone's body language, and I tried to imagine what it would be like if I had the same affliction. I sat in my little abode, trying to pretend that I too had a twitch, until finally the ache in my neck begged me to stop. After coming to the realization that head twitching was quite painful, I had only empathy for her and tried to make her feel welcome.

Her boyfriend had a lazy eye. I never knew which eye to look into, and when you're six, it's hard enough to look a grown-up in the eye, so I gave up. If I spoke to him I would gaze at the seat or the window; I didn't want to be rude and look into the wrong eye.

Between the twitch, the eye, the cramped space, and the gamy hygiene, our guests were wearing thin on us. Fortunately, they departed after three days.

My mother and Jesus camped out every night; Rachel would sometimes join them, or choose to sleep with us. Alexandra and I would lock ourselves in the van at night, she in the bunk and I in the very back, which I christened "The Boobida" (pronounced exactly as spelled). I have no idea why I called it that or where the name came from, but it stuck from the moment I claimed it.

I grew to love the Boobida; it was my very own little space, cozy and safe. I set up my rabbit and lamb, my soft blanket, and created a world for myself that no one could enter. I sat looking out the rear window when we were driving and waved at all the cars behind us.

One goal on the trip was to take a detour to Normandy to see Mont-Saint-Michel. This was the only planned event on our itinerary. My mother just *had* to experience what she had heard was one of the most spiritual places you could ever encounter. Mont-Saint-Michel lures 2.5 million people to its magnificent cathedral ceilings every year. Its conception started in the year 709. It is a wonder to the Western World as it forms a tower in the heart of an enormous bay invaded by the highest currents in Europe. In 966 a group of Benedictines established themselves there at the request of the Duke of Normandy, and the pre-Romanesque church was built there before the year 1000.

It was nightfall by the time we arrived. In the dark, the campers set out to sleep under the stars alongside the road while the children locked themselves in the van.

When we woke up the next day we found ourselves next to a field of sunflowers, and just over the tops of these magical golden stalks, far off in the distance, we could see the towers of Mont-Saint-Michel, glistening in the light, inviting us in.

From Mont-Saint-Michel we drove to Spain. Jesus Christ, who had been with my mother for only two months before we went on the trip, was kicked to the curb in Barcelona. The demise of that romance was instigated by the sudden authoritarian edge Jesus had taken about us kids eating snacks in the car. He couldn't tolerate the noise of the wrappers or the smell of the food while he drove. That didn't sit well with my mother. Jesus would have to find his own way home.

"The truth is, I didn't know him all that well, he was much younger than me, and once I got to know him on our trip I realized I didn't really like him at all. He had to go," my mother told me years later.

From Barcelona we drove down the coast of Spain, free from unwanted guests and tyrannical boyfriends, happy to swim in the blue waters that beckoned us from the hot, sticky van. My mother dropped us off at the airport and put us on a plane to Portugal, where my father awaited our arrival.

Once she dropped us off, she drove on alone to a beautiful hotel in Algeciras, where she met her next beau, Michele, who hailed from Canada. That romance took her, via the Strait of Gibraltar, back to England, where she sold the van, packed up the rest of our belongings, and headed back to the States.

When I asked my mother how she managed to afford all this travel, she marveled: "I have no idea! We didn't have much money. I didn't even have a credit card, we used American Express traveler's checks. I suppose I was very thrifty. I can't believe I did all of that, but, you know, life back then was much simpler."

# i wanted to be just like them

At the end of the summer we moved back into our house on Renfrew Road. For the first time in my six-year-old life I had my very own room. When my mother asked me what color paint I wanted on the walls, I insisted on light blue, with wall-to-wall blue carpeting. Rachel chose a strong yellow with a yellow shag rug; Alexandra had a white room, the largest of the three. I loved that house. It was modern and fresh, and I kept hearing "We're home!" We were home.

My windows looked out over the woods in the back of the house; the porch wrapped all the way from the kitchen around the living room, past my mother's bedroom to mine. I had sliding glass windows that I could open up and climb through right onto the porch. I felt so grown-up in my own room, and I was excited to start first grade.

My first day of school I wore the Laura Ashley dress Vicky had bought me in London, cream with dark red tiny flowers all over it, pretty puffed short sleeves, pinched in at the waist with elastic embroidery. When I got to school I quickly realized that I had chosen the wrong outfit. All the kids were in jeans and sneakers. I looked down at my navy blue leather sandals and felt completely out of place. Not only that, my accent was all wrong. The three years it had taken me to perfect a British accent were for naught. How would I be able to figure out how to speak like my new classmates? I was very aware that I had a huge task ahead of me. I needed to change immediately if I was going to fit in.

My mother had proudly let all the teachers know that I was fluent in French, and I'm sure my new French teacher was trying to make me feel special by having me stand up on a chair and recite a French poem for the rest of the class so they could hear my perfect pronunciation. I wanted to crawl into a hole and disappear.

That first week of school was torture. Kids coming up and asking me, "How would you say 'Mommy'?"

"Mummy," I would reply.

"Say it again!" They would giggle, enthralled by my British accent.

I didn't want to be different, I wanted to be just like them.

In a very short time I turned things around. I left my Laura Ashley dress crumpled on the floor of my closet and adopted a new look: jeans, T-shirt, sneakers. After a few months I developed an American accent and a new outlook on who I should be: a tomboy. While Alexandra was auditioning for the School of American Ballet and Rachel was learning how to play the violin, I was playing baseball, climbing trees, and excelling in gym class. Any sport introduced to me became my new passion. When asked what I wanted for my seventh birthday, I told my father I would like a football. On my eighth birthday I asked for a workshop: rasps, saws, sandpaper, vises to hold the wood. I set up shop in our garage and endeavored to make wooden bowls, animal figurines, salad forks and spoons. I was never very good, but it gave me a certain sense of power. I could shape and mold the wood into objects I could give people. My mother still uses one of the wobbly salad spoons I made her.

I sought attention by pretending I was tough and could fight. Some of the boys nicknamed me Julianimal because I would do what they asked, tearing through the woods after less popular kids and terrorizing them. In class I was loud and obnoxious; I interrupted teachers and found ways to get the kids to laugh, being disruptive any chance I could get. I thought being the class clown was cool and would make me more popular.

When I was in second grade my mother was called in for a conference and was shocked to discover all of this about me. At home, I was the same sweet Sunshine Girl my mother knew. I did as I was told, set the table, made the salad for dinner, cleaned up. "What? My Julianna? Can't be. She's sweet and gentle and obedient; you must have her confused with someone else."

Around this time, the fights between my mother and my eldest sister were escalating to the point of no return. Alexandra had become a student at the School of American Ballet, where my mother had studied in New York City, and her schedule was rigorous. Her discipline outmatched any of ours. My mother was enrolled in a five-year course studying Eurythmy during the week, and waitressing at a restaurant near the George Washington Bridge on weekends to make ends meet. Alexandra was barely thirteen, and living in the same house with my mother proved impossible for her. She disapproved of every choice my mother made; every boyfriend warranted a sarcastic response; the fights were endless.

I remember the screaming match between them that last night. My sister called my father in Manhattan and told him, "I'm not going to live like this anymore, you need to come and pick me up right now, I'm moving in with you. I can't live with that woman!"

As she packed her bags, Rachel and I stood in her doorway

watching. I was crying, begging her not to go. Rachel was somber and quiet, standing next to me, holding my hand.

"I'm sorry, I just can't do it anymore, I'm so sorry, but I have to go. You guys will be okay," she promised us. "I'll see you on weekends when you come to visit Dad."

She moved in with my father that night and never came back to live with us.

The house felt so empty when Alexandra moved out. Her bedroom sat vacant, the door ajar. I had to pass her room to get to mine at the end of the hallway, and I would peek inside as I walked by, straining to see her in my mind's eye, mourning her departure. I never told anyone that my sister moved out because she and my mother couldn't live together. Instead, I used the excuse that ballet school had become too demanding and she needed to live in the city to study. There was some truth to that, of course; with each passing year SAB eliminated students who didn't show promise. My sister kept on going to the next level until eventually she had to go to the Professional Children's School in order to fit school into her ballet schedule.

She moved into the guest room of my father's apartment on East Seventy-ninth Street. On their return from London my father and Vicky had rented the apartment from his friend Stan Dragoti, a big-time commercial and film director who was married to the model Cheryl Tiegs. When we would visit Dad on weekends I would spend hours on the marble floor of their mirrored hallway. Mirrors everywhere, on the backs of the doors to the den and master bedroom and bathroom at the end of the corridor. If you closed all the doors you were in a magical mirrored kingdom. I sat for hours watching millions of me as I moved about to see how many images of myself I could count. Going to their apartment always felt extravagant. Rachel and I slept in the den, which had a pullout couch and a TV. My mother still didn't own a television set. We were allowed to watch TV until my dad and Vicky woke up on Saturday mornings. We would fill big bowls of cornflakes and eat them watching cartoons. Heaven!

I got to see Alexandra some weekends, although she wasn't at the apartment all that much. My father was buried in his work and Vicky was not maternal in any way, so Alexandra learned to be independent in the blink of an eye. At thirteen she knew how to get around the city and fend for herself. By the time she was fifteen she had a boyfriend and her own life. She seemed so grown-up to me, so sophisticated. Her new romance woke me up to the idea that maybe I liked boys too. Maybe boys weren't only my opponents in sports, maybe they could be *boyfriends*?

By fourth grade I began to have crushes on some of the boys in sixth grade. One day as I was walking past the librarian's desk I overheard her talking to Paul Onderdonk, a blond, blue-eyed boy in the sixth grade whom I had a mad crush on. I remember so clearly hearing her say, "Oh, Paul, you are my favorite student."

That was all I needed to hear. I switched gears overnight. If I was going to get the attention I wanted from Paul Onderdonk, I was going to have to change my ways. I needed to get into the librarian's good graces. I had fantasies that she would invite me and Paul to a special luncheon, only for her two favorite students. I didn't want to be on the team of boys in my class anymore, running wild at recess and causing a ruckus, I wanted to be on Paul's team. I began to study hard and sit up front in the classroom so I could pay attention to every word the teacher said. I dove into being a good kid with the same determination I'd had when trying to fit in with the rough kids. My report cards reflected my newfound identity. I began to excel as a student and loved the feedback, still hoping that Paul would notice me. I was ten, he was twelve. I lived for the fantasy of him falling in love with me. He never did, but my crush on him straightened me out at school and set me on the right path, away from the "Julianimal" nickname, and no longer having to live with two identities.

———

Following our time in Europe, after five years in Spring Valley, I finally felt like I was part of a community. I fit in. I had friends, I loved my teachers, my neighbors; there was a routine to my life and I was thriving. Most weekends were spent in the city with my father; family was nearby, only a forty-five-minute drive. My two great-aunts, Marley and Bernice, and my uncle Dinny lived on lower Fifth Avenue. If we were visiting my father for the weekend, we would often take lox and bagels down to them for Sunday brunch. Uncle Michael and his wife, Aunt Judy, lived in Scarsdale with my two cousins, Arthur and David. My grandma Isabel lived in Brooklyn. My paternal grandparents had retired to Florida, but we would fly down to see them at Christmas. I finally had a sense of family, of belonging.

I had perfected my American accent. I even had a cat that I'd found at a school fair, the runt of the litter, half Siamese and half Persian. I had to beg my mother to let me have him, promising that I would take full responsibility for him and she wouldn't have to do a thing. She was scared of cats, and Rachel was allergic to them, but somehow at the age of eight I convinced them both that the cat was a good idea. I named him Tonto because he had black markings around his eyes that looked like a mask. While we didn't have a TV, I had heard of the show *The Lone Ranger*. The only thing was that I confused the Lone Ranger (who wore a mask) with his sidekick, Tonto. No one bothered to correct me, so the name Tonto stuck. He was an indoor-outdoor cat who would come to my window at night, tapping on the glass with his little paw. I would slide open the window as quietly as possible so my mother wouldn't hear, and Tonto would jump up on my bed and sleep with me all night, his soft, furry body stretched out across my neck, his sweet face near my ear; listening to him purr was my favorite way to fall asleep. I would stay in that one position all night long so he wouldn't leave; even if I was drenched with sweat under the warmth of his fur, I didn't move, afraid that the smallest gesture would send him flying off the bed.

To make my life even better, I was crazy about my mother's boyfriend, Tony Diorio. He was the gym teacher at my school, the one "cool" teacher all the kids adored. His uniform consisted of the perfect faded Levi's jeans, white sneakers, and a navy blue cashmere sweater. He had a cool seventies mustache and wore his thinning blond hair pretty long, a bit wild and loose. He was short and compact but very athletic. He was fun to be around and his love for children was abundant. He fell head over heels in love with my mother starting when I was in the second grade, and he openly showed his love for me and Rachel. His nickname for me was "The Bean," because I was always testing myself to see how high I could jump. When Tony came over we weren't shooed away, we were always welcome to join him and my mother. When we stayed in Spring Valley for the weekend instead of going to see my dad, Tony and I would get up early and drive to Pakoula's bakery in Nyack in his light gray Fiat to get fresh bagels, hot out of the oven, and bring them back for everyone.

He taught me how to work the stick shift in his car. From the passenger seat I would put my hand on the knob of the wooden gearshift, and just as he pushed in the clutch he would say, "Now!" I would shift into second, and then, when he picked up speed, he would give me the go-ahead and I would shift to third. I felt incredibly cool knowing how to shift gears, and then he would drive a little too fast so I could shift into fourth. A smile would spread across his face when he saw how delighted I was that he was driving over the speed limit.

Those Sunday drives with Tony were some of my happiest memories as a kid. Listening to the Top 40 songs on the radio and singing as loud as we could. In my mind he was the perfect boyfriend for my mother. He was hip and cool, he treated all of us with such love and respect. When my mother had to waitress on Saturday nights, often Tony would come to babysit us. He genuinely liked our company. His friend Jaimen rented our basement, which he had turned into a makeshift apartment. Jaimen was a music teacher and taught Rachel how to play the guitar and me how to play the flute. We would all hang out in the living room, singing songs while they strummed, playing cards or board games. I remember thinking how lucky I was to have them both in my life.

Because Tony was so beloved by all the students at my school, I became one of the cooler kids by association. Everyone knew my mother and Tony were an item, which made me feel like I had suddenly arrived somehow, that I wasn't out of place, that this was where I belonged.

Around this time, my father rented a picturesque country house in Roxbury, Connecticut, for a few years. When it was his turn to have us on weekends, he would pick us up after work and we would drive out there, arriving late on Friday nights. I loved falling asleep in the car squashed between my two sisters in the backseat, Tonto on my lap, the hum of the engine and voices fading in and out as slumber overtook me.

One Saturday in Connecticut my father casually asked me if I would like to try horseback-riding lessons. I jumped off the couch and immediately said yes! He found me a wonderful riding teacher named Anne; her barn wasn't far from the house. I fell in love with riding the moment I sat in the saddle. Right away I had a connection with horses; there was something so majestic about them, strong but gentle and sensitive, slightly frightening but at the same time so graceful and intelligent. I felt free and in control when I rode. I liked the challenge of learning how to post smoothly when they were trotting and how to move with them gracefully at a canter. Anne taught me how horses can sense fear, so if you are calm, they are calm, and it always amazed me how well they responded to my commands.

Anne was a wonderful teacher. She had been a show jumper and was quite an accomplished equestrian when she was younger. I think I reminded her of herself when she was my age.

She still had all her riding gear from when she was little, and when I got to enter my first competition, she let me borrow her show clothes. My dad, Vicky, my sisters, and even my grandparents had come to watch. It was a lead-line class, which meant you were literally lead by someone else holding on to the horse. Only three kids were entered in the competition. I was so excited to be in my very first horse show I forgot everything I had learned. I jutted my arms out straight instead of bending at the elbow, my heels lay loose in my stirrups when they should have been pressed down with my toes pointing upward, my mouth spread into a gaping smile while I pranced around the ring, looking more like I was on a merry-go-round than in a horse show. I came in third, earning a bright yellow ribbon, which I proudly hung in my room.

I took riding very seriously after that. My father gave my mother extra money so I could have one lesson a week after school, and I rode every weekend when we were in Roxbury. Any chance I got I would compete, adding each ribbon to the growing collection on my wall. I hung up a long piece of string on two nails and watched with pride as my collection of ribbons grew. Blue, red, yellow, white, pink, and green for sixth place. My mother didn't discourage me from riding, but she didn't encourage me either. She was afraid of horses and even more afraid that I would hurt myself: "Oh, honey, your body is your instrument! What if something happens to you?"

My father gave me my first riding helmet for my ninth birthday. A black velvet hard hat that was a little too big for my head, but with time I would grow into it. At that point in my riding career I was jumping (only foot-high hurdles), and Anne felt I was ready to compete in jumping. She took me to my first jumping competition. Still dressed in her riding gear, but now with my own helmet, I entered the ring full of jitters but with aching excitement.

I got to my first jump and landed perfectly, rounded the corner at a slow canter, but as I did so I felt my large helmet shift on my head; the brim was coming down into my eyes. I needed to move it so I could see. I took my hand off one rein and tried to push the brim up, but when I did, I steered the horse crooked into the next jump and fell to the ground, landing on my back. I was so stunned by the fall, I just lay there, not moving. Paramedics were called; they brought in a backboard, slid it under me, and strapped me on. Before I knew it I was in the ambulance headed to the hospital. I couldn't speak, which probably made them think I might have broken my back. In reality I was just badly winded. Anne couldn't go with me to the hospital because she was in charge of all the other kids from her barn who were competing. My father hadn't come with me that day, so I was on my own.

I had never been in an ambulance or a hospital. I was more scared of being alone, among all the hubbub happening around me. They cut off my jodhpurs from the ankle up, while they warned me not to move. They X-rayed my back, and there was no sign of injury. Soon afterward the East Indian doctor taking care of me handed me a small plastic cup and said in a thick accent, "Urinate in the cup and leave it in the bathroom." I was left alone in the room wondering what "urinate" meant. I had no idea. When the doctor came back in and saw me still sitting in the same place with the empty plastic cup in my hand, a blank stare on my face, he put two and two together and said, "Pee-pee in the cup." *Ohhh, why didn't you just say that in the first place?* I thought as a toddled off to the bathroom.

My father, Vicky, and Rachel arrived at the hospital just as I was coming out of the bathroom. They threw their arms around me, relieved that I was okay. While I was simply sore from the fall, the concern on my father's face told a different story, one more like panic, like something really bad *could* have happened. As we were leaving, my father took off his safari jacket and wrapped me up in it. All my clothes had been cut to pieces; the only things I had left to wear were my white cotton ankle socks. We padded out of the hospital together, and when my dad offered up a fast-food place for lunch, I knew he must have been really worried about me. We *never* ate fast food.

We went to McDonald's for the first time in my life. I had a cheeseburger, fries, and a chocolate milkshake. Sitting in a booth with my father's jacket hanging down past my ankles, my stock-inged feet dangling above the floor, I was the happiest kid in the joint.

The fall did not deter me from riding, and my father surprisingly encouraged me to get right back on the horse. I did so without fear or reservations. By the time I was ten, riding had become my life. I was interested in anything that had to do with horses. I begged my parents to send me to a horseback-riding sleepaway camp. My sisters and I had been going to sleepaway camp since I was three. The first one had been in Switzerland for three weeks. (Later, when I became a parent, I asked my mother in an incredulous tone what she could have possibly been thinking, sending a three-year-old to sleepaway camp. "You wanted to go! Your sisters were going and you insisted on going with them," she told me as if *I* were the crazy one.)

The years between three and six I don't recall going to camp, but by the age of seven I went with my sisters to a Christian Community Camp somewhere in Pennsylvania for three weeks; the year after that I went to the Harlemville Camp in Upstate New York with Rachel. All of these camps had a crunchy-granola feel, like our Steiner schools. Most of them were on farms where we milked cows and made our own butter, picked vegetables in the biodynamic garden, ate only healthy, organic foods and natural sugars, from fruit and honey.

At ten I put my foot down. I wanted to ride horses.

We found a camp in the Adirondacks called Camp MacCready. My father signed me up for the first four-week session. I loved it so much that when I found out I would be missing the extra two weeks most kids were staying for, I called him begging to let me stay.

I loved the routine of getting up in the morning and caring for the horse I was assigned to: mucking out the stall, grooming, and feeding. I loved hearing the bell clang for breakfast, walking down through the woods to the dining hall with my friends. I loved the order of activities for the day: riding lessons, tennis, track and field, archery, lunch, rest period, more riding, dinner, singalongs by the bonfire at night, counselors telling ghost stories, sneaking out of our cabins in the middle of the night to the boys' camp, canoodling with them under the moonlight by the lake and then raiding the kitchen.

I even loved inspection, when the counselors would come and examine the bunks to see whose was the cleanest, because whoever won got to choose the evening activity. I loved the competitiveness. Horse shows on weekends, trips to the Dairy Queen on our way home while we sang on the bus, and then just at the right spot we would burst into our camp song, so that by the time we pulled into the driveway the last verse rang out: "But the camp we love the most of all is Camp MacCready!"

I loved every single thing about camp.

On the last day, as we were standing by the homeward-bound bus with our packed trunks, we would cry and throw our arms around one another, so sad to leave. Before getting on the bus to depart, I would tearfully kiss each horse goodbye. My friends and I wrote endless letters to one another all year long, excited that we would be one year older when we got back to camp the next summer. I went to Camp MacCready for five summers in a row, until I was fourteen. They were among the best times of my childhood.

As fifth grade wound down and I looked forward to heading off to Camp MacCready, my mother graduated from Eurythmy school. I assumed she would begin teaching in Spring Valley, or somewhere nearby. I hadn't given much thought to what she would do after her training. I was about to turn eleven and I was going to camp; that was all that mattered to me. I was going to spend the rest of August with my father in the Hamptons, where he had rented a small farmhouse in Amagansett for the month.

As I was packing to get ready for camp, my mother came into my room and sat down on my bed. She cleared her throat and told me that she had been offered the opportunity of a lifetime. She had been asked to go to Nuremberg, Germany, to work with some of the best Eurythmists in the world.

"Isn't it exciting, honey? We're moving to Nuremberg!"

I couldn't comprehend what she was saying. Germany? My body reacted like a popped balloon limply deflating to the floor, and then the floodgates broke open as my eyes filled with tears and I flew into a rage. Screaming, flailing my arms in the air, pounding my fist into the carpet, hyperventilating as I writhed on the floor.

"I'm not going, I'm not going, you can't make me go!" I screamed.

I ran out of my room into the kitchen. I wrapped my arms around the refrigerator so tight they turned purple. "You're going to have to cut my hands off to make me move there—I'm never letting go!" I wailed as I held on tighter to the yellow Frigidaire.

I was inconsolable. My mother tried everything to calm me down until she became enraged herself. "Stop this nonsense right now, Julianna. We are going and that's that. Don't be ridiculous!" And she stormed off, leaving me strapped to the fridge, listless and spent.

Why did she want to ruin my perfectly good life? How could she be so selfish? Only her life mattered; mine meant nothing. And what about my father? When would I see him if we lived in Germany? And Alexandra? What about Tonto and my friends? My teachers? What about Tony?

It turned out Tony was so in love with my mother that he had quit his job at the Green Meadow School and was moving to Germany with us. Well, that was something, but it wasn't enough. Nothing could ever be enough.

When we both calmed down, my mother explained that she couldn't go on spending her life in the suburbs. "I need to expand my horizons, honey, can't you see that? I'm an artist. This is no place for an artist."

She had never planned to live in Spring Valley longer than she had to. "I always knew that once my training was over we would leave," she said. No one had ever let *me* in on that plan. I never knew that our life in Spring Valley had a ticking clock.

I went to camp that summer with the Nuremberg cloud hanging over me, not quite comprehending what was ahead. I decided to ignore it; maybe my mother would change her mind, maybe my father would stop her from taking us, maybe someone would save me. I hung on to that hope and threw myself into my camp activities, lapping up every minute like a thirsty puppy.

After camp I went to Amagansett to be with my father, Vicky, and my sisters. We had been coming to the Hamptons every August since we got back to the States. Renting little farmhouses in Bridgehampton, East Hampton, or Amagansett. I loved the ritual of our family being together for one month a year. I learned to swim in that unpredictable ocean, my father telling me: "Always go with the tide, honey, you will never drown if you go with the tide. You might get swept down shore, but if you don't fight the water, it will carry you."

I adhered to that logic and would sit back even in the roughest of tides, trusting that his words would carry me to shore. They always did.

My sisters and I spent hours dodging those waves. I would run back to our spot on the beach, flop down on our fluffy beach towels blissfully exhausted, and doze off in the afternoon sun, hearing the distant voices of my siblings and my father as I was lulled into sleep. To this day, when I am having trouble falling asleep at night, that's where I go in my mind, picturing the vast sandy stretch of beach, hearing the waves crash down on the shore, closing my eyes while my salt-soaked body drinks in the rays of the sun, knowing my sisters and father are right next to me. My happy place. My safe place.


The house my father rented wasn't fancy. At that time the Hamptons were much more relaxed; you didn't have to be a millionaire to rent a place for the summer. There was an innocence back then;

even though there were fancy estates tucked away, the Hamptons didn't have the upper-class affectations they seem to have adopted more recently. We rode our bikes in shorts and flip-flops to the beach and into town after dinner, gathered on the sidewalk to eat our ice cream with other kids, had barbecues in the backyard with fresh corn from the farmers' stand on Route 27.

August in the Hamptons was all about family and friends, Saturday night games of charades in the living room. Or KEEK, an Austrian game one of Vicky's ex-boyfriends taught us. It involved candy from the penny store. We would lay all the candy out in a large circle, then one person would leave the room while the rest of us picked the one piece of candy that would be the KEEK. We would invite the person back into the room, and the idea was to take as many pieces of candy as you could before landing on the chosen KEEK. The player would strategically lower their hand over each piece, but when they landed on the wrong one, we would all yell "KEEK" and their turn was over.

When Vicky's parents came to visit, Boris, her father, who had been a seven-time backgammon champion in Yugoslavia and had been teaching me backgammon since I was six, would challenge me to a tournament. He was an imposing figure, just under six foot four, with a full head of white, wavy hair and a thick accent. He played backgammon only on wooden boards, his small dice kept in his shirt pocket at all times. He would slam the playing pieces down on the board with tremendous force, making a loud bang for dramatic effect. He always won. The one time I beat him, when I was eleven, he held me captive at the table for four hours until he won five games in row. My father had to come and rescue me. "Boris, she's just a kid, it's time to stop now," he said gently. The idea that an eleven-year-old girl had beat him was humiliating. Boris had to prove to himself and everyone there that he was boss.

While we were in the Hamptons that summer, my mother rented out our home and ventured off to Nuremberg to find us a place to live and set us up for the coming school year. I assumed that she had found someone to care for Tonto until we got back from Germany. It wasn't until I saw my mother again that I found out she had just abandoned him, figuring someone in the neighborhood would find him and give him a home. The same way she thought our birds would be fine out in the wild, she figured Tonto could take care of himself. The image of my sweet cat, who had brought me so much happiness, alone in the streets with no shelter, no warm bed to sleep in at night, not knowing where his next meal would come from, shattered me. I couldn't believe she could be so thoughtless. What upset me the most was the idea of Tonto thinking I was the one who had abandoned him. The only way to find comfort when I thought of my cat was to pretend that he *had* found a new home and that someone was feeding him. I had no choice but to live in that fantasy and prayed that he knew I would never have done that to him.

My father had bought two one-way tickets for me and Rachel to join my mother in Germany at the end of August. I know he wasn't thrilled with the idea of us leaving, but I don't recall any conversations where we implored him not to let her do this. I don't remember asking him anything about it. I think I was always scared to talk about my mother with him because I knew he disapproved of all her choices. I didn't have to ask; I could see it on his face. There was enough drama in my life when I was with my mother, I didn't want there to be drama when I was with my father, so I stayed silent.

All three sisters were there that last night in Amagansett. Rachel was playing her guitar and the three of us were singing *I'm leaving on a jet plane, don't know when I'll be back again* . . . We sang in harmony; I liked to pretend we were the Simon sisters. Carly Simon was my favorite singer, and thanks to Alexandra, I listened to all her albums over and over again in her room.

We were crying as we sang, knowing that in the morning Rachel and I would be flying off to an unimaginable life in Germany. In the middle of our song, the phone rang. It was my mother. She was crying, and she told my dad her plans had changed, Nuremberg was awful—her exact words: "I couldn't bear that place, I felt like Hitler was in every corner."

My mother erred on the side of drama at all times. Germany unhinged her, there was no way she was going to have her children speaking German in a German school. She instructed my father to change our plane tickets to England. In her desperation to get out of Nuremberg, she had flown to England and found a job teaching Eurythmy to mentally challenged kids back in Sussex, where we had lived five years before.

"The kids can go back to the Michael Hall School, I have found us a temporary apartment, but school starts in two days, so they need to be here by tomorrow."

My father grumbled something under his breath and shook his head in disbelief. My mother's decisions exhausted him. I don't know why he didn't say, "Well, it sounds like you don't have a home set up for our children and they need a solid foundation, so why don't you just let me take them? You can't expect me to change plans at the drop of a hat and send them off to uncertainty." Instead, he called the travel agent and that was that. Rachel and I were on a flight to England the next morning. No questions asked.

## FIVE

# let's just stick it out for the year

We disembarked at Gatwick Airport early in the morning, half asleep on New York time. When we got to passport control, the customs officer asked us why we were coming to England.

"To go to school," we said. "Our mom has a job teaching kids and we are going to the Michael Hall School."

"Do you have papers?" he asked.

"Umm . . . no."

"Is your mother picking you up?"

"Yes."

"Where is she?"

We didn't know where she was, we didn't clearly understand where *we* were, but we assured him she would be there soon. She wasn't. No one had given us a number to call or an address to go to. We had no money. Rachel was fourteen, I was eleven; we didn't have the foggiest idea what we were supposed to say or do. We just shuffled our sleepy feet, jet-lagged and hungry, staring at the floor. We waited there by the customs officers for a while, but there was no sign of my mother. Finally they took us to a fluorescent-lit room at the back of the baggage claim area and told us to stay there. Before they left they told us we had two months, they even stamped it in our passports. TWO MONTHS!

Rachel and I couldn't figure out what that meant, two months of what? Had we said the wrong thing? Should we not have told them Mom had a job? Was that illegal? What papers were we supposed to have and why had no one told us? I began to panic. I wanted to cry but I was trying so hard to be brave. Rachel tried to calm me down, imitating their accents and saying in a deep voice: "TWO MONTHS!"

I don't know how long we waited. It felt like a lifetime. Just when I started to imagine what I would look like in an orange jumpsuit, shackled to my sister on my way to prison, we heard a hysterical woman running down the hallway. We peered out the glass window, and there she was, our mother, wild, unruly black hair flying in all directions, sobbing and shrieking at the same time: "WHERE ARE THEY? WHAT HAVE YOU DONE TO MY CHILDREN?" She was in a state, enacting quite a dramatic scene for this sleepy airport in the middle of Sussex.

Turned out my mother, who was not used to driving on the left side of the road, nor did she understand her new car, a green Citroën that had a stick shift but no clutch, kept driving in circles unable to enter the airport. She couldn't figure out the roundabouts that are so common in England. She would see an entrance, and the next thing she knew she was on the A22 again, heading back where she came from. Round and round she went, until finally she couldn't take it any longer. She found herself crying on the side of the road. Some kind soul must have helped her find her way to the parking lot, but at that point she was already over an hour late to pick us up and we weren't at baggage claim when she came charging in to get us.

She was volcanic by the time she was told where we were being held. A ferocious howl came spewing out of her, not something the tight-lipped British officers were accustomed to. Our mouths hung open in embarrassment as we witnessed her. My immediate response was to try to calm her down. The customs officials were too stunned to do anything but hand us over. She wrapped her arms around us and wept into our necks. "Oh my God! I thought I would never see you again!"

My mother was still crying when we got to the car. I clocked the way the Citroën rose up on its tires when she turned the ignition key.

"I'm just so happy, so happy to see you!" she kept repeating. It had been over two months since we had been with her. As we drove toward East Grinstead she began rapidly talking about her nightmare in Nuremberg and how relieved she was that she found a job in England.

"I mean we couldn't go home, we rented out the house, where was I supposed to go? Let's just stick it out for the year." Her tears were letting up and her smile was coming out as we pulled into a gloomy-looking, large institution-like structure. This was the Peridure Home School, a boarding school for mentally challenged children.

I was so relieved not to be in jail that nothing she said really landed until we opened the door to our new home. I knew how bad it was when we walked into the kitchen, because my mother, who like my father was a health food fanatic, had stocked the cupboards with chocolate biscuits and other sugary treats to distract us. Something was surely amiss.

The "flat" was part of the school. My sister and I were to share a tiny room with horsehair cots shoved into the corners, barely enough space to walk between. Mom had a dank room at one end of the cramped corridor; the other room belonged to a hippie couple who were studying biodynamic farming. There was one small bathroom at the other end of the hallway that the five of us were to share. I don't remember much about the hippie couple other than that they kept to themselves for the most part and smelled a bit like manure. I'm sure sharing living quarters with two American kids and their eccentric mother was not ideal for them either.

The apartment was dark and dreary, shaded by large trees on every side, light struggling to shine through the windows. We were right next to the dorm rooms, an easy escape for the kids living in them. One day I came home from school to find one of the students in my bedroom. She had gone through our paint-chipped dresser and was dancing with a pair of my underwear on her head. I had no words.

Five years had passed since we had last attended the Michael Hall School. A few things had changed: uniforms were no longer required. The upper school had no formal dress code, but the lower school insisted all the girls wear skirts. I didn't own a skirt.

The day after we arrived was our first day of school. I alerted my mother that I had nothing to wear. Trying to make everything seem okay, my mother cheerfully handed me her denim skirt with snaps up the front. "Well, what am I supposed to wear with this, Mom? I don't have the right shoes or the right top, I just have jeans and sneakers," I snapped.

My mother suggested I wear my tan leather sandals and my riding jacket. "It will look just like a blazer, perfect," she stated.

With it already being September, an autumn chill in the air, my sandals were too summery to wear without socks. I put on my navy blue knee socks, my riding jacket, and my mother's big skirt. I cinched the waist with a belt, doubled over the extra material so the skirt wouldn't sweep the floor, and headed downstairs for breakfast. A creeping feeling of nausea followed me to the kitchen.

I stood in front of my mother and my sister and burst into tears.

"I look like a Hasidic Jew!" I cried.

There was a moment of silence, and then they couldn't help it, they both burst out laughing. They tried to compose themselves and tell me I really looked fine, but I knew they were lying. I wanted to crawl into a hole and die.

My mother promised she would take me shopping after school and find me the appropriate clothes. In the meantime I had to get in the car and go to school looking like Bielke, from *Fiddler on the Roof. Let's just stick it out for the year.* My mother's painful words echoed in my ear.

When my mother dropped us off at school she stayed in the car, telling us as we opened the door, "Be brave, go find your classroom, before you know it you will feel right at home." And off she drove to work.

We were late, as usual. I was in a dreamlike state, jet-lagged and still shocked I suppose by the fast turnaround. Two days before this moment I had been with my father, enjoying the comforts of his company, the warm, salty beach air surrounding me, the calm, reassuring feeling of familiarity. Now I was being tossed to the wolves, fending for myself in the cold, damp, misty morning of West Sussex, trudging up a gravel path I no longer recognized. There was an eerie silence, no sign of a living soul except my sister and me.

As we made our way toward the school we heard music coming out of what looked like the main hall. We ventured over, following the sound, peeked our heads inside the door, and were summoned in by a stern-looking teacher, finger to her lips silencing us before we even spoke. All the students were sitting in chairs facing the stage, where the welcoming ceremony was in progress. We were ushered to a side bench, and each time we tried to ask the teacher a question she shushed us with her pinched lips and pointy finger. We sat down on the hard wooden bench. Rachel took my hand and I squeezed as tight as I could without breaking her fingers.

After assembly all the students rushed off to their classrooms. The witchy teacher finally let us speak and told us to go to the main building. We followed the marching crowd. Rachel was much more familiar with the school than I was. She was old enough to remember some things from the last time we had been there. Now that she was in ninth grade, she was allowed to wear pants to school. I remember so clearly wanting to be in her shoes. She went off to the upper school building in search of her classroom and maybe a few friends she could reconnect with. I, in my Hasidic ensemble, hesitantly shuffled my feet in the direction of what looked like the middle school building. I had no idea where I was; the last time I had been to this school I was in kindergarten, and that building was way up on a hill in a completely different area.

I stood facing the front doors, trying to find the courage to walk in while a lump in my throat started to rise. I turned around quickly and glanced at the hedges in front of me. I couldn't bear the thought of anyone seeing me cry, and the last thing I wanted was to draw attention to myself. While I stood staring at the hedges, willing myself not to break down in tears, I heard someone call out to me. I turned around with a glimmer of hope in my heart that someone had recognized me from kindergarten, but when the redheaded girl who called for me saw my face she said, "Oops, wrong person, sorry," and went running off with a gaggle of girls.

Eventually I found the courage to make it to the first floor of the building. I asked a teacher where the sixth-grade classroom was.

"Well, there are two, are you in six-A or six-B?" the teacher asked.

I had no idea. I shrugged.

"Six-A is on this floor to the right, Mr. Ashe's class. Six-B is upstairs to the left, Mr. Masters's class."

I nodded and scuttled over to 6A. I poked my head into Mr. Ashe's class and saw a large man with a bushy red beard and a full head of ginger hair. He looked like a Viking and had a bellowing, deep voice. He was shouting at the students to be quiet and get to their desks. His loud voice and bullish manner stopped me in my tracks; he was frightening. I slowly stepped away, backing out of the door, praying he didn't see me, and ran up the stairs to 6B.

I stood in the doorway of Mr. Masters's class. He was a tall, willowy man with gray hair, wire-rimmed glasses, and a gentle disposition.

"Hello," he said with a smile. "And who might you be?"

I told him my name, but nothing registered on his face. For a moment he stood still, frozen in midsentence, then, after a few moments of silence, he smiled again and said, "Welcome to six-B, take a seat."

I found out years later that my mother had never enrolled us; she hadn't even called the school to let them know we were coming back. She just assumed that since we had been there five years ago we could walk right in as if we had never left. We weren't on any roster or roll-call sheet, school fees hadn't been talked about, let alone paid, and no one said a thing.

Day after day I searched for the one person I remembered from my time in kindergarten, Nina. I didn't know her last name. I had been so little the last time I had seen her, but I was determined to try to find her, thinking that if I did I might be able to rekindle our friendship.

My search seemed futile; no one I asked claimed to have heard of her. Maybe she had moved away? No one seemed to know who I was talking about. When I finally gave up the search, I focused my energy on the girls in 6A. I became obsessed with them. At morning recess and lunchtime I would watch the girls in that class, peering into their classroom from the hallway. They all seemed so much cooler than me and the girls in my class. I cursed the day I chose 6B.

The girls in 6A all looked like they were best friends. I watched as they laughed and shared secrets I couldn't hear. They also looked much older than me. They had budding breasts, and some of them even had curvy hips. I overheard them talking about periods. Periods? I was shocked. None of my friends in America had gotten their periods. I was a tomboy when I was eleven, like most of my friends back home. I was straight and narrow, flat as a board and much smaller than these girls. I was into sports and Adidas sneakers.

They had perfect Farah Fawcett haircuts, "wings" we used to call them; you could just flip your head and your hair fell perfectly around your face, feathering back like little angel wings. With my long, wavy, thick hair (the frizz started at fourteen), I was in a constant state of envy. I watched these girls intensely, yearning to be part of their clique. I wanted to look like them, sound like them, and dress like them. I was too shy and embarrassed to try to talk to any of them, partly because of my looks and inappropriate attire, and partly because of my American accent. I had worked so hard to perfect it the last time we moved back from England, and now I was determined to get my English accent back.

I began to resign myself to the fact that I would never be invited to their party. I needed to start finding friends in 6B. I imagine my 6B classmates must have thought I was a bit of a snob, never interacting with anyone, or even trying to befriend them. What was the point? We were only there for the year and then we would be going home; it made more sense to me not to get attached. But I was lonely. Rachel had reconnected with her best friend, Esther. I was envious of her ability to seamlessly blend in; at least that's how it looked to me. Through Esther she had a group of friends right away. She had a social life I longed for, and she got to wear jeans. *Oh but to be, oh but to be . . . my older sister,* Carly Simon rang out in my head.

When I finally made an effort, the girls in 6B turned out to be very sweet. Mary Hitchcox, Alison Adams, Deb Ashe, and Christina Goodwin; they were kind to me, and once I got to know them they became my friends. Mary Hitchcox remembered me from kindergarten, and one day we were reminiscing about all the kids that had been in our class and I asked her if she remembered Nina. Mary gave me a funny look and nonchalantly said, "Oh yes, I remember you and Rowena always called each other Nina, I never understood that, she's in six-A."

My heart was beating so fast I could feel it in my throat as I ran over to 6A during lunch that day to see if I could tell which one was Rowena. I sucked up some air for courage and walked into their classroom. I saw a tall, beautiful girl with straight, light brown hair, fringe (bangs) that feathered out perfectly around her huge almond-shaped brown eyes. She had breasts and a tiny waist, and perfectly small, rounded hips. I was immediately intimidated by her. I shuffled over to her, looking at the ground, afraid I would lack the courage if I caught anyone staring at me. I asked her if she remembered me from kindergarten and explained our "Nina" exchange. She threw her head back, laughing sweetly, and told me she did remember and couldn't believe it was me. From that day onward we were inseparable, except of course that I had chosen 6B so we were never in the same classes. Every recess and at lunchtime I ran over to her classroom, and after school we would walk back to her house and hang out.

Rowena's family was the ideal family, in my opinion. Their house was only yards away from the school, just a short walk from the main building on Priory Road. The house was called Priory Mead and had an inviting large garden in the back that her mother tended beautifully. Her brother and two sisters were all two years apart, Eunice being the eldest, then Adrian, Rowena, and Karin. Her parents took in boarding students, so their house was always full of life. Kids ranging in age from eight to eighteen wafted in and out of the rooms. The boarding students were from Germany, Sweden, France, Holland, Switzerland, always interesting and different from anything I knew. Dinner at Priory Mead was no fewer than ten people around the dinner table and always at six o'clock. I longed to be invited over every day of the week and have sleepovers on the weekends. I would wait with bated breath to see if I was invited for dinner, and if I was I went out of my way to help her mother, Angela, prepare the meal, set the table, clear the dishes, wash them if I could, hoping my assistance would convince them to invite me back the next night.

I wanted to be just like Rowena. I even went so far as to try to copy her fringe. One night, when my mother wasn't home, I asked Rachel if she would cut my hair into bangs. She thought it was a great idea and with the kitchen scissors lopped off the front part of my hair, leaving a huge bushy hedge on my forehead that took two years to grow out.

Physically, Rowena was much more advanced than I was, and

the upper school boys were crazy about her. I was considered more her little sidekick. When we went to parties, the boys were all vying for her attention; no one gave me a second glance. I sat and watched her slow-dance and even witnessed her first make-out session with Jeroen Markies, a tall, strikingly handsome boy in ninth grade who came from a Dutch family. Years later I would be her maid of honor at their wedding.

Because we lived at the Peridure Home School, I never invited anyone to my house. I was too embarrassed. It was far easier for me to integrate into Rowena's life than she into mine. And when I was in her world, I pretended that mine didn't exist. I allowed myself to live in a fantasy when I was with Rowena; missing my father, my home, my school lessened in her company.

About four months into sixth grade, my mother finally found us an apartment. She moved us to a place called Hoathly Hill, in a village much farther away from the school called West Hoathly.

Our new dwelling was a small one-bedroom flat with uneven floors. My mother slept in the living room; my sister and I shared a small bedroom. The kitchen was our communal space. Highly inadequate compared to the house we'd left behind in Spring Valley. The floors were so slanted that pouring a full glass of milk, we learned quickly, was impossible. We shoved matchbooks under the kitchen table legs to try to even out the surface, but nothing worked. The bright side was that it was our own; we didn't have to share the bathroom with strangers and no one was rummaging through our drawers, dancing with our undergarments on their heads. It was definitely a step up from our previous residence.

Our apartment was on the second floor of a large housing complex that must have been one huge home at some point but now was divided into ten separate flats. Surrounding the large main house were several smaller houses, most of which housed Waldorf teachers, students, and their children. The place was brimming with Anthroposophists. They seemed to float about the property with their heads in the clouds, their speech slightly affected with a lilting quality, almost singing their words rather than just speaking normally. Everyone in the community was a health food enthusiast like my mother. Antibiotics were frowned upon. The holistic approach to any ailment was always first choice. Arnica cream, arnica ointment, arnica pills were always on hand at our house. If I had a headache my mother would massage my feet; if I had a fever she would say this was my body telling me I needed to rest. Chamomile tea with honey beat out cough syrup every time. The first time I ever had an antibiotic was for strep throat when I was fourteen. The idea was to build the body's immune system so it could fight for itself. There was no television. "It drains the creative forces," they would say.

West Hoathly itself was a sleepy little village with one grocer and little else. I think there may have been a pub and maybe a fish and chip shop, but it wasn't a center for socializing. We would do all our food shopping in Forest Row, and if we needed anything more than food we would venture into East Grinstead or Tunbridge Wells, much larger towns than these quaint little villages but quite a drive from our new home. Hanging out at Rowena's after school was no longer an option; our new apartment was in the opposite direction and a good forty-minute drive from school.

I didn't like living at Hoathly Hill, even though it was better than the Peridure Home School. I found it depressing. I was desperate to find something to cling to, something that would drive my thoughts away from the constant ache in my belly yearning for home. There were two girls who lived in one of the houses on the periphery of the property, and I found out they both owned horses. One of the girls, Paige, was my age, and her sister, Loraine, was a few years older. I gravitated toward their house every day, walking through the back gardens of the property, dodging the biodynamic vegetables at my feet. Each day I garnered enough strength to go a little farther until I finally met up with them and shyly asked about their horses. They were delighted I was interested and brought me to their stable, about two miles down the road. When they saw how well I interacted with their horses we bonded instantly. They let me help take care of the horses, probably thrilled that they had found someone willing to do the hard tasks without asking for anything in return, except on occasion the opportunity to ride. We became fast friends, and the stable became my new home.

One day, when the three of us were out in the woods playing, I spotted a pony way off in the marshy field beyond the wooded area. I slowly started toward the pony, who looked wild and scruffy, un-cared for and filthy, marsh mud caked to his coat. His forelock had grown long over his eyes and his mane was scrappy, hanging down past his neck. I could see he was a beautiful bay pony, dark brown with a black mane and tail. I kept inching closer to him, very slowly, I didn't want to scare him away. I held my hand out to him and started singing very softly. To my surprise he didn't move; he al-lowed me to get so close to him I was able to pet him.

He wore no halter, there were no signs of ownership. I looked to see where he may have come from, and off in the distance, a long way from the marsh, I spotted a barn. I started to walk in that direc-tion, sure that this pony must belong to someone. As I walked, the pony began to follow me, occasionally gently butting the backs of my thighs with his head as if urging me to move faster. We walked like this all the way across the field. I was nervous heading up to the nearby barn but too curious to stop. I popped my head in the barn door and saw a farmer working in there. I asked if he was the owner, and he told me he was but that the pony was too stubborn, they had let him run free in the marsh. He was declared untrain-able; no one paid him much attention. The pony's name was Bar-onet. I quickly asked the man if I could try to train him. I said I would take good care of him and have him back to the farmer at the end of the school year. I don't know what I was thinking, or how I summoned up the courage for such a huge undertaking, but the farmer gave me an amused look and told me Baronet was mine if my parents agreed.

I rushed back to our flat with butterflies in my stomach, so ex-cited to tell my mother. I had rehearsed my speech on my way home:

I could keep him in the extra stall at the barn where the other girls kept their horses. I would take care of him all by myself, I knew exactly what to do, and I would never, ever ask for any help. Paige and Loraine told me that they wouldn't charge much for boarding him, and they assured me they would help me train him. All I needed to pay for was food. They had extra bridles and saddles they could lend me.

When I burst through the front door, I started talking so fast my mother had to ask me to slow down. I ran through my list . . . "how easy, perfect setup with the barn and Paige and Loraine, how she wouldn't have to do a thing . . ." My mother was worried about the expense of the food, but she could see how elated I was. This was the happiest I had been since moving back to England, this could be the one thing that saved me, this could be the one thing that could make a horrible year into a wonderful year.

She called my father and asked him for a little extra money so I could have the pony. He said yes.

I woke up every morning at five and walked the two miles down to the stable. I mucked out Baronet's stall, groomed him, fed him, and tried to ride him. In the beginning it was rough going. The poor thing had lived out on the marsh for so long he wasn't used to eating oats or sleeping under a roof. His severe diarrhea and stomach problems warranted a vet visit, but I knew that would cost too much, so I relied on the girls for their wisdom, and continued every day with much determination. I fed him by hand, standing in front of him, his soft, warm nose in my palm. I spoke to him as if he could understand me, and slowly, one handful at a time, he ate his oats and began to recover from marsh life.

I was so focused on getting him healthy that the hard work didn't bother me; in fact it helped ease my anxiety. I had been having stomach problems of my own, something I developed when we moved back to England. I would be ravenous and try to eat, but every time I did I felt a strange acid form in my belly and the food wouldn't go down. I remember my mother taking us to a burger joint, something that was allowed only on special occasions. This was a regular school night. My mother treated us now and then to a classic American meal: burgers and fries, trying to make us feel less homesick, I suppose. Sadly burgers and fries in Sussex tasted nothing like they did in America. It was still a treat though, to eat out; we didn't have that kind of money, so it always felt like a special occasion.

I ordered a burger, but when the food came and I dug in, I couldn't swallow; when I tried I felt the food move back up my throat. I would get a burning sensation in my stomach that left me writhing on the floor in pain. I looked longingly at my burger but couldn't eat it. This sensation would come and go; sometimes I would be fine and able to consume a meal. The acidic feeling crept up on me at odd times, and I was never prepared for it. The pangs of hunger were easier to deal with than the burning sensation, so I just wouldn't eat. Looking back I am amazed that my mother never took me to a doctor to see what the problem was and how to rectify it. She would give me chamomile tea before bed and tell me I would feel better in the morning. We never went to the doctor. I'm not sure we even had one in England. I know for sure we didn't have a dentist; I went two years without visiting one.

Baronet took my focus off myself. He was all that mattered. A few weeks after caring for him, my stomach issues subsided completely. The hollow ache in my belly dissipated, I woke up every morning excited to see him, and after school I ran down to the stable to be with him.

Once his health was restored I tried to train and ride him. Every time I got on his back, he would buck me off and bolt as far as he could go. I spent the first few months thrown to the ground every morning or hanging on to him for dear life as he galloped up the road, away from the stable, refusing my commands.

In time, with the help of Paige and Loraine, he learned to trust me and I was finally able to ride him. He didn't shy away anymore when I saddled him up. He stood still and allowed me to secure myself in the saddle, waiting for the small push from my calves signaling for him to walk. We made a good team. I even managed to enter him in some local horse shows. We didn't win much of anything, a ribbon here or there, but we had come such a long way and he had given me the biggest gift I could ask for: a sense of purpose and belonging.

Giving Baronet back at the end of the school year was excruciating. In my haste to take care of him, I hadn't thought about the consequences of not having him in my life anymore. My heart broke into a million pieces. I had no idea what to do with my emotions. On the one hand I was so desperate to get back home and see my father, go to camp, and have my life back to normal; on the other, saying goodbye to this pony was harder than anything I had ever done. I couldn't fathom not seeing him again—all that hard work, all that care and love, what would I do without him? I had no choice, I rode him back to the barn he had come from and returned him to his owner. His coat was shiny and healthy, forelock trimmed, his mane perfectly brushed along with his tail. I whispered in his furry black ear that I would be back, tears running down my face. I think we both understood that this would never happen. I reasoned with him and told him at least we'd had each other for the time that we did. I told myself I would have to be okay with that. I couldn't stop thinking about Tonto, abandoned on Renfrew Road, imagining the worst of me.

My mother hadn't figured out where we were going to live that following year. With school ending and her girls flying back to New York, everything was up in the air. She wanted to stay in England; I wanted to go home to Spring Valley, to our life as we knew it, to my dad and Alexandra. We couldn't keep living at Hoathly Hill; even she hated it there. She told us that if she couldn't find us a decent place to live we would go back to Spring Valley. My heart soared; I took that to mean we were going home. I packed my bag and flew to New York. Alexandra helped me pack up my trunk for camp as she did every summer, ironing labels onto my clothes, organizing my camp list, making sure everything was neatly folded. Off I went, thrilled to be back in the States, elated to be going to camp.

Halfway through the six-week session parents were invited for visiting day to see our progress. My father came and watched me ride, amazed at how far I had come. I was jumping three-foot fences by then. We did archery together, and played tennis; he toured the camp with me. Parents were allowed to take their kids out for a decent meal, so my dad took me to a nice restaurant and halfway through lunch I asked him where I would be living come September, looking at him with hopeful eyes, ready for the answer I thought I already knew.

He looked down at his food and quietly said, "Well, kiddo, looks like you're staying in England."

I couldn't believe it. I didn't want to believe it. I was so sure we would be back home.

"Your mother is putting the house in Spring Valley up for sale; she doesn't want to live there again. But she told me she found a very suitable home for you to live in in Forest Row, close to the school. This year will be so much better than last year."

I withdrew in defeat. I knew I couldn't protest to my father; I didn't want our remaining time to be ruined. I also knew that if I complained or spoke ill of my mother I would just be cementing what he already felt about her: she was selfish, self-centered, and put her needs first at all times. I wanted my father to love her, to think she was a wonderful mother. I'm not sure why I was always protecting her from my true feelings when I was around my dad. I didn't want to burden him with my problems; he always seemed so overwhelmed by all the things he had to take care of already, I didn't want him to think that I was a problem. I wanted him to see me as only easygoing so we could just be together without any anxiety. If I stayed silent, I couldn't condemn my mother. If I didn't condemn her in front of him, maybe he wouldn't think less of her.

But I was never going home again, that much I understood.

——

That summer after camp, when I was twelve, I went to East Hampton, where my father had rented a gray-shingled house with a bubble gum pink living room. After ten years together, my father and Vicky had decided to get married. They had rented the same house a few summers before and planned to get married there. This would be my father's third marriage.

When Rachel and I had come back from England, my father gathered the three of us in Alexandra's bedroom to tell us about the pending nuptials.

"Why?" we all asked. "You've been together for ten years, why now?"

I didn't like the idea of it. As long as my father wasn't remarried there was a glimmer of hope that one day my parents would get back together. I knew it was silly to think like that, but I couldn't help myself. I had always secretly hung on to the dream that they would come to their senses and reunite. It wasn't that I didn't like Vicky. I did—she was always fun to be around—but she wasn't my mother, and the way I saw it, she stood in the way of our family's reunion.

"Well, Vicky has always wanted to marry, and it's helpful to be married for tax purposes," my father said.

I could tell that he was waffling. What a bizarre answer to a simple question. Shouldn't he have just said, "Because I love her, and she loves me, and we want to be married"?

He put all the onus on Vicky, which made me think he didn't want to marry her; he was just doing it to please her. And taxes? What? I didn't even know what taxes were at that age.

"Are you going to have kids?" I asked.

"No, I don't think so, honey. We talked about it once, a long time ago. When she wanted to I wasn't ready, and when I wanted to she wasn't ready, and now it's probably too late." Vicky was already forty-eight, three years older than my dad.

The wedding was planned for August.

I wasn't happy about the marriage, but I was, strangely, looking forward to a wedding. I had never been to one before, having only seen them in the movies. Weddings to me sounded like fun, and I was kind of impressed that I would be the daughter of the groom; something about that would no doubt be special.

When Vicky arrived at the house and saw that the owner, Faith Popcorn (thus we called it "The Popcorn House"), had painted the living room bubble gum pink, she burst into tears. "I can't get married in that!" she exclaimed. Vicky was all about appearances. She dabbled in interior design and was very particular about how things looked. Her aesthetic was English charm, chintz-covered walls, double-backed silk curtains, antique tables and chairs, silver frames of various shapes and sizes on every surface, with pictures chronicling their life together. She was not going to get married in a bubble gum pink living room.

Instead they decided to get married at the 1770 House on Main Street in East Hampton. It was a charming inn that dated back to 1663, with the original architecture and colonial charm. This made Vicky very happy.

She found a white Mexican wedding dress, simple and pretty with a square neckline and bell sleeves. My father would wear a white dinner jacket and gray flannel trousers. Vicky took us shopping. I picked out a pale purple cotton skirt with a light blue billowy blouse; Rachel, a strappy red sundress with a full skirt. Alexandra was eighteen and had lived with Vicky for six years by this time, so her outfit reflected her opinion: jeans and a blue silk kimono.

What I remember most about their wedding was asking Rachel if I could borrow her black eyeliner. I had never worn makeup before. Rachel helped me put it on, just a little under my eyes. I thought it made my green eyes pop, I felt so sophisticated. When we went outside to get into the car, my father looked at me and said, "What's on your face?"

"Just a little eyeliner."

"You're too young to wear makeup, Julianna." He turned to my sister. "She's too young to wear that!" Rachel shrugged. That comment stayed with me all day. I kept wondering if he was mad that I was wearing eyeliner. Or upset that I looked so grown up. I loved the way I looked. I couldn't believe how just a little eyeliner could transform my face. I walked into the 1770 House feeling a little older, a little prettier, and somewhat worried that my father had disapproved.

During the actual ceremony, I don't remember my father smiling very much. Instead, he had a pained expression on his face, like he had just sucked on a lemon. It wasn't a huge wedding, maybe sixty people. Vicky's family was there, her mother and father, a bunch of their friends. I never understood why my uncle Michael, aunt Judy, and my grandma Henrietta weren't there. Maybe my father felt they disapproved because Vicky wasn't Jewish? Or perhaps he was embarrassed that this was his third wedding? The occasion seemed to belong to Vicky; she was beaming from ear to ear the whole day. I didn't spend too much time worrying about anything; I was having a ball. I had never been to such a huge party, especially not one where I felt like I was a small part of the main attraction.

My best friend from camp, Lexa Stern, came with me and stayed for the weekend while my dad honeymooned in Montauk. Rachel, at fifteen, was our babysitter. Alexandra went back to the city with her boyfriend the minute the wedding was over.

At the end of August, my father put us on a plane back to Gatwick Airport.

This time our arrival was less dramatic. My mother was there on time, waiting for us as we disembarked. She was excited to show us our new home: 3 Ashdown Place, right on the edge of the Ashdown Forest and the local golf club.

The flat was in a beautiful mansion with manicured lawns and blue hydrangea bushes surrounding the windows. There were three bedrooms, a large, level-floored kitchen. The living room was big but cozy with couches and stuffed chairs in gentle hues of ivory and taupe. Every room had wall-to-wall carpeting, keeping out the damp draft that we had become accustomed to at Hoathly Hill. Rachel's room was off the kitchen, my mother's room and my room were on the other side of the flat, down a wide carpeted corridor. My room had flowery blue and purple wallpaper with a mauve carpet, a proper bed, no horsehair cots in this place. I had to admit it was a million times better than where we had lived the year before. Finally, this was a home I could actually invite friends to; this place begged for sleepovers and friends at our table.

The best part of our new living quarters was that we could walk to school, which meant I would never be late again. I didn't have to wait for my mother to find her keys or Rachel, who was not a morning person, to get dressed. I could leave when I wanted and arrive on time.

After breakfast I would walk down the quarter-mile-long gravel driveway, turn right onto the main road, walk about ten minutes to the cow path that cut through the fields, cows happily grazing on either side of the fence, on to the school. In all, the walk was about twenty-five minutes, depending on my clip.

Seventh grade was a breeze compared to sixth. Determined to have a social life, I enjoyed the freedom of inviting friends over after school. On weekends we would roam around the golf course behind our house, stop at our place for a snack, maybe stay there listening to my sister's albums on the record player, or walk over to Rowena's house. Jeroen and Rowena had become boyfriend and girlfriend. His house was off the cow path, easy to get to from mine; we spent hours in his room with his friends, Rowena comfortably in the crook of his arm while I longingly gazed at Ed West, a blond, blue-eyed boy who had absolutely no interest in me whatsoever.

At twelve I was still not as developed as the other girls; I was lithe and athletic to their curves. I was desperate to grow up, to mature into a woman the way they seemed to have. I wanted attention from boys, but found myself always on the outside of that. I think those ninth-grade boys viewed me as fun to have around but not to date.

Abba's *The Album* and Supertramp's *Breakfast in America* were the albums we played over and over again. Rowena and I could recite every word. Gloria Gaynor's "I Will Survive" came out that year, and we would sing that song at the top of our lungs, dancing to it at every party.

Now and then Rowena and I would take the train from East Grinstead to London, disembarking at Victoria Station and wandering around Sloane Square and the Kings Road in search of trendy clothes we couldn't afford. FU's jeans and Kickers (shoes) were all the rage. I don't remember how I purchased them, but finally I bought bright red Kickers and the tightest FU's dark denim jeans I could find. When I wore them I felt like I had finally arrived. Biba makeup was becoming a trend with teenage girls: glittery eye shadow and glossy lips; hair was in a high side ponytail. I was getting the hang of it; at twelve I tried to dress like an eighteen-year-old, fantasizing all the while about having a boyfriend to call my own.

I had a social life, I was beginning to feel like I fit in. My friendship with Rowena grew daily, but I missed my dad. He wrote letters every week and put sweet paper angels inside each one. I taped the angels to the wall above my bed, creating a little halo of angels around me. With each letter I would add another until by the end of seventh grade I had four feet of angels surrounding me. The busier I was the less I felt his absence, and even though we were doing much better than the year before, we still implored our mother to move back to the States.

My father visited us once in the two years we were away, when we lived at 3 Ashdown Place. It was Easter break at school, and my dad came to take us to London for the week. He still had a lot of friends there from the first time we had lived in England, and one of them had given him their apartment for the week. I remember him coming to pick us up in his rental car. I was so excited to show him my room and all my school art projects. It was a rushed visit; he scanned the flat, looked at my room, and gave my mother a polite hello before ushering my sister and me into the car.

I remember how much fun we had. Vicky was waiting for us in London; we had dinners out at fancy restaurants and saw *The Mousetrap,* an Agatha Christie play that I loved. There was a dinner party one night with old friends at the apartment we were staying in. With the adults talking long into the night in a celebratory atmosphere, I remember my father tucking me into bed. "Leave the door slightly open please," I asked him. I always had to sleep with the door ajar; I liked to see the hall light falling into my room. As he walked down the hall, I heard the laughing voices wafting from the dining area. I remember thinking to myself how much I loved the feeling of being there, how I never wanted to leave, I felt so safe and secure. I fell asleep with a smile on my face.

My mother had found her stride in her work, not only in teaching but creatively as well. She was part of an artistic Eurythmy group that performed in London, Brighton, and Tunbridge Wells. Artistic Eurythmy is performed to poetry or music. Her costumes were silk tunics with flowing diaphanous veils over them. She would move gracefully about the stage, veil shadowing her every gesture. This was what she had waited for, her moment to shine onstage. Her work was her life and her life was in England and she loved every aspect of it.

With the new location of our apartment, she was free to live a life less occupied with shuttling us around. We always had dinner together; her rule was that dinner was a time to sit and catch up with one another. Occasionally her boyfriend Jorgen would join us. He was an architect from Denmark. Not very tall, with blond, thinning hair, a bushy beard, and blue eyes. He wasn't awful, he was nice enough. His interest in us was minimal and vice versa. Now that I finally had a life of my own, my mother's relationships didn't weigh so heavily on me. One thing about Jorgen did bother me though: he had a strange smell, an unwashed smell. I glanced at him one morning at the breakfast table and noticed his undershirt sticking out of his sweater at the nape of his neck; it looked dirty, slightly brown where it should have been white, and I wondered how my mother didn't notice.

That night I brought it up at the dinner table and instead of getting angry with me, which was the reaction I was expecting, she burst out laughing. "Oh God! I will never be able to look at him the same way again!" She was laughing so hard she was crying.

"He smells a bit too, Mom, don't you smell it?" I said, thrilled now to know that I had made her laugh instead of angry.

"Well, you know men here don't wash the same as men do back home, and washing your body too much gets rid of all the essential oils your body needs, so I do understand that, but I didn't realize he smelled bad." She was still laughing. Her laugh was infectious, the three of us howling around the kitchen table, stomachs hurting we were laughing so hard.

I gathered Jorgen wasn't long for her world when he gave her a clay saltcellar for her birthday. I could see it in her eyes as she held up the heavy, gray pot, turning it in all directions, trying to figure out what it was.

"Francesca, it's a saltcellar," he explained.

My mother cocked her head as she reexamined it. "But you can stick your whole hand in here, I don't understand," she said as she put it down. I knew in that instant she would break up with him.

As the school year was winding down, my mother received an offer to teach in America.

"Oh my God, Mom, that's fantastic, we're going home!" I was elated.

"Well, not home home, but home America home."

"Where?" I asked, figuring that wherever it was wouldn't matter, I would still be so much closer to my dad than in Forest Row.

"We're moving to New Hampshire."

# barely there branches

My mother had secured a job at the Pine Hill Waldorf School in Wilton, New Hampshire, a small town in Hillsborough County. Nestled in the Monadnock region, which is tucked in between Peterborough and Nashua, the New England hamlet had a population of barely three thousand.

The Pine Hill school welcomed children from kindergarten through sixth grade. Rachel and I would be attending the High Mowing Waldorf School, eighth through twelfth grades. There were thirteen kids in my eighth-grade class, four girls including me.

My mother had reconnected with Tony Diorio, who was now the gym teacher at High Mowing. After she'd left him stranded in Germany when she changed her mind and moved to England, he tried to follow her. I remember him coming to visit us in our lopsided apartment at Hoathly Hill. I was so happy to see him. He had flown from Germany to surprise us. The dinner we had with him

seemed to be a joyous occasion, a light in the midst of our bleak surroundings. He stayed only one night. I overheard them the next
morning behind the closed door of the living room, where my
mother slept. I heard muffled arguing and then, "I just don't love
you anymore!" She was done.

I sat on my horsehair cot, silently weeping. Tony was the best
boyfriend my mother would ever have as far as I was concerned.
Why was she doing this? When he came out of her room, his eyes
were bloodshot and swollen. I felt so sad, my heart broke in two. I
threw my arms around his neck. "Please don't go, Tony!" I begged,
sobbing into his tobacco-smelling navy blue cashmere.

"There's nothing I can do, Bean. I gotta go, sweetie." He held me
for a long time, his hand gently resting on my back, trying to soothe
me, letting me cry into his chest. I could feel his own body shaking
as we held each other.

There was nothing he *could* do. Once her mind was made up, my
mother was immovable. He flew home to America and found a teaching job in Wilton, New Hampshire. He contacted her when he heard
of the job opening at the Pine Hill school. Two years had passed since
that morning in Hoathly Hill. I was so happy when I got out of the
car and saw him standing there, looking a little chubbier than I had
last seen him, but smelling the same, cigarettes mixed with soap.
I jumped into his arms, and he twirled me about in his driveway.

"I don't know if I can call you Bean anymore, honey, you've
grown so tall." He looked down at my red Kickers and smiled.
"One day you're going to grow into those feet too!" He laughed.

Tony lived in a two-family house on campus. We lived with him
for the first three months; my mother hadn't found a place for us
yet. Rachel and I shared an upstairs bedroom, Tony gave my mother
his, and he slept downstairs in the living room on the couch. I secretly prayed they would get back together. I think Tony did too; he
did everything he could to make us comfortable, but I knew as I
watched him devour junk food and inhale Marlboro cigarettes that
my mother would be turned off.

Tony had a sweet tooth that could never be sated. I observed in amazement as he poured chocolate milk into a glass of Coca-Cola "It's the closest thing I can get to an egg-cream soda," he told me with a guilty laugh. He always had a supply of sweets stacked on top of his refrigerator—chocolate-covered donuts, boxed coffee cake—and cartons of cigarettes.

My first day of school I wore my FU's jeans and my red Kickers with a blouse tucked in. I felt incredibly chic as I walked into my eighth-grade classroom, only to observe that everyone was decked out in plaid flannel shirts, baggy pants, and yellow Timberland boots. "Jesum Crow!" one of them said to me when they sized up my ensemble. I had no idea what "Jesum Crow" meant. Was that good or bad? It meant "Jesus Christ," I later found out. I had to learn a whole new language.

In between classes I ran back to Tony's house to change my shoes, as my once coveted red Kickers were now a source of embarrassment. I threw on my sneakers. When I got back to school, I was a few minutes late for my Latin class.

"Youa taady!" the teacher said as I entered the classroom.

"I'm what?" I replied, not understanding her in the slightest.

"Taady," she said, annoyed.

"Sorry, I don't know what that is," I said as innocently as I could.

"T.A.AH.D.Y, taady."

One of the kids came to my rescue and told me she was saying "tardy"; I was late.

That day after school, I lamented to my mother that we had finally moved back to America but I couldn't understand anyone all over again! The kids in my class seemed so immature compared to Rowena and the boys in Jeroen's class. I hated New Hampshire.

"You'll get used to it in time, sweetheart," my mother said, brushing off my complaints.

I kept thinking I had made a huge mistake. I should never have told my mother I wanted to come back to the States. We'd had a nice apartment in Sussex, I had friends, I knew the school and the people. I missed Rowena desperately. This was not going to be a good year. How could I live in a place where people said "Jesum Crow"?

Aside from Tony, the only good thing about moving to New Hampshire was that I got to see my father again on weekends. Friday after school, my mother would drive us to the Manchester Airport, about an hour from Wilton, and we would fly to LaGuardia to spend weekends with my dad. It was only an hour flight and worth the travel to spend time in the city with him. I was thirteen and allowed to take the bus by myself down Fifth Avenue to see my friend Lexa, who lived on Bleecker Street. At least being in the city I was able to feel somewhat myself. I liked being familiar with my surroundings, I liked knowing how to get from A to B. I wanted to have that feeling all the time. In New Hampshire I felt like I was biding my time. I knew there was no way my mother would last in this tiny, unsophisticated town. What was she thinking?

And then my mother bought a house. A passive solar house in the middle of a bedraggled apple orchard, down a long, dusty driveway, eight miles from our school. When she first told me about the house I felt a surge of excitement. A home of our very own! I had been a gypsy for the last few years, carrying all my belongings in a suitcase back and forth from Sussex to New York. I hadn't had a room of my own with my own belongings in it for two years. Everything until that moment had a "temporary" stamp on it. The thought of hanging up a framed picture, putting my books on my very own bookshelf, unpacking the boxes that were God knows where from Spring Valley and finding all the things that reminded me of home, leaving them permanently in a fixed drawer where I could find them exactly as I had placed them thrilled me. Suddenly New Hampshire didn't seem so bad after all.

Because our new home was passive solar, the main source of heat was the giant granite fireplace that stood smack in the middle of the house. The idea was that the sun would come in through the massive glass windows during the day, the granite would soak up the rays of the sun, and then it would release the heat at night.

The house was only a few years old, very modern, with an open kitchen, dining room, and living room, laid out around the huge chimney. The ceiling in the kitchen rose all the way up past the third level, leaving a wide open space that was bright and sunny. Rachel and I had our own bedrooms on the second floor; the third floor was a balcony-like space we never knew what to do with. You could stand next to the wood-slatted banister and peer down into the kitchen from there. The third floor was carpeted and airy; the chimney loomed up along the side of the balcony from the ground floor. My mother's master suite was on the fourth floor.

The passive solar concoction looked great on paper, but it never really worked. The house was always bitter cold with the expansive windows butting up to the cold New Hampshire winters. We heated with a woodburning stove that was attached to the chimney. Every morning, we threw wood in the stove and stood next to it to warm up. There was a furnace, but my mother didn't like to use it because of the draining cost. Once in a while, on the bitterest of nights, we were allowed to turn it on, wallowing in the warm air that came up through the vents into our bedrooms.

Our furniture from Spring Valley eventually arrived. The deep-wine-colored velvet couch, our round wood dining room table, my mother's Tiffany lamp with its beautiful hues of olive green and gold. Everything was on a dimmer; my mother was adamant about lighting creating a warm ambience. The beautiful oriental rug my parents bought when they were first married was laid out under the couch. The house was beginning to resemble a home I once knew. Having these objects around me offered a certain amount of security held by the past.

I traded in my Kickers for L.L.Bean boots and began to dress more like the kids at school. Plaid flannel found its way into my closet. Halfway through eighth grade I began to feel more at ease, trying to make the best of the situation.

Our flights to New York to see my dad dwindled to once a month; the cost of the tickets, plus the hour drive to Manchester and back, was beginning to weigh my mother down. "I can't spend my weekend in the car, chauffeuring you around," she said, slightly annoyed.

I took what I could get and went whenever there was a chance. Still, we were in America. I could talk to my dad regularly on the phone; he was finally back in my life, at least more than twice a year.

Jorgen, my mother's Danish boyfriend from Sussex, came to visit us. I thought they had broken up after the saltcellar incident but apparently I had misjudged. My mother set him to the task of painting a huge orange and golden tree on the wall above the kitchen. "Veil painting" it was called, where you could see layers and layers of watercolor paint, one hue on top of the other, and you had to wait for each layer of paint to dry before adding the next, a long, arduous process. But before he finished this gigantic tree, my mother ended the relationship. I don't remember why she finally had enough of him, I just remember Jorgen was asked to leave and we were left with a half-painted diaphanous trunk and some gold barely there branches that stayed like that till the day I left, five years later. Whenever someone came to the house and looked up at the mural, their first question was "What's that supposed to be?"

"It's a long story," I would say, diverting my eyes from the yellow and orange tangle that hung rough-hewn on the wall.

By my freshman year my life was beginning to take on a consistency that I liked. Rachel was a senior and very popular. I felt a sense of pride being her sibling; entering high school, I already had a golden ticket by association. High school was a different playing field than middle school. There were a hundred students, almost thirty per grade, which felt huge to me after having been one of thirteen. The high school was a boarding school with the exception of a few day students like us. Students came from all over the country, some from Europe, very few from Wilton. My world grew exponentially. There were activities every weekend: school plays, events, skiing on Wednesday afternoons. I didn't want to leave on weekends, I wanted to be a part of the school, go to parties, enjoy the social life I was starting to build. I entertained the thought of having a boyfriend, a real proper boyfriend, for the first time in my life. That didn't materialize in ninth grade, but there were a few starts and stops. The boys in my class were too young and immature in my opinion; however, the boys in eleventh and twelfth grade were much more appealing.

I dated a senior, Doug Elliot, for a few months. Our romance began when the whole school went to see the epic film *Doctor Zhivago*. Somehow I managed to wriggle my way into the seat next to Doug, whom I had been admiring from afar since my first day of freshman year. I was giddy with excitement. A few minutes into the film his fingers crawled over to my hand and rested there. My heart jumped into my throat. I couldn't believe he was actually holding my hand. We sat that way through the whole movie. I couldn't hear anything other than the sound of my heartbeat pulsating through my body. That was it as far as I was concerned, we were now a couple. What I didn't know was that he was also holding the hand of Anka, a junior from Germany, sitting on the other side of him. Of course she had no clue that he was holding my hand at the same time. I don't remember what exactly transpired except that I really thought I was his girlfriend. We had make-out sessions in his room (he was a boarding student), but I was so naïve and inexperienced I didn't know how to behave with him, what to say or how to respond. I only thought if I made myself available to him and he showed me affection then we must be a couple. One morning when I walked in for roll call, which was a tradition where the entire school met in the Big Room to check in for the day, I noticed his ex-girlfriend Maggie, in Anka's class, wearing his sweater. I went right up to Maggie and asked her if that was Doug's sweater, and she replied, "Oh yeah, I had to borrow it this morning when I snuck out of his room, it's so cold outside."

"Are you guys back together?" I asked, feeling my cheeks redden.

"Yup, not sure what I was thinking breaking up with him, he's the best," she said with a glassy smile. And that was that. Doug and Maggie were back together and I was dumped without so much as a note to let me know.

In a strange twist of fate, years later when my father was living in the Berkshires and needed his TV installed, Doug was the guy who showed up at his door and became his technician, installing all his electronics. I was home on a break from shooting *ER* and Doug was there working. I was actually happy to see him, and I greeted him with a huge smile. "Oh my God! Doug! How are you? It's been years. What have you been up to? Are you married? Kids?" I truly was genuine in my happiness to see him and catch up. Looking very uncomfortable, he asked if he could speak with me outside. We stepped out on my father's front step.

"I just wanted to tell you how embarrassed I am at how I treated you when we were in high school," he said, looking down at his feet. Then he looked up at me and said earnestly, "That wasn't right what I did, and I have always regretted not being able to apologize to you."

I laughed. I honestly had not given him any thought. I was living in L.A. with my boyfriend at the time, working as an actress, and Doug Elliot had not crossed my mind in years.

"Oh wow, ummm . . . please don't worry about it, Doug. It was so long ago and you were a teenager, I get it. Dear Lord, I was only fourteen; you were right to break up with me."

"But I should have been more graceful about it. I think I hurt you badly."

"Isn't that what high school is all about? Getting hurt and learning that your world won't end and you actually will go on living?" I offered with a smile.

Later that night I thought about how sincerely terrible he'd felt all those years later for something I could barely remember. I was touched by his regret.

I had always been a disciplined student, and I liked the work in high school; I found it interesting and challenging. I wanted to do well in school; because if I succeeded and got into a respected college, I thought my father would be proud of me. Neither of my parents insisted on good grades, this was something I put on myself.

I remember visiting my dad one weekend when he was living on Eighty-ninth Street and Madison Avenue. I brought my report card, all A's and one A–. I proudly handed it to him, waiting for a pat on the head like a good little puppy. We were standing in his living room. I watched in anticipation as he read.

Then finally he put down the report card and looked at me. "Well, Juli," he said with a chuckle, "if you had a B and maybe a C somewhere in here, it would make all these A's really stand out."

I was gutted. What was he saying? Why wasn't I being hailed as a brilliant student, raised up on a pedestal? Where was the celebratory dinner? What more could he want from me? His response made me angry. *What does that mean?* I silently sulked and walked away.

Years later I asked him what he'd meant by that remark. He put it simply, and as an adult and a parent now myself I can understand why he said what he said, why he was giving me a chance to fail once in a while. He was worried for me. "I could see the pressure you were putting yourself under. I didn't want you to miss out on enjoying your high school years. I wanted you to see that I would love you whether you got A's, B's, or C's, or even failed now and then. That's what was important to me: your well-being, not your perfect scorecard."

I wish he had told me that when I was fourteen. Most of my high school academic career I beat myself up, never happy unless there was a plus beside the A. A twenty-five-page research paper I wrote for my senior-year thesis ended up in a muddy puddle, thrown with dramatic effect when I received my final grade, A-.

I was so hard on myself I developed a rash. When I took my SATs, I was covered in red patches of hives from my legs all the way up to my neck, scratching myself until I bled because the itch was relentless. The more I stressed over my exams, the more I scratched.

I found a report card recently from my high school guidance counselor that said, *I wish Julianna could enjoy herself more.*

By the end of my freshman year a confluence of events had rocked the steady path I thought I was finally walking. My father announced that he was moving back to London. He had been offered a job as the creative director at Ted Bates International, and the opportunity was too good to pass up. He would be moving during my sophomore year, selling the apartment on Eighty-ninth Street and setting up shop in London with Vicky.

"We could have stayed in England!" my mother spewed, furious as if she had been tricked into moving to New Hampshire. The irony. There was no moving back to England now; we finally had a home that we owned, she had a steady job, we were slowly adjusting to our new life, our surroundings, our school, our friends.

New York, which had been a huge light in my life, would be over. No more trips on weekends to see my dad, or my sister Alexandra. We would be stuck in New Hampshire all the time, floating on an isolated island of Jesum Crows.

I was turning fifteen at the end of freshman year, too old to go to camp, too young to be a counselor; my camp life as I knew it was over. That which had been the other steady ray of light in my life was now also gone.

Rachel was graduating from high school and would be heading off to college in a few short months. I would no longer have her to cling to, as I had been accustomed to doing my whole life. Who would I check in with when my mother was in despair, or her boyfriend was annoying, or her choices inappropriate? Who would be there for me to turn to when I needed a sane answer, one I trusted?

I felt unmoored, left behind, scared, and angry.

I decided the best course of action would be to get a job and start making my own money. I knew that money meant freedom and independence. It also meant that I could have more control over my life. I needed to start earning and saving. I certainly wasn't going to stay in New Hampshire for the summer. I had to figure out a way to get a job and find a place to live. I started scanning the want ads in the back of *New York* magazine.

"Mother's Helper Wanted!" Perfect. I had never taken care of a baby, but how hard could it be? One weekend when I was visiting my father, I called the number that was listed and went on my first job interview.

I walked across Central Park to the address the woman had given me, on the Upper West Side. I was nervously practicing my pitch. I wanted this job more than anything. Ninety-five dollars a week plus room and board in the Hamptons for two months—it was perfect. I could save money, live in the Hamptons for free, swim in the ocean I knew so well, and at the end of the gig I would still have time to visit Rowena in England. Two years had gone by since I had seen her; we were devoted letter writers and had promised ourselves that this summer we would finally see each other.

I got the job. I couldn't believe it! The baby was eight months old. His parents were EST seminar leaders. One of the first questions they asked me was "Do you know what EST is?" Piece of cake. I had witnessed my mother's introduction into EST. She had taken a seminar in Boston one weekend led by the founder, Werner Erhard, a self-help guru whose mantra was "BE HERE NOW!" When they asked me, I didn't think twice. I had witnessed everything from Hare Krishnas and EST devotees to Anthroposophists and Scientologists; all of them had been wafting in and out of our home since I could remember. I met each and every one with an eye roll. My mother was always searching, always digging deeper to find her "true self." My constant argument with her as I got older was that she was so caught up in finding herself that she forgot to do the important things in life, like picking her daughter up from school on time.

"Your head is so high up in the clouds, Mom, you forget we are actually supposed to have our feet on the ground so we can walk!" I would hiss.

I found all of the self-searching to be a load of crap. All talk, no do as far as I was concerned. Before my teenage years, I didn't really feel one way or another about my mother's journey to find her spiritual life. I suppose it wafted over me because nothing seemed to really stick except Anthroposophy. I had been going to Waldorf schools since nursery school, I understood what Anthroposophy was and would tell her that she didn't need to preach it to me. I was living it every day at school. But as I got older, and once I was in high school, I found her spiritual development tedious and annoying. I looked at it as yet another distraction from *real* life. All these people from my viewpoint yammered on about how to find our place on this earth, but it seemed to me that no one was actually doing anything, they just liked to hear themselves talk. Empty words.

I didn't care that my new employers were EST seminar leaders; all I could see was the job. And I had to admit, I was pretty impressed with myself for finding it. I turned fifteen, finished the last days of school, packed my bags, and headed to the Hamptons.

Their house was in the Springs, a wooded hamlet on the bay side of East Hampton. When I got there they showed me the lay of the land: I was to sleep in the baby's room, wake up in the middle of the night if he needed anything, feed him or change his diaper. I was not to wake the parents until 8:00 A.M. My job was not just feeding, bathing, and playing with the baby; I was also required to teach him math and reading. The father made his case very clear to me on the night of my arrival: this child was on schedule to be a genius and he would learn to read and multiply before anyone else his age.

From the moment I got there I had a lump in my throat. The fantasy I had envisioned—walking the baby in the stroller to the beach, strolling on the sidewalk in East Hampton with the baby on my hip, talking to all the shop owners who were familiar to me, taking the baby into the ocean and splashing around, having friendly conversation with the mom at the kitchen counter, maybe learning to cook with her, playing some backgammon, hanging out in the living room while all their interesting friends came for a visit—that fantasy was quashed the first night I got there when I realized that these people were nuts.

The house was dark and foreboding; in among the tall pine trees, little light shone through the windows. I felt isolated the moment I stepped over their threshold. The town was a good fifteen-minute drive from the house. There would be no walking with the baby to get a coffee in the morning, or to the beach, which was even farther away. I never realized how lonely it could be, sharing a room with an eight-month-old. Waking up in the middle of the night to soothe a crying baby is hard for any parent. When you're fifteen and the hired help, it's torture.

The mother was not warm and fuzzy as I had imagined her to be the first time we met; she seemed to want to keep me at a distance. She was short and compact, dark hair cut in a no-nonsense style. She seemed exhausted all the time, which I couldn't understand as I was the one waking up two to three times a night with the baby. I had never been so tired, which made everything all the more difficult.

The father was there only on weekends; during the week it was only me, the kid, and his mom, who didn't seem to want to spend too much time with her child either. No friends popped by for visits. There was an eerie silence in that house, it seemed as though no living souls were around. The three of us were stuck in a dark, shadowy, joyless house. I had never felt this kind of lonely, not when we lived at the Peridure Home School, not when we lived in Hoathly Hill. At least there I had my mother and my sister to comfort me, to make me laugh. There was no laughter in this house.

I kept hearing my grandfather: *Grin and bear it.* When anyone asked him how he managed to live with my bullheaded grandmother, he would say with laughter in his eyes: "I just grin and bear it." I would try to do the same.

However as each day went by, the loneliness grabbed on tighter and tighter. I kept trying to shake it off, but I couldn't. I heard my mother's refrain: *Let's just stick it out for the year* . . . But I was miserable, overwhelmed by lack of sleep and isolation. I was searching for a human being to connect with. The longer I stayed there, the bigger the lump in my throat became. I cried every night into my pillow for fear of waking the baby. I would tell myself that this wasn't the rest of my life, it was just a moment, but each day dragged on so slowly I couldn't imagine I would ever be myself again, have my life back, my friends, my family. I couldn't find my anchor, and I was slipping into a depression I had never experienced before.

I managed to get through the first two weeks, willing myself every step of the way, thinking of the money I would have by the end of the job. Finally, with my weekend off looming, there was a light in the distance. I couldn't wait for my father to come and take me out of this toxic environment. Something about the way the mom looked at me was frightening. She would size me up and cock her head. I had the feeling she was angry with me all the time, even though I did my job and kept the baby out of her way. I just wanted to escape from there.

My father knocked on the door, and I ran as fast as I could to let him in. My weekend bag was packed and in my hand. He introduced himself to the mother and we left. As soon as I got in the car I burst into tears. My father listened to me rant and rave about how horrible the past two weeks had been. How hard it was to teach an eight-month-old to read and do math when he couldn't even speak yet! My father drove, focusing on the road, while I spewed.

He took me out to a diner. By that time I had calmed down, cried all the tears I had, and was so grateful to be with him. We ordered our meal, and when the waitress left the table my father looked at me very seriously. "You're not going back there, Julianna. There's something off in that house. We are going to have a nice weekend" —he was staying with friends out in Amagansett—"and then we will go back there on Sunday, get your stuff, and you will quit."

He told me even though he'd met the mother only briefly, he could feel that something was amiss. He didn't want me in that environment.

All through my childhood, I thought I had to prove myself to everyone. I could take care of myself and manage just fine, no matter how difficult the circumstance, no matter how isolated, lost, or insecure I felt, with each move to a new school, town, country. I thought I would be letting people down if I showed any vulnerability or weakness, if I was unable to finish what I started. I had this ongoing recording playing in my brain that I wasn't a quitter, I was a survivor. I was strong, dependable. Looking at my father in that moment at the diner, I was overcome with emotion at his empathy and understanding. I was grateful for his advice, and, to be perfectly honest with myself, I was surprised and delighted to see him so protective of me. He had never fought a battle for me before or stood up in my defense. The truth is that he hadn't been around to do it. I was with him only on weekends or holidays. I felt his love, but I never knew he felt protective of me. This was a side of him I was experiencing for the first time in my life. And I loved it.

We went back on Sunday. I can still feel the butterflies that were in my stomach as we approached the driveway. I was so scared to tell my employer I was quitting. My dad came in the house with me and stood in the doorway as I told her in the kitchen that I couldn't keep working for her, I would be leaving that day. She concentrated on my face and crossed her arms over her chest. She reminded me of a squat pit bull. "Well, that's just great, fucking great, thanks a lot!" She was fuming. "This is the last time I ever hire a fucking teenager."

I apologized profusely, packed up my stuff, and got the hell out of there.

---

The relief I felt when I left that job was immeasurable. Within days my old self started to come back. I couldn't believe I had ever taken for granted a full night's sleep. I savored every minute in bed, shuffling to the kitchen in my father's apartment in my bare feet as the aroma of fresh-brewed coffee beckoned me. Everything felt luxurious; just a walk down Madison Avenue was blissful, freedom. I was free.

Since I had no plans until August, when I would visit Rowena in Sussex, I went to stay with my friend Lexa in Sag Harbor for a week. I loved her family, who had always welcomed me as one of their own. Lexa had been going through a long and painful stint with braces and headgear. I remember her efforts to sleep with that strange contraption strapped around her head as she desperately tried not to drool. Since we were kids, braces had been a part of her life; that summer she was in her fifth and final year of dental trauma. She would always tell me how lucky I was to have been born with naturally straight teeth.

One night her mother suggested we ride our bikes into town for pizza and ice cream. We jumped on our bikes, all five of us: Lexa, her sister, her mother, her stepfather, and me. I felt so free and alive, so grateful and happy to be there.

On our way back from town, the night air had settled into a deep black velvet coating. Always the competitive one, I rode my bike as fast as I could to get ahead of the pack. As I pedaled faster, hearing the *Chariots of Fire* soundtrack in my head as I rode, I realized that the fog had risen off the water surrounding us, and between the fog and the dark night, there was barely any visibility. Just as I was thinking it would be wise to lessen my pace, the front wheel of my bike slammed into a pothole. I flipped over my handlebars and skidded for a good three feet on the pavement. The bike spun up like a penny being flipped in a bet and landed on top of my back.

I lay there motionless, stunned and winded. I thought maybe I had broken my back. I was afraid to even try to get up. I felt a trickle of blood drip from my lip. I started to realize that it was my face that had taken the brunt of my fall. Panic set in as I began to discern what I had done to myself. I sat up slowly, pushing the bike off my back, afraid to touch my face with my shaky fingers. I didn't want to know how bad the damage was. As the shock from the fall was wearing off, I started to feel a horrendous sharp pain in my mouth.

When Lexa and her family caught up to me, they tended to me as best they could in the dark, but when I tried to speak I knew something awful had happened. Aside from the blood mixed in with gravel and saliva, when I moved my tongue I realized my tooth was gone. I starting screaming: "MY TOOTH, MY TOOTH IS MISSING, FIND MY TOOTH, PLEASE FIND MY TOOTH!"

On our hands and knees, in the dark, we looked everywhere, turning over every hard pebble in the road, no tooth.

We got back to the house and they applied first aid to all my cuts and scrapes. I didn't care about any of that, as I kept sliding my tongue over the front of my teeth. One tooth had been completely knocked out, the perfectly straight teeth on either side of the missing tooth had been chipped. My lip was split and starting to swell like a fat, ripe tomato.

They called my father in New York City and arranged for me to go home the next morning to get medical attention.

That night in bed, lying next to Lexa, trying to see the silver lining, I joked. Thank God it was me and not her. After all her years of braces, that really would have been a catastrophe. Inside I was spiraling downward, down into a rabbit hole. *Why me? Why me?*

In the morning I didn't recognize myself when I looked in the mirror.

I used to pretend to enjoy watching boxing matches with my dad; this was my way of spending alone time with him. He loved boxing; he had been a boxer in high school and college, and he was good too. He did it for the sport, not to hurt anyone; he was fast and agile. When I saw my face, I thought of Muhammad Ali and what his opponent looked like after a fight I had watched. I could barely see out of one eye the swelling was so bad; my lip had blown up to the size of a crusty maroon popover. I could barely open my mouth. The pain shooting up, past my gums, straight into my head was what I imagined it must feel like when a knife is jammed through your gums all the way to your brain.

Alexandra picked me up at the bus stop with her boyfriend. She saw my face and opened her arms, holding me for a long time while I cried. When I finally lifted my head, she told me the plan was to go to my dad's dentist so he could assess the situation and fix me up. My dad was at work and would meet us there. I refused to open my mouth to let her see my teeth. I was so mortified and angry with myself for letting this happen.

The prognosis was depressing. I had to have a root canal right away. The gigantic, crusty popover on my lip made it difficult to get in there, and the pain was sickening. After the root canal they would try to see if they could replace my tooth; in the meantime I needed to heal.

Alexandra took over caring for me. She used to love mothering me. After my parents' divorce she stepped up to the plate every time, even though she was only seven or eight. She was a natural care-taker, always has been. I stayed in her room at my dad's apartment. She insisted I use vitamin E oil from a capsule to ward off my scar-ring. Every night, she would prick the capsule with a needle, squeeze out the oil, and gently apply it to all the parts of my face that had been beat up by the concrete road.

My mother flew in from New Hampshire to make sure I was okay. She said she had to look at me "with my own eyes, poor angel." Witnessing my mother and father in the same room together made me impossibly uncomfortable, especially if my stepmother was around. The tension was always palpable. I was almost grateful for the distraction of my accident. I was in too much of a self-pitying slump to care.

I had made a vow to myself that I wouldn't open my mouth to

speak to anyone until my tooth was replaced. I never realized how important teeth were, and I mourned the loss of one of mine every minute of the day. I stayed in bed and watched soap operas. Disappearing into the lives of the folks in *All My Children*'s Pine Valley made me forget my woes for a minute, until Erica Kane smiled that dazzling toothpaste commercial smile of hers and I would be racked with tears all over again.

I couldn't eat, too painful. Everything hurt. I would wake up in the morning after a fitful night's sleep and forget for an instant that anything was wrong, but the moment I started to yawn, my cracked mouth would swallow me up for another day of doom.

I don't know how long I lay in my sister's bed consumed with self-loathing and self-pity, probably a week give or take, at which point my father came into the room with a yellow legal pad and ballpoint pen. To know my father was to know that all his writing began on a yellow legal pad. He had them everywhere, and always with a blue ballpoint pen, never black, always blue.

He sat down on the bed beside me and gently laid the pad and pen down next to me. "I know you're hurting, honey, and you've been through a lot, but I want you to start thinking about all the good things that have come out of this accident. I'm going to leave this notepad here for you, and you may not think of one good thing yet, but in time, you will. You will be amazed at the list of good you will discover."

And then he left.

*There is nothing good about any of this. Period. I HATE EVERYTHING!*

As the weeks went by, the scabs started to fall off and scars miraculously disappeared where my sister had attentively applied vitamin E oil. It was around this time that I realized how lucky I was to have a big sister who cared for me so beautifully. I grabbed the legal pad and wrote it down. Then it dawned on me that my mother had stopped everything she was doing just to fly to New York to make sure I was okay. Once I started writing I couldn't stop. So many people had called, concerned when they heard. Flowers had been sent. My stepmother would come into the room with a goofy smile, arms loaded with trashy magazines, trying to distract me from my plight. Rachel came and tried to make me laugh with her funny jokes and sweet songs. Once I started to write it all down, the amount of love I felt from all the people in my life was immeasurable. The last thing I wrote was how lucky I was to have my father in my life, encouraging me to find the good in what I surmised would be the worst tragedy I would ever face.

# grin and bear it

When I came back from visiting Rowena in Sussex at the end of August, I stopped off in New York on the way to New Hampshire. I wanted to see Alexandra before she moved to California with her fiancé, and my father before he moved to London with Vicky. I was anticipating a sad farewell; I knew I was entering a new phase of my life, without Rachel by my side, without Alexandra or my father in New York anymore. The blow of their absence was buffered by the fact that I did have a familiar home to go to, and at least my mother was there. She and I were still very close; my teenage years so far hadn't amassed too much animosity toward her. She still embarrassed me from time to time, but that was nothing new. She was well liked in our New Hampshire community, and my friends loved coming over to our house for a home-cooked meal and thought-provoking conversation.

When I was younger I had had fantasies of what it would be like to have a mother less expressive, more conservative, less egocentric, more doting, less dramatic, more tame. By the time I got to high school those fantasies had faded for the most part because my friends really liked my mother. I, in turn, began to accept her for who she was, with all her quirks, her spiritual agenda, her constant search to find herself. I reasoned with myself, Wasn't this better than having a parent who *didn't* ask the hard questions? I could tell my mother everything, ask her anything, and never feel judged. She was completely open to who I was. I knew how fortunate I was having a parent I could talk to. I never shied away from asking her questions about sex, drugs, boys. Most of my friends were afraid to talk to their parents about that stuff, but with my mother I could be an open book. I hid no secrets from her.

What I hadn't anticipated on my return home was her new relationship.

When I walked in the door to my father's apartment, Alexandra told me that my mother's new boyfriend had moved into our house.

"Mom has a new boyfriend?" I asked, having heard nothing about this.

"Yeah, and it's not good, honey, he's twenty-one!"

*"What?"* I spit out with a half laugh. "How long have they been together? He's living in the house already?"

My mother always had boyfriends; this was nothing new, but they never lived with us. They stayed over, sure, but living with us was never on the table. And twenty-one? Even for my mother this was a new low.

My heart fell into my stomach. The plates in my brain started to spin so fast I couldn't keep up with every thought that zinged through my head. *Oh my God, my father, what will my father think of her now?* I had always tried to defend my mother, she was my loving mama and I was her girl. I needed her, loved her, and could forgive most anything, but this, this was unforgivable. How could I defend her to anyone now? And what about me? Hadn't she considered my well-being in this new living situation? Wasn't I worthy enough to be asked if this was okay? Wasn't this my home too? How could she do this? He was one year older than Alexandra. What part of her thought that this was healthy for me? Or did she not think of me at all?

My father said very little about it as he put me in a cab to the airport. I could tell what he thought by the look on his face, the same look he often had when confronted with uncomfortable situations, as though he had just bitten into a sour apple and couldn't get the taste out of his mouth. I wasn't sure if he had spoken to her, or if he just accepted this new information and thought I would be able to handle it. Nothing was said. I was too scared to tell him how upset I was; even then I didn't want him to see her in a bad light. But how else could he see her? I was furious at my mother for putting me in such an uncomfortable position with my father.

When I arrived in Manchester, my mother was there to pick me up. She was bubbling over like a high school girl, newly in love. I stared out the window observing the ugly cinder-block mini-malls strewn on either side of the road as she prattled on about how wonderful Charlie was, and how much I would like him. Her words drifted over me. I couldn't engage; there was only enough air in the car for her. I was silently stewing in my newfound identity: the indignant teenager. *I will make his life hell . . .*

As we drove down the driveway, I noticed the apple trees drooping, not because they were full of abundant ripe fruit but more as if they were trying to crawl back into the ground they had sprouted from. *What sad trees,* I thought, remembering how my mother had been so excited to live on a small apple orchard in our New Hampshire town. All forgotten now. *They'll just die, like everything else,* I murmured to myself, not listening to a word she was saying.

We rounded the last corner, and there he was. I saw his bleached blond hair before I could see his face. As we pulled to a stop I inspected more closely and saw acne on the side of his cheek, seeping down to his chin. *He has acne! Jesus, he's so young he has acne!* He was waxing his gold 280ZX Datsun. *How apropos.*

He stopped waxing his car and came over to give my mother a wet kiss. *Repulsive.* She introduced us; her voice, I noted, seemed a little too high-pitched.

"Nice to meet you, sir," I said. I wanted to make him uncomfortable immediately.

"Oh, no need to call me sir."

"Yeah, I think it suits you," I retorted as I took my suitcase out of the car and headed to my room, offering no further interaction; I was not going to indulge them in some warm welcoming party. They needed to know right off the bat that this was going to be a rough ride. *Just try me.*

My mother had planned a dinner for the three of us. She pulled out all the stops to cook a lovely meal. I watched Charlie silently while I pushed my food around on the plate, not contributing one word to the conversation, making them work overtime to fill in the awkward blank slate I was proffering. I observed how he ate, his wide mouth open as he chewed, the melted butter glistening on his pimpled chin. *She would never let me chew like that, can't she see how he's eating?* Table manners in my mother's house were a rule: *Close your mouth when you chew, don't slurp your soup, napkin on lap*... The two of them were in their own little world, I was outside looking in, figuring out how I could manage to survive them.

This was the turning point in my development as a dutiful daughter. Charlie drove a wedge into my relationship with my mother, wrecking the sanctity of our home. I saw clearly that she had put her own needs first, and she needed him, not me. I would have to forge my own way because I was *not* going to share her with him. That much I knew.

That night in my room I devised a plan: I would walk to school every day. That way I would be out of the house before they woke up. Since my mother had broken all the rules, I decided to make some for myself.

I woke up at five every morning, put the kettle on, brought my tea to my room. While it steeped I warmed up my body with forty push-ups and sit-ups, then drank my tea while I got dressed and was out of the house by six.

We lived on Curtis Farm Road, a hilly, winding dirt road that ran six miles before it reached town. From town I had a two-mile trek uphill to school. On bitterly cold days I would hitch a ride with teachers on their way to class, although I preferred not to. The last thing I wanted was to have to explain why I was walking to school in the first place. I didn't want anyone knowing about my mother's boyfriend, plus I liked my independence. At a fast clip I could make it to school in a little over an hour.

I decided to join the soccer team, another good excuse to stay away from home as long as possible. I wasn't very good, but I was fast enough that no one questioned how I became the only girl on the team. I knew Tony was throwing me a bone by letting me join. He was well aware of the circumstances at home and that I was basically hiding from my mother. I would go to his house after practice and tell him how much I hated Charlie, how embarrassed I was by him. I couldn't invite anyone home anymore; I didn't want them to meet him. I was fully aware that people knew about my mother and her twenty-one-year-old boyfriend. One sighting of them canoodling at dinner in town had resulted in the whole campus finding out. I was horrified but held my head high, as though nothing unusual was going on.

Tony was always kindhearted toward my mother. Even though she broke his heart, even when I spoke ill of her, you could see the sparkle in his eyes when her name was mentioned. He loved her still. He would try to ease my torment by telling me that it wouldn't last very long; he believed she would tire of Charlie soon enough. She didn't. Not for the three years I had left before I went away to college. She would tell me how crazy she was about him, how he made her feel young and alive. My mother was forty-six when they got together; maybe being loved by a man less than half her age gave her the security she needed as she faced middle age. Tony had known me since I was six years old; I'd grown up in front of him. He knew how much I loved my mother; he was there when she called me her Sunshine Girl; he'd witnessed our bond. When I was fifteen, he watched as I began to build a protective armor around myself, making sure she couldn't get in. I was determined to never need my mother again.

The tricky part of my plan, staying away from the house as long as I could, was the ride home. I couldn't walk eight miles in the dark after practice. Tony had hired an assistant coach, Kuel, to help with soccer practice. He had graduated in Rachel's class my freshman year and had always been a popular figure on campus. Now, with most of his friends either away at college or back in their home-towns after graduation, he cut more of a lonely figure walking around the school that once was his.

He would join me and Tony after practice and we would eat to-gether, hang out, talk. Tony's house became my sanctuary. Kuel was an added bonus. There were two factors at play here:

1. I had a mad crush on him, with his dusty blond hair, which he wore with a side part, grazing over his baby blue eyes. He was handsome and fun to be around. I don't think he had noticed me one way or the other my freshman year, but now he seemed at-tentive and I was craving attention.
2. He owned a car and began driving me home every night from Tony's.

During our car rides we talked about everything. Kuel's mother had died when he was three; his father raised him on his own, some-times moving every few months. One year they lived in their car. He was nineteen now and lived alone in a house he and his father had built but never finished. He barely made ends meet working odd jobs as a carpenter and a mechanic. There was nothing he couldn't fix. It thrilled me when his car would break down and he'd pull over to the side of the road, insisting that I stay inside. He'd tinker under the hood and have it running again a few minutes later. He made me feel safe.

I poured my heart out to him on those rides home. Spewing unpleasantries about the boyfriend, lamenting how different my mother was around him, how hard it was for me to be in the same room with them. Kuel listened with empathy. Each ride home I fell a little bit more in love with him, wondering if he thought I was just a kid, or old enough to consider as a girlfriend.

One night we drove home in a snowstorm, barely making it to my front door. I invited him in. My mother was having a romantic dinner with Charlie, candles flickering, the Tiffany lamp at the lowest setting on the dimmer, a fire roaring, quiet giggles intercut by clanking silverware. I announced from the doorway that it was too dangerous to drive and that Kuel would be spending the night. This caught my mother off guard; she struggled to sound authoritative when she said, "Okay, Julianna, but he sleeps in the guest room."

I replied nonchalantly "Uh-huh" as we crept off into my bedroom.


Just before my father moved back to London, I went to visit him one last time on Eighty-ninth Street. I was in Alexandra's old room, talking on the phone with her in California, complaining for the umpteenth time about my life with Charlie and my mother and how much I hated him. After dinner that night, my father knocked on the door and asked to speak with me.

"Juli, I overheard you talking to your sister. I've been thinking a lot about this, and I want to offer you some options." He paused, looking so uncomfortable I thought he would stop himself and bolt out the door.

"I don't think it's healthy for you to be living with them, but there's nothing I can do or say that will change your mother's mind." He looked at the floor, slowly shaking his head. "So I think there are three choices here, and you can make the decision. Whichever one you choose I will support. One: You can become a boarding student at the school you are going to now. Two: You could go back to the Michael Hall School in Sussex and board there. Three: I bought the house where you live now, so it's ultimately your house. I have the authority to tell your mother to leave and you can live there on your own."

I listened to my options, my fifteen-year-old self, trying to picture me alone in that house. Knowing full well I could never, ever do that to my mother. *Is he serious? He would be okay with my mother out on the street and me living in that place all by myself?* I knew I didn't want to go to boarding school; for me that wasn't an option. All my friends hated boarding school. Watching them yearn for the freedom I had as a day student made that clear. *These weren't options, they felt more like prison sentences.* The air was heavy in the room. I didn't want my last visit with my father to be weighed down by my mother and her unacceptable behavior.

"It's okay, Dad," I said with an awkward smile. "It's really not so bad, I'll just grin and bear it. It's only two and a half more years; I can handle that." The conversation made me want to rip my skin off and flush my remains down the toilet.

On the plane back to New Hampshire, I ruminated over my father's options. *He didn't ask me to come live with him.* I put my hurt feelings in a drawer somewhere in the back of my brain and didn't pay too much attention to the rejection, possibly because at fifteen I didn't know how to handle it, but most likely because all I could think about was Kuel. I was deeply, madly in love with him.

Kuel became my anchor, my safe harbor. There was nothing my mother could say. How could she enforce any rule when she had broken every one?

I spent most weekends at Kuel's house. On Friday after school he would pick me up in one of his "fixer-upper" cars or, if the weather permitted, his motorcycle. Nothing made me happier than wrapping my arms around his waist, resting my head on his back, and watching the world go by as we rode to his house for the weekend. I admired his independence and his "I can do it myself" attitude. I saw the two of us as kindred spirits, somewhat abandoned by our parents but determined to keep pushing forward.

Surprisingly I never turned to drugs or alcohol during this time. I knew that I needed to stay focused, alert, do well in school so I could make something of my life. I wasn't sure what it was exactly that I wanted to do as an adult, but I wanted every option open to me, and I knew that achieving a high grade point average was my ticket to success, whatever that success would be.

Kuel taught me how to drive, and at fifteen I was driving without a license. When we went to parties I was the sober one driving everyone home, Kuel in the passenger seat guiding me. I knew most of his friends, and even though I was always the youngest in the room, they depended on me to get them home. I loved the feeling of being needed, of belonging to a group of people, a tribe.

One of Kuel's best friends, Stephane, was a senior at school, and also a day student. On the days Kuel couldn't pick me up, Stephane and I would hop in his mint green Gremlin and drive out to Kuel's house. Fridays were the only days after school I allowed myself to let my hair down, relax a little, and just be with my friends without thinking about homework or responsibilities. I could just be. One weekend Stephane and I arrived at Kuel's house, where a large party was already in progress. A group of friends had just come back from a cross-country trip and were staying with Kuel for the weekend.

Music was blasting, a keg of beer was pumping out large drafts, and the smell of brownies permeated the air. I was starving. The second those brownies came out of the oven I scarfed three of them down.

I sat at the round kitchen table feeling the bass line vibrate through the wood. People were standing around laughing, talking, having a great time. My friend Emily was sitting across from me. She was a couple years older, a slight girl with jet-black, thick hair she wore parted in the middle and tucked behind her ears. We weren't best friends, but we were close enough. I was about to start a conversation when suddenly I saw, at the crown of her head, two small horns, one growing on either side of her part. I sat there with my mouth slightly open ready to say something, but I couldn't find my voice. As I watched, the horns got bigger and bigger. I looked around me to see if anyone else had noticed this phenomenon. No one was paying attention. I was transfixed.

I knew I should stop staring before she recognized that I understood who she truly was, but I couldn't look away. She stared right back at me, a long, prodding glare, and I knew instantly what she was saying with her eyes: *If you tell anyone what you're seeing I will kill you.*

She was Satan, or a devil. I could see everything, I knew her secret, her horns gave her away, but why was it only me that could see them? My heart began to race, pounding in my temples. She snapped her head away, and when she turned back to me her eyes grew darker, smaller, black-eyed peas. She was warning me that if I made one false move I would suffer her wrath.

I abruptly stood up from the table, noticing the sweat that had pooled under my arms and behind my knees and was dripping down my forehead. I held on to the table, sure that my legs were not attached to my body.

"Jules?" I heard someone say, but they sounded like they were underwater, talking in slow motion.

"Did she eat those brownies?" another voice called out from the water tank.

Kuel came over to me. "Julianna, did you eat the brownies?"

I was too afraid to speak. I nodded, still staring at Emily and her ever-growing horns.

It turned out the cross-country trippers had bought some home-grown weed on their travels and baked it into the brownies. The stuff was so strong that one brownie would have given a large man a good time, but three of them were enough to put a girl my size in a padded cell.

Kuel carried me to his bedroom because my legs refused to function. He laid me down in his bed and put a blanket over me, telling me I needed to sleep it off. He left the room, shutting off the light as he closed the door, and went back to the party.

Plunged into darkness, I desperately tried to erase the images that kept morphing behind my eyelids. This only made them more animated. Gargoyles grimacing at me, yellow fanged teeth piercing through their stretched lips, making threatening sounds. I opened my eyes, gasping for air. I tried to focus on solid things: a chair, the curtains, a bedside lamp. Nothing worked; each object became a deathtrap, luring me to the dark side. I was in my own horror movie with no way of escaping. Everything around me was evil; the more I tried to focus the worse it became, until finally I knew I had to get out of there. If I stayed in that room one minute longer I would surely die.

I called out, begging God, or someone, to help me, but no one could hear me over the loud music. This was my worst nightmare. *Please don't let it end this way, please help me, please!* This was my first experience with drugs; I was sixteen and I was sure I would die.

Somehow I managed to get out of the bedroom. The house was split level with open, unfinished slatted staircases made of plywood. I stood in the doorway looking down through the slats to the kitchen, where everyone was. I couldn't let Emily see me; I was scared to death of her. I maneuvered my way quietly down the stairs unnoticed, past the kitchen, down the next flight of stairs to the front door, and ran out of the house. The ice-cold air immediately made me feel better; it was so cold it shocked me out of the nightmare. I gulped as much of it into my lungs as I could at one time, and then again and again, breathing so hard I thought my body would burst open. And then I just stuck out my thumb at the first car that passed by. I wasn't thinking rationally, I didn't care, I just needed to get away from that house. I would rather have died in a snowbank on the side of the road than go back to that house.

I have no idea how I got home. I don't remember the car picking me up when I stuck out my thumb. I don't know if I was crying or trying to act like everything was fine. I have no idea what I said or who picked me up, I just know I made it home. Late on a Friday night in the middle of nowhere, New Hampshire, I made it fifteen miles back to my house.

I opened the door, and soothing classical music washed over me; a small fire hummed in the fireplace. The house was warm and inviting. I ran to my mother, who was sitting on the couch, threw myself into her arms, and held on as tight as I could. "Mom, I ate three pot brownies and I am having a really bad trip. I swear to you, if you can just get me through this I will never do drugs again. Please make it stop, I just need it to stop!"

She cradled me close, holding my head to her bosom, stroking my hair. A babe, nestled in her arms, the safest place on earth. She calmed me down, soothing me with her beautiful, clear voice. "You're okay, sweetheart, you're going to be just fine. Breathe, big deep breaths, just breathe."

When I calmed down she brought me up to my room, gave me fresh, clean pajamas, and put me into bed. She warmed a washcloth and gently washed my face, erasing the tears. When she felt I was calm enough, she went to the kitchen, then brought up hot soup and buttered toast. I was still shaky and couldn't hold the spoon. I let her feed me, comfort me, mother me until I fell asleep with the affirmation that I would be okay, I wouldn't die, not tonight anyway, not under her care.

The comfort my mother gave me that night was bigger than my anger. After the brownie experience, my heart softened and our relationship healed . . . a bit. I became a little more accepting of Charlie. I didn't throw him a welcoming party, but I was kinder; my cruel edges dissipated. I wanted him to be there for her when I was gone. I wanted her to be happy. I didn't go so far as to engage with them. I still walked to school and took my dinner to my room when I was home, always with the excuse that I needed to study. The three of us shared the same house but didn't necessarily live together. This felt manageable. Not ideal, but better than it had been.

## EIGHT
# time well
# spent

I was accepted to Sarah Lawrence College. As excited as I was to
further my education, I was also in need of a break from academic
life. With the support of my parents, I deferred my entrance for one
year and decided to take my gap year in London. The plan after I
graduated high school was for Kuel and me to take a trip through
Europe for a month, after which I would stay in London for the
year and he would go back to the States.

I wanted to be near my father. I had seen him only twice a year
for the last three years, and I wanted to get to know him better. I
wanted to meet his friends, have dinner with him on a weeknight,
see where he worked, whom he worked with. I think subconsciously
I was inserting myself into his life, making him wake up and pay
attention to me.

Rowena and I had always fantasized about living together in
London for a year, and this seemed like the perfect opportunity. My

father agreed that taking a year off before going to college was a smart decision, one he wished he had made. His rules for my year off were that I had to work, make my own money, and find myself a place to live. He would give me one month of free living at his house, after that I was on my own.

Kuel and I stretched our pennies as far as we could on our trip, taking the train from London to Paris, traveling through France, Germany, Switzerland, and Belgium. In August we came back to my father's house in Knightsbridge, bid a teary farewell to each other, knowing it would be four months until he came back at Christmas for a visit. Saying goodbye to Kuel wasn't as difficult as I'd thought it would be. I loved him dearly, but I was ready to be on my own and excited to finally have time with Rowena. She and I moved into a frilly pink guest room on Hasker Street. The clock was ticking; we had one month to set ourselves up.

Our first task was finding work. I was told that jobs were few and far between in England, and the ones you could find paid so little it was impossible to live on. We were determined to beat the odds. We decided the best place to work would be a clothing store; you really didn't need experience and how hard could it be? We headed to Kings Road, a few blocks from my dad's place, with all the shops we loved. We trudged up and down, both sides of the street, and filled out applications at every store that was looking for help. Nothing.

Every day we ventured out a little farther beyond Knightsbridge and Chelsea, applying to any store that looked half decent. Finally we ended up on South Molton Street in Mayfair, a pedestrian precinct with a lovely cobblestone walkway that runs from Oxford Street to Brook Street, right near the Bond Street tube station.

Rowena put in an application at a shoe shop called Bertie, and I filled one out at a clothing boutique called Friends. They were two doors away from each other, and miraculously we both got the jobs.

I lied to the store manager when she asked me for my National Insurance number; I told her that I would be getting it any day now, my father's lawyers at Ted Bates were working on it. Of course they weren't; I don't think my father even had a lawyer. I figured if I worked really hard and showed her how invaluable I was, somehow she would let me keep my job without papers.

We were paid in cash every week, including bonuses to whoever sold the most clothing. Being the stepdaughter of a former stylist, I knew exactly how to get women to buy clothes. When they were trying them on in the dressing room, I would tell them how thin they looked in the outfit. That was all they needed to hear. Oftentimes I would say, "Wow, the last lady who tried that on couldn't pull it off, but it's as if it was made for you, you look amazing!"

I became an expert folder, organizing items in color order. With the hanging garments I took five sleeves at a time, holding each one in the vee of my fingers, bringing them up and then slowly settling them back down so each shirt was equidistant from its neighbors.

I made sure I was always on time and never complained, holding my breath for the day they would ask me for my papers. They never did.

Rowena and I found an apartment on Oakley Street, at the high end of Kings Road. A one-bedroom flat on the fifth floor of a walk-up. It was a decent size with high ceilings, a large living room, a small but functioning kitchen, and a bathroom that you had to step up into through a door fit for a Hobbit. The ceiling in the bathroom was so low, if you stood taller than five foot eight you had to duck.

Our friend Gwendolyn came to join us. We knew her from the Michael Hall School; she had transferred there in the seventh grade. Gwendolyn came from a well-off family and had an allowance I had always been envious of. She didn't really need to work, but she got a job at a chic boutique on the Kings Road, which lasted about two months, until she got fired for never showing up on time. She slept in the single bed, and Rowena and I shared the double bed. Rowena and I hadn't planned to include her in our year together; as much as we loved her, she had a tragic quality about her, probably moored in the fact that she didn't really have ambition of any kind;

everything was handed to her. I witnessed that year how crippling it can be for a young person not to need a reason to get out of bed in the morning. What was the point of going to work when she really didn't need the money? She lived for glossy magazines and Hollywood movies. She spent her days in the Hobbit bathroom, soaking in a bubble bath, smoking cigarettes while she read *Glamour, Vogue,* and *People,* and fantasized about falling in love with film stars. She was stunning, her aquamarine eyes piercing. She was always up on the latest fashion and all the "in" places to go. Rowena and I followed her around like little puppies when we went out at night.

The electricity in the flat was dependent on a coin-fed meter. Rowena and I religiously stacked ten-pence coins on top of the meter so we would never run out of power, but inevitably Gwendolyn, too lazy to go to the bank, would take the money to buy cigarettes and magazines. Rowena and I would come trudging home after a long day of standing on our feet, looking forward to cooking dinner and finally being able to relax, and nine times out of ten, just as we were about to finally sit down, the lights would go out. Gwendolyn, in the bath, cigarette dangling out of her mouth, would yell, "Sorry, guys, I don't think there's any more money for the meter, had to use it today, will pay you back." She drove us nuts, but her wicked sense of humor and her share of the rent were reasons enough to include her in our sojourn.

Getting to work and back every day proved to be challenging. We could either walk fifteen minutes to the bottom of Kings Road and take two trains or take the bus a block away and get off at Oxford Circus. The bus took over an hour, the tube less time but more walking. The irony of Rowena working in a shoe shop was that she suffered from bunions on both feet. Her lot in life was never being able to wear fancy shoes. At sixteen she had had both bunions removed and wore casts from her feet up to her knees, for two months hobbling about with a cane, only to discover, when they finally sawed the casts off, that her bunions had already grown back. If we took the tube home at night the poor girl would be limping up the street to our flat, her bunions aching by the end of the day. I would lovingly imitate her as we made our way home, dragging my one leg behind me like Igor, hands dangling down in front of me, hunched over.

Some mornings I would get up extra early and meet my father at his house so we could walk through Hyde Park together on our way to work. Our walks gave me time alone with him.

Wherever my father lived he walked to work. When he lived on Eighty-ninth Street in Manhattan he walked through Central Park to his office on Fifty-ninth Street every day. In London he did the same, leaving a half hour early to get his exercise in. He had a heavy brown leather briefcase he would hold out to the side, arm raised up. He would carry it that way for twenty steps and then switch arms, his way of incorporating some kind of weight training into his daily exercise. I find myself doing the same thing when I am pressed for time, holding my groceries out to my side as I walk home.

What I loved most about my year in London, aside from living with Rowena, was not having this constant fear of running out of time. I was a year old when my father moved out; time with him felt too precious. Weekends were not enough to delve into anything uncomfortable for fear of our time together ending and things not being resolved. In London I could engage with him in a way that I had never been able to. We talked about everything, and for the first time in my life I wasn't afraid to disagree with him or make him angry; we had time to talk through it, see each other's point of view.

One of our biggest disagreements was about abortion. At eighteen I was finding my voice as a woman and believed (and still do) that a woman has the right to choose whatever she feels is right for her; my father agreed with me on that point but asked me to try to understand it from another perspective. He was looking at it through a spiritual lens: "It's not that women shouldn't have the right to choose, they should, but for me, when that child is conceived I believe that the spirit of the child came long before the pregnancy."

"So if Jack the Ripper raped me and I got pregnant, you would want me to have the baby?"

"That's not what I'm saying. I would want you to do what you felt was right for you and I would support you in anything you chose to do, but I think that baby was meant to come into this world because I believe that child comes from the spirit long before there is a physical body."

These were our discussions as we made our way to Oxford Circus via Hyde Park. We would agree to disagree, to see things differently; that was an anomaly for me, liberating in my relationship with him. I could see that he enjoyed my passion, my thoughts, my ideas. Before my year in London I assumed I was supposed to think like him, agree with everything he said, accept his beliefs as though they were mine. My time with my father had been so skeletal I wanted it only to resemble a happy relationship. I could afford to argue with my mother, disagree with her, because we lived together. Even when we fought there would be plenty of time to make up. For the first time as a young adult with my father, I thrilled in having a difference of opinion. I liked the debates; whereas before I shrank away from them, now I welcomed them.

By the end of May, Rowena and I had saved enough money to go on vacation, at least enough for round-trip tickets to Tenerife, a tourist destination bursting with sunshine. Tenerife is the largest and most populated of the eight Canary islands, teeming with sunburnt tourists from England, Denmark, Norway, Germany—all the nearby countries where winters rule long and dark.

After working a nine-to-seven job six days a week for nine months, we were ready to let loose and feel free. Gwendolyn decided to join us when her parents agreed to give her the money, a slight thorn in my side after feeling so accomplished that Rowena and I had saved every penny we earned to deserve this vacation; the upside was that Gwendolyn could lead the way when it came to our social life.

The three of us rented a studio apartment; I shared the bed with Rowena, giving Gwendolyn the couch. We knew our money wouldn't last for the whole month, so we went about searching for easy jobs, which we found thanks to Gwendolyn, who easily navigated her way through all the hip clubs. Doors opened to her immediately. I don't know if it was her upscale outfit or her attitude that got us in everywhere we went, but we were grateful. We fell in with some owners of a nightclub that needed people to sell tickets to tourists for their special events on the beach. During the day we slathered vinegar on our bodies, a trick we learned from the locals, to get as dark as possible, and at night we hung out for free in the nightclub.

I copied everything Gwendolyn did. When she put Sun In in her hair to bring out her highlights, I did the same to my dark curls. Sadly I have no natural highlights; my hair took on a burnt orange hue. Back then getting a deep, dark tan was all the rage; the tanner you were, the better. When I stepped off the plane at Heathrow Airport on our return, my father took one look at me and said with his sour apple face, "You left here with dark hair and light skin, you came back monochromatic orange." I didn't care; I thought I looked great.

My gap year was coming to a close; in a few months I would be venturing into my college life back in the States. I was ready. In my year off I had accomplished what I had set out to do. I cemented the connection I had been craving with my father, and that brought me tremendous joy. My time with Rowena solidified our friendship for life. Working every day, out in the real world, made my appreciation for a higher education even stronger than it had been in high school. Now the idea of waking up and walking into a classroom to learn felt like summer camp compared to the hustle and bustle of trying to make a living. I was looking forward to the next four years of my life.

# *in the boom boom room*

I spent the night before my first day of college with Rachel in New York City. She lived on Twenty-seventh Street and Second Avenue in a rented apartment with a roommate. Sarah Lawrence College was twenty minutes away by train. We would catch the Metro-North from Grand Central the next morning and head up to Bronxville. My mother had broken up with Charlie the year I was away and sold our house in Wilton, moving to Keene, New Hampshire, where she had a teaching position at the Waldorf school there, a place I had absolutely no connection to. Bronxville would become my new home, college my new life.

I don't really remember how I processed the news when my mother told me about the breakup. I can't recall if I was furious that I had suffered three years so he would be there for her when I was gone, or if I was relieved I would never have to see him again. My guess is a bit of both. At the time I was too concerned with my own life. I wanted to settle into college and figure out what I was most passionate about so I could focus on my future. I must have filed the information away in my drawer of grievances to save for another day, knowing that one day, when I opened the drawer, it would smack me in the face. For now, I needed to put one foot in front of the other and get through my first semester.

Rachel helped me schlep my old camp trunk through Grand Central, each of us holding on to the worn leather handles on either side. I was nervous and so grateful to have my sister by my side. In a flash we got to the Bronxville train station and dragged the trunk onto the platform, wondering how we would get it up the hill to my new dorm room. It was late August; the thick air lay heavily on the denim shirt I'd opted to wear. It had been my father's and was over-size and threadbare. I loved that shirt; when I wore it I felt pro-tected. But now I cursed at myself for putting it on that morning as sweat began to run down my body, marking the armpits with dark halos. The black cotton leggings I had on began to droop and sag in an unsightly fashion, making my rear end look like I was carrying a heavy water balloon.

We found a taxi and made our way to campus. As we struggled to get my luggage out of the grease-stained trunk of the cab, a gleaming white limousine pulled up in front of us. I watched as an elegantly dressed man stepped out, opening the door to an out-stretched dainty hand that belonged to a young woman decked out in a white linen pantsuit with an impressive straight blond bob fall-ing just perfectly to her chin. She stood up out of the car and pulled out a cigarette; her father (I assumed) dug in his pocket and brought out a silver lighter. I was dumbstruck. I stood and stared at what I thought must be a scene out of a movie.

My hair was tied back in a loose ponytail, the humidity creating a burnt orange ball of frizz. *Why didn't I think to dress better?* I thought to myself as I looked down at my saggy knees, utterly self-conscious. Not that I owned a white linen suit, but anything would have been better. Rachel saw me crumbling before her eyes and whispered in my wet, soggy ear, "Don't worry, honey, she'll be in jeans and a T-shirt the second he leaves."

We found my assigned room; my roommate was already there, unpacking with her mother. The bed by the window was already made up with beautiful, soft flowery sheets, her desk by the only other window in the room neatly organized with leather binders and a blotter, matching cup to hold her pens and pencils already sharpened and ready for use. My sister quickly sussed out the situation and came to my rescue.

"I think we need to rearrange the room so Julianna can have a window too, don't you? Only fair, really."

"Of course, of course," her mother replied with embarrassment. "What was I thinking?"

We went about reconfiguring the furniture so that my bed was in a cozy nook by the window, looking out toward the trees. I was so relieved, so thankful to my sister for speaking up for me.

After helping me unpack and sort things out in the room, Rachel kissed me on the cheek and said goodbye. Left alone with my new roommate and her mother, I began to panic. I didn't belong here; this was a rich person's school, a school where parents lit their kids' cigarettes with silver lighters. Where mothers bought high-thread-count sheets and made their kids' beds. I clocked my roommate's dresser: bottles of Clinique moisturizers, cleansers with cotton pads piled neatly on top of one another in a glass container made for just that. A bottle of Chanel No. 5 perfume propped up to the side like a trophy. My dresser in comparison looked sparse and unadorned, holding an old toiletry bag with my discount moisturizer, a jar of Vaseline, and a travel-size tube of toothpaste. What was I doing here? I forced myself to push my anxiety down, feeling it hovering in my abdomen as I tried to make conversation. *I'm not going to last the semester,* I told myself.

During the first few weeks of school I spent every weekend at Rachel's apartment. When my last class was over on Friday I couldn't get to the train fast enough. I'm sure I overstayed my welcome, sleeping on the couch Friday to Sunday. I didn't care if Rachel went out on Saturday night; I was content to sit at the table and write my papers, or watch TV, as long as I didn't have to be at school. Rachel kept trying to assure me that it would get better, I would make friends, I just needed to give it time. That first month was excruciating. I missed Rowena, even longed for our makeshift apartment and my long days at the clothing store.

I threw myself into my studies, amazed when the professor told us we had three weeks to write one paper. I got it done in two days. I took a few theater classes that first semester. I had such a heavy academic schedule I thought it would be a good change for me to do something creative. I was toying with the idea of going into law like my grandmother. I thought following in her footsteps would give me the opportunity to make a difference in the world, push the female agenda forward, respect the path she had diligently forged ahead of me.

On my way to acting class I saw a sign-up sheet for a play the seniors were doing. They needed underclassmen to fill in the smaller roles. The play was *In the Boom Boom Room* by David Rabe. I decided to audition, assuming I wouldn't get the part but had nothing to lose. I got the part: Melissa, a go-go dancer. I had four lines in the play, the rest of the time I was in a go-go cage dancing.

The first day of rehearsals I sat off to the side, listening, watching, taking everything in. I loved the rehearsal process, a safe place where you could experiment, saying the same line a million different ways before you found the right tone, pitch, meaning. A community of people collaborating, all there for the same purpose. Rehearsals allowed me to finally feel like I belonged somewhere, fit in, was appreciated. Every day I would run from my last class to be with this newfound group. No linen pantsuits, no Chanel perfume;

all that mattered were the words, the ability to make people believe what you were saying.

When the lights came up at our first performance, I remember standing in my thigh-high boots and hot pants looking out at the audience in my two-by-two go-go cage, thinking, *I'm home!* I had never been so sure of anything in my life. It was a lightning bolt moment that hit me so hard I wanted to cry I was so happy.

After the play ended I signed up for as many acting classes as I could. I wanted to learn everything. I had always been in school plays or acting out plays at home. With no television, playing charades had been our go-to source for entertainment, but I had never studied the actual process; acting was just a part of our family's life. I had been around creative people all the time but never really gave it much thought. My mother and sister were both dancers, Rachel a singer-songwriter and musician, my father a writer. Acting made sense to me.

I started reading plays like I was eating potato chips, one after the other, never getting enough. I dove into the world of theater, excited for every class, discovering a place to finally release all these emotions that I had bottled up for years: Anxiety I had pushed down when I was a kid always on the move to uncertain places. Anger I had swallowed when my mother took me away from my father and my sister. Rejection I felt from my father but never expressed. Fear I subconsciously carried around like a heavy backpack, that if push came to shove my mother would abandon me for a man. All these feelings I had somewhere inside of me, but I had never allowed myself to address them because I never wanted to appear "difficult" or "ungrateful."

I realized once I let myself go, I could tap into my emotions at the drop of a hat without being afraid to show them. Being able to express myself without the fear of being thought of as too weak, too emotional, or judged was ultimately the most freeing experience I ever had. Even better, to express this through a character, finding out what motivates them, how they see the world, to walk in someone else's shoes, was liberating beyond belief. To peel off my own skin and take on someone else's—what better way to learn about yourself than by freeing yourself from your own constraints?

About halfway through my first semester my fake tooth from my bike riding accident began to bother me. It had been four years since my father's dentist had seen me, sending me out of his office with a fake tooth that never fit properly in my mouth, a little darker than the rest of my teeth and leaving a gap where once there was none. The bonding he had adhered to my chipped teeth was always falling off. I shoved them back on, once even trying to attach the bonding to my teeth with Krazy Glue. My mouth had been a constant source of discomfort since the accident. I developed a habit of putting my hand in front of my face to hide the ugly gap and discolored tooth when I smiled or laughed. I got used to it; it was better than not having a tooth at all. But now it was bothering me, and when what began as a slight throb turned into a painful ache, I knew I needed to have it looked at.

I couldn't remember the name of my father's dentist, and for some reason, probably because phone calls abroad were so expensive, I didn't call my father to ask. Instead I took out the yellow pages. I remembered that he was located on Central Park South and he had a Jewish name. Much to my surprise when I looked for a Jewish sounding dentist on Central Park South, I found about five hundred listed. I scanned the names and picked out three of them randomly. I made appointments and took the train into the city. None of them turned out to be my father's dentist. I went to the first appointment, and after looking at my mouth briefly, the dentist told me the only way he could fix the tooth was to replace eight of my front teeth with new caps. This would cost upwards of ten thousand dollars. I went to the second dentist, who told me the same thing. By the time I walked into the third and last appointment, I was on the edge of hysteria. *I won't be able to act if I can't open my mouth. I'll never be able to pay for new teeth. I like my other teeth, I only want one new tooth! What am I going to do?*

I waited to be called into the examination room, swallowing the emotion that was bubbling under the surface. Finally my name was called. A kind man with a trimmed beard sat down next to me. He asked me what the problem was and I told him the whole story, about the accident, how the tooth was never fixed properly, how I had fallen in love with acting at school and needed to fix the bad tooth. He gently asked me to open my mouth and took a good long look inside.

"Well, you have naturally beautiful teeth. It's going to take a little time, but I think I can make you a perfect tooth to match the others and give you the right kind of bonding on your chipped teeth. You won't be able to tell the difference once I finish."

I paused, a little confused. Not prepared to hear good news, I was skeptical.

"But I've been to two other dentists, and they both told me I had to replace at least eight of my teeth," I said, beginning to get emotional.

"That's because they aren't artists," he said with a mischievous grin. He assured me that he was the right man for the job and that he would give me back the smile I once had.

For a brief moment I felt unbridled joy, until it dawned on me that he hadn't told me the cost.

"Do you take payment plans?" I asked as casually as I could. I didn't want him to abandon me. "I can pay a small monthly sum, and I promise I will pay you back every penny, it's just . . . I don't have a lot of money at the moment."

His response shocked me. He laughed sweetly and told me not to worry about the payment; right now all he wanted to focus on was doing a great job, the rest would follow.

Relief flooded over me when I left his office, and it wasn't only because my tooth would get fixed; it was because he showed me such kindness. A total stranger cared about me. He seemed so invested in my happiness and was offering to help.

He did fix my fake tooth and my two chipped teeth. We spent a lot of time together. He drove me in his own car all around the city to different dental labs, making sure the color of the new tooth would match perfectly. He took such pride in his work, which astounded me. He cared so much about what he was doing, and I was the lucky recipient of his artistry. In only a few weeks I was smiling, hands free, no gap, no cheap bonding falling off in my sandwich. He gave me back my smile, just as he'd said he would.

He became my regular dentist as well. When I went in for check-ups I would ask him not to bother with X-rays, I couldn't afford them. He would look at me seriously and say, "I'm pretty sure one day you will be able to afford them, so for now let's just make sure you have healthy teeth." He was my guardian angel. Whenever I came into the city I made sure to go to his office to say hello. I loved talking with him. He became my confidant. I cried over boys in his office, lamented my overloaded academic schedule, complained about my father being so far away. I felt safe with him, trusted him, and always left his company feeling happy.

He watched me struggle as I endeavored to get work as an actress, never doubting my ability. He came to every play I was in, watched everything I did on television, went to every movie I made, good and bad, and always called to tell me what he thought. He celebrated all my successes, and at every step of the way he would say, "I told you so."

As I got older our friendship grew. I became *his* confidante when he was going through rough times, and I was able to give *him* a shoulder to cry on. I am so blessed to have him in my life. We joke that he is my surrogate father. He spoke at my wedding, yet never got in the way of my relationship with my father; in many ways he helped me understand my dad a little better because he could speak to his point of view, helping me see things differently than I would have.

When my father died unexpectedly in 2014, I was devastated. I didn't expect my dentist to come to the funeral; it was three hours from New York City. But as I left the podium after reciting one of my father's favorite poems by Mary Oliver, "When Death Comes," I looked up and there he was, standing at the back of the chapel. He locked eyes with me and without speaking let me know that he would hold me up until I could walk on my own again. And he did. Every step of the way.

His name is Marc Lowenberg, I found him in the yellow pages when I was nineteen. Just by chance.

Christmas break freshman year, I flew to London with Rachel to be with my father. While we were there he told me about some Sarah Lawrence students he had met at a health food restaurant he frequented in Oxford Circus, near his office. He overheard them talking at the table next to him. They were on their junior year abroad, and not being able to help himself, he butted in and told them that his daughter Julianna was at Sarah Lawrence as a freshman and they should look me up when they got back in the fall. I listened to my dad relay this story, slightly embarrassed that he had injected me into their lunch. *As if they will ever look me up,* I thought, letting it go, hoping he hadn't been too nosy.

As freshman year was coming to an end, I found a job waitressing in Southampton for the summer. Through the grapevine I heard that a guy who had been in Rachel's class at the Michael Hall School was managing his father's restaurant and bringing with him a few of the guys I knew from school. My father had given me the gift of paying for my college education, but I was responsible for my books, meals, and spending money. I needed to work in the summer, and I needed a job that would pay well. Conscience Point Inn was a hot spot, a restaurant until 11:00 P.M. that then turned into a nightclub.

Chris Greenwood, whom I knew from Jeroen's class, was coming to DJ; Richard Big, who was in Rachel's class, would be the bartender; and Sandro, son of the photographer Mike Reinhardt, would manage the place. Chris was two classes ahead of me in school, and I'd hung out with him a fair amount when Jeroen and Rowena started dating, so at least I knew someone. I wouldn't feel like a complete stranger.

I put most of my stuff in storage, packed a suitcase, and took the bus out to the Hamptons. Chris had written to tell me I could stay in his room on the floor above the restaurant until I found a place.

I would start working the day I arrived. I had waitressed before but in small local places, nothing as upscale as this. On the bus ride out there I tried to remember all the dos and don'ts of the job. Before I got on the bus I purchased extra pens and a corkscrew, praying I remembered how to open a bottle of wine properly.

I arrived at Conscience Point Inn and said a warm hello to Chris. It had been a while since I had seen him. He showed me to his room, where I dumped my bag, scanning the lone mattress in the corner, the scuffed-up hardwood floor, the slight musty smell accompanied by salty air, body odor, and dirty socks. I didn't have time to worry about my accommodations. I changed into my white shirt, black skirt, took out my pens and corkscrew, and headed downstairs.

After introducing myself to the chef and the other waiters, memorizing the specials, learning where everything went, how food orders were handed to the kitchen, where to put the bar slips, how to work the credit card machine, I walked over to the hostess to introduce myself. She looked to be around my age, with beautiful wavy brown hair that hung long past her shoulders; she was wearing a chic dress, minimal makeup. This was Dini. We made small talk, realizing a few common themes in our lives. She went to Vassar, my cousin David went there; oh yes, she knew of him, she told me. Then she said, "I'm having a birthday party next weekend, you should come."

"My birthday's next weekend too, not sure what my plans are yet."

"Really? What date, June eighth?"

"Yup."

"What year, 'sixty-six?"

"Yes!"

We had the exact same birthday. After we discussed being Geminis, Dini asked me where I was staying.

"Not sure yet, I just got here today. I'm crashing in Chris's room tonight and then hopefully I will figure something out tomorrow."

"Yuck, don't stay there, come stay at my house. My mom isn't out here yet, I have the place to myself."

It was a crazy night, all of us flying by the seat of our pants, not prepared for the onslaught of people, nothing running smoothly; I spilled beer on a customer, broke a cork in a very expensive bottle of wine. We didn't have enough napkins or silverware; the bar was so crowded waiters couldn't get through to bring cocktails to the tables. The wait for everything—food, drinks, checks—was ridiculously long. By the time we cleared the tables out of the dining room and turned it into a nightclub, Chris was up in the booth spinning records. No one seemed to care, everyone was having a great time.

Finally finished for the night, I ran to get my suitcase and threw it in the back of Dini's car. We were exhausted. My feet throbbed, my back ached, I hadn't sat down in ten hours. As we drove to her house I felt like I had just gone through some sort of bacchanalia, the loud music still reverberating in my ears.

When we pulled up to the house, my jaw dropped. It was beautiful and enormous, with perfectly cut hedgerows keeping out the lookie-loos. Once we were inside my eyes widened at the expanse of the tastefully decorated rooms; soft silk rugs welcomed my tired feet; the kitchen had a fully stocked fridge. We were both so tired, Dini showed me directly to the guest room, a few doors down from hers. There was a plush bed, made up in soft hues of cream and white, fluffy carpet, thick drapes, my own clean bathroom. I was so overwhelmed by my good fortune I could barely speak.

I thanked her and closed the door, looking around the peaceful space that was mine for the night. I unpacked as little as I could, extracting a T-shirt and boxers to sleep in, knowing that in the morning I would just have to pack up again and start hunting for a room to rent. *Why was this girl being so generous by letting me stay here for the night? We barely knew each other.*

Just as I was getting into bed Dini knocked on my door. In her pajamas, she walked in laughing. "Okay, so this is a little weird, right? I mean we barely know each other and you're sleeping at my house!"

I was relieved to hear her say it but too tired to stay on my feet, so we both got on my bed and began what turned into a gab fest, talking through the wee hours of the morning until we couldn't keep our eyes open. We ended the conversation agreeing that it was as if we had known one another all our lives. As Dini went to the door, she turned and said, "Why don't you just stay here for the month of June? My mom doesn't come out till July, and I could use the company. We can drive to work together." I fell into a blissful sleep.

The next morning, I woke up late to the sunlight streaming through the curtains. I padded downstairs and saw the lush green lawn in the backyard. Off to the right was an Olympic-size swimming pool. Dini and I had our coffee out on the porch, surrounded by shading trees, an array of flowers planted with purpose around the lawn, the light glistening off the glassy water. *How did I get so lucky?*

That week, Elizabeth, another waitress from the city, came to work with us. We hit it off immediately and Dini invited her to stay at the house too. The three of us were inseparable, driving to work together, Elizabeth and I waiting tables, Dini greeting guests and seating them. During the day we hung out at the beach or the pool, lounging about this beautiful home that was ours for the month.

When Dini's mother came out, Elizabeth and I found a room to rent near the restaurant so we could walk to work. The guys at the restaurant labeled us the Fusilli Heads, because all three of us had curly, dark hair. Once we got the hang of things, the restaurant ran smoothly, packed to the rafters every night with enthusiastic customers willing to dole out large tips for good tables. I was saving more money than I had ever thought I could, socking it away in the bank with plenty to spare for my abundant social life.

Kuel and I had broken up when I got back from London; a year apart had been too strenuous to keep what we had going. It was time for me to try new things, have different adventures. I dated a few guys that summer, none of them particularly worth noting; what they had in common was a lack of commitment. Just when I was getting comfortable, each of them disappeared like a king crab searching for food. I didn't crumble when these relationships ended. I had Dini and Elizabeth by my side, making me laugh and keeping me in good company. Our friendship has lasted over thirty years now.

During the first semester of my sophomore year I was cast as Queen Isabella in an original production of *Three Hand Solitaire,* written by a senior playwright, David Grimm, based on the life of King Edward II. The play was an instant hit on campus. My role was complex. David had written Queen Isabella as becoming a drunk once she finds out that her husband, King Edward, is sleeping with his manservant. The fights between king and queen were deliciously ferocious. My character goes down a tawdry path of destruction, devouring men and spitting them out, all the while drinking with abandon. In the end, she collapses, a puddle on the floor, drowning in her own tears as the audience realizes all she ever wanted was the love of her king, which she will never have. There were so many juicy twists and turns I could sink my teeth into, I jumped in headfirst, unafraid to explore every aspect of this woman.

After our final performance, the cast threw a party to celebrate the success of the show. Students I had never met before were mingling among the actors, congratulating all of us on a job well done. Two handsome men came up to tell me how much they loved my performance. Alec and Bill were seniors and had been abroad their junior year. Bill studying at Oxford, Alec in London at the Royal Academy of Dramatic Art. Although I had never met them before, I liked them instantly. Alec was funny, dapper, and elegant; Bill was playful, introspective, and a little disheveled, like he had dressed in a hurry and forgotten to button his shirt all the way.

We talked until the party ended and made plans to get lunch the next day. The ratio of women to men on campus at Sarah Lawrence, formerly an all-female college, was ten to three. I hadn't met too many guys there that interested me. I had a hunch Alec was gay but was certain Bill was straight.

We started hanging out regularly. I realized Alec was in Song Class with me, and I couldn't understand why we hadn't connected before. Bill was a painter, studying art, theology, and English literature. The three of us became a fixture on campus; whenever we had free time we were hanging out in one of our dorm rooms. They introduced me to their friends, took me with them to the city to parties alumni were throwing. College life opened up to me with Alec and Bill, and with each day my crush on Bill grew a little bigger.

There was an annual school gala, which I had purposely missed the year before thinking it wouldn't be any fun. Alec and Bill assured me otherwise and insisted I go with them. We gussied up, Alec in his father's 1960s suit, perfectly tailored; Bill in his slightly baggy khakis, a blue blazer, and a pink shirt. I had one of my mother's black velvet dresses from Paris, bought a pair of long white gloves from a thrift store, painted my lips red, and off we went, the three of us, arm in arm, down the hill to Bates, the school's cafeteria, which had been magically transformed into a beautiful dance hall.

I was dancing with Bill as reflections of the red and blue lights spun off the mirrored ball hanging in the middle of the room. I had never experienced college like this, at a dance, having fun with my friends, taking little sips of vodka from a flask someone had brought. We were all having a great time when Bill spun me around and threw me into Alec's arms. "You two should be dancing together!" he said, and scurried off the dance floor in search of a drink.

Alec and I danced for a long time, and when we finally stopped to rest I looked around for Bill.

"Do you know where Bill went?" I asked Alec, with no particular urgency.

"He's probably outside on the lawn, making out with Jim."

"Wait, what? Bill's gay?"

"Yeah, you didn't know?"

"Um . . . no. I thought *you* were gay. You're gay, right?" I said, praying I wasn't offending him.

"Nope, not gay."

*Shit, I'd offended him.*

Obviously my radar was completely wrong. I was so sure that Bill was straight and Alec was gay. I needed a few days to wrap my head around that one. I had no choice but to accept this new information. It actually made things less complicated in the long run. There would be no breakup; we could be friends for the rest of our lives. The idea of that made me happy.

A few weeks after the dance, we were hanging out in Bill's room when out of nowhere he announced: "You and Alec should try dating!" Alec had let Bill know he was sweet on me from the day we met but was too shy to tell me. I was a little thrown. I looked over at Alec, who seemed utterly mortified, furious at Bill.

The several men I had dated since Kuel had a macho quality about them. Inattentive, more concerned with themselves, acting as if I should be grateful they were giving me any time at all. I ruminated on that as I looked at Alec, wondering if it wasn't time for a change, time to be with someone who was kind, gentle, and present. Maybe that was just what I needed. Alec was funny and smart and fun to be around, easy to talk to and a good listener. *Why shouldn't I give it a try?*

I don't remember exactly how it started, but Alec and I began dating.

We were crazy about each other. Not in a sexual way, but in the most loving way I had ever experienced. He didn't try to change me, he loved me just the way I was. He was affectionate and tender, vulnerable and sweet. We loved being around each other.

The sexual side of our relationship was more strained. We tried to be intimate, but it felt clumsy and unnatural. We were uncomfortable talking about sex; it was easier to enjoy what did work rather than delve into what didn't. And strangely I was okay with that, at least for a while. Alec's love and friendship was enough for me. I hadn't acknowledged how much I was craving this kind of attention until we got together. He showered me with affection like no other man had ever done. My friends became his friends, his friends became my friends, I belonged to a tribe that I loved.

It had been almost a year since my father told me the story about the Sarah Lawrence students he met at the restaurant in London. Alec, Bill, and a bunch of other friends were hanging out one night when someone asked me about my father. I gave them a brief synopsis, telling them he lived in London, describing him as a vegetarian who would rather go to his favorite health food place by himself with an esoteric book on philosophy than be forced to dine with other executives at three-martini and steak lunches.

As I was speaking, Alec looked at Bill with his mouth agape. "Oh my God! You're Julie-Anna!"

"What?" I asked, confused.

"We met your dad at a health food place near Oxford Circus. He told us to look up his freshman daughter when we got back, told us your name was Julianna, we wrote it down like Julie-Anna and tacked it up on our fridge when we got home. You became a little bit of a joke: *Let's make sure to look up Julie-Anna when we get back.* Once we packed up and went home we forgot all about it! You are Julie-Anna!"

I called my dad in the morning and said, "You're never going to believe this one, Dad. You know those students you met last year from Sarah Lawrence? Well, I'm dating one of them; we just figured it out. You met him before I did."

"Well how do you like them apples?" my dad said with a chuckle.


Alec and Bill graduated at the end of my sophomore year. That summer I got a job waitressing at the River Café in Brooklyn Heights four nights a week, and during the day I worked in a clothing store on Columbus Avenue. I rented a room on 116th Street and Riverside in a beautiful apartment that belonged to the family of one of the students from Sarah Lawrence. Bill found a place to live on the Upper East Side, and Alec lived in Prospect Park with another friend from college. We had the summer together in New York City, all of us working and hanging out together on our days off. I was saving money for a sojourn in Italy.

I had always known I would take my junior year abroad; Sarah Lawrence encouraged it as did my father, and I knew this was a once-in-a-lifetime opportunity to study abroad. I had decided to go to Florence. I wanted to study Dante. I had become infatuated with him my senior year of high school. I painted a huge mural (not very well) of Dante's Inferno, nine circles of Hell, for one of my senior projects. I was convinced that I needed to go and study the man in his hometown, immerse myself in his world, walk the streets he walked, try to understand him better. Since I had already lived in England and France, I thought I needed to challenge myself. My girlfriend Blair was going to the Sorbonne in Paris and tried to get me to go there with her. I thought that sounded too easy since I had already lived in Paris as a small child. What a mistake.

While Blair was having a blast in Paris, I was experiencing PTSD from the time I had been a nanny in East Hampton. All the students had been placed with families, and for some reason they placed me with a woman in her late sixties who had just gone through a brutal divorce. Her husband, a judge, had left her for his much younger secretary. She walked around her empty hallways more like a widow than a divorcée. The apartment was very nice, but the large uninhabited rooms felt impossibly lonely. She holed herself up in her bedroom most of the time; her children were grown and out of the house. She didn't speak a word of English and I didn't know any Italian. There was a lock on the telephone; only incoming calls were permitted. I lived in what must have been the maid's quarters when the house was brimming with children and full of life. I had my own bathroom and small bedroom.

In the morning she left coffee and a pastry on the kitchen table for me, as breakfast was part of the deal. But there was never any sign of life. Her despondency cast a shadow that extended all the way to my room. If I wanted to call anyone I had to walk a mile into the main square in town, stand on line at the post office, and wait my turn, sometimes taking over an hour. I missed Alec so much. By this time he and Bill had found an apartment together on Third Avenue and Eighty-seventh Street. I longed to be there with them. I felt achingly isolated and called Alec every chance I had just to hear his voice. Other students in my program came to school reminiscing about the fun dinners they'd had with their host families, the kids showing them around town, teaching them Italian. I came home at the end of the day and hid in my room.

Also, there were no classes on Dante; the itinerary was only on art history, which I had studied throughout my sophomore year in order to be eligible for this year abroad.

I felt defrauded.

I was cold. I had sent my winter clothes on ahead of me in a cheaply packed box to save room in my suitcase, only to discover the box never arrived and there was no way of tracking it. Every day I wallowed in regret that I hadn't chosen Paris or Oxford. I called my English professor at Sarah Lawrence and begged him to help me switch programs, but to no avail. I was stuck in Florence with my sad signora.

One night the phone rang and it was my father. I was so happy to hear his voice. But he was calling with bad news. This was 1987, the year of the stock market crash. He had lost a lot of money, and some of my college funds were gone, so I needed to get a job. Not speaking Italian, I was going to find this very difficult. I racked my brain to figure out how to make some money. I decided that teaching English was my best bet. I put up flyers all over town to teach conversational English. To my surprise two people called me for lessons.

One of my students was an elegant Swiss woman, married to an Italian banker. I loved going to her house, which was warm and welcoming, furnished exquisitely, modern but comfortable. When I arrived she served tea and cookies at the kitchen table, and I would raise the cup to my lips and say, "cup," point to the table, "table." Every item in the kitchen became a part of my lesson. Fork, spoon, knife. With each class we moved around the house: couch, rug, fireplace. It wasn't so hard. I pointed, said the word, and made her repeat it. Then we would string sentences together and I would act them out for her and watch her imitate what I had just said. I looked forward to our meetings twice a week.

My other pupil was a law professor. We met in his office. He was a tall, gray-haired gentleman with wire-rimmed glasses and a kind, open face. He spoke a little English, so I began our lessons with sentences.

I enjoyed teaching. It provided a welcome distraction and connections that made me feel a little less detached from my surroundings.

One evening after my lesson with the professor I was slowly walking back to my rented room, taking the long way home through the piazza. A woman came up to me and in English asked me if I was American. Yes, I said. She asked me if I had ever done any hair modeling; she was looking for hair models for a show that was coming to Florence. I was familiar with hair shows; during my gap year I had been approached to model my hair at a salon near my shop on South Molton Street. To tell the truth, it was a complete sham; they had me strut down the runway and told the audience that my hair was the result of their perming solution. They paid fifty pounds and the whole thing was over in less than an hour, a great way to make extra cash. I always felt slightly guilty that they were lying about my natural curls, but I justified this by telling myself if it wasn't me it would be someone else and I really needed the money.

So, when this woman asked me to model my hair for one hundred dollars, I jumped at the chance, skipped school the next day, and showed up at the address she gave me.

The woman who ran the show was a short square figure, with white hair cropped close to her scalp. She didn't speak English, but even in her Italian I could tell she was icy. Her assistants instructed us to put on the costume in the dressing room and come out to be assessed by her. I found a ridiculous silver spandex jumpsuit in the cubicle they gave me, put it on, and went to stand next to the other girls, about fifteen in total.

The Ice Queen walked around us, sizing us up as she went, and then rattled off something in Italian to her assistant and went to start the show. I was told to wait in the wings and come out when my name was called.

I watched from the sidelines as each girl was called to the stage; they walked down the runway to where Her Majesty waited. I felt bad for every girl as I watched how brazenly she chopped at their hair, giving ridiculous haircuts that even high-paid models couldn't have pulled off. I was a little smug, standing there pitying the poor fools who allowed her to do that. I knew the drill, I would walk down the runway with my mane of wild, curly hair and she would announce to the audience that I was the result of her magic perming solution. Maybe I would even make it back for my afternoon classes.

Finally my name was called. I strutted down the runway to the end, trying to pretend I didn't feel absurd in my silver cat suit. As I walked I could hear her talking about my face, something about my jawline, I couldn't make out the rest. When I got to her she lifted my hair from my face and ran her cold finger down the side of my jaw. Then in one fell swoop, without any warning, she lopped off everything; more than a foot of my hair came tumbling down, landing at my feet like a discarded carcass. There was an audible gasp from the audience as I entered an out-of-body experience, floating up to the ceiling, completely detached from my physical body. I looked down in utter despair as her sharp steel scissors butchered what was left of my mane. I was frozen in place, sure that I was going to wake up soon and it would all have been a dream. She sheared one side of my head, leaving the hair on the other hanging chin length, an asymmetrical cut, à la Vidal Sassoon.

When the execution was over, I walked zombielike back to the dressing room, still waiting to wake up, certain that this couldn't be true. And then I looked in the mirror. I didn't recognize myself. I started to cry, huge loud sobs, *Oh my God, oh my God, what did she do to me?* The more I looked, the harder I cried, until I was so hysterical people came running in. I was hyperventilating, so someone gave me a paper bag to breathe into. I swatted it out of their hand. The Ice Queen walked over to see what all the fuss was about and with disdain said, "Don be sech a bebe!" Then she turned on her heel and marched out.

In a daze I got dressed and ran out of there, not knowing what to do with myself; there was nowhere to go for comfort, no one to run to for safety. When I walked outside, the cold air smacked my neck like a whip. I had been so protected with my woolly mane; I wasn't used to my neck being exposed, making me feel even more vulnerable. I cried my way to a store, bought a bottle of cheap Chianti, and locked myself in my room, drinking until I fell asleep.

The next morning, waking up in the same clothes I had worn the day before, hungover from the cheap wine, eyes bulging out of my head from all my crying, I decided that was the last straw. I needed to go home. I started walking to the bank to withdraw the little savings I had and buy a ticket home. On my way I passed a barbershop. *Well, it can't be any worse than this,* I told myself. I walked into the shop, where one lone man was standing in an apron. In my bad Italian I tried to tell him what happened to me; finally I was forced to pull out my passport and show him what I had looked like twelve hours ago.

"Yesterday I looked like this!" Seeing my photo made me start crying all over again.

The man put both hands up to his cheeks. "Madonna!" he exclaimed as I stood there, shoulders slumped in despair.

He sat me down, put a cape over me, and started snipping away. He kept shaking his head as he worked, mumbling under his breath, the universal language for "what a shame."

He was the first human being I had made contact with since it happened, and I took a little comfort from his gentle manner. He evened out both sides, which meant he cut my hair very short all over, and then he used gel to slick it back. When he was done he smiled and said, "Better, yes?"

Well, it was better, but the damage had been done. I couldn't brush off the intense feeling that I had been attacked, violated, deceived. I needed to talk to Alec. I needed to hear his voice. Before going to the bank I ran as fast as I could to the post office and got on line.

Thank God he was home.

"Alec, my hair is gone! They chopped it off." I was crying so hard I could barely pronounce my words.

"What, honey? What do you mean?"

"I did a hair show and without even asking me if it would be okay, she just lopped off my hair. I look so ugly!"

"You could never look ugly, my angel. How short is it?"

I reached around to the back of my head.

"Shaved-at-the-neck short!" I was working myself into a frenzy as I heard the words come out of my mouth.

"Oh, honey, you know what? I bet you look gorgeous. It's about time you stopped hiding behind your hair; now you get to finally show the world your face. I've always told you you would look great with short hair, and now you have it. You never would have done it otherwise. Maybe this was a happy accident?"

Hearing his voice began to calm me down.

"I want to come home now, Al, I can't take it here anymore. I feel so alone and so fucking cold; none of my stuff arrived and now my neck is exposed and I'm even colder then I was before. I want to come home. I was on my way to the bank to take out money so I could buy a ticket home."

"Sweetheart, if you do that you're going to lose a whole semester of credits. It's October already, you'll be home in two months, that's really not so long, honey. Trust me, you will be so upset if you lose a semester. You're gonna be okay, you're just in shock, and I bet you look so beautiful; you just can't see it yet, but I know you do."

We spoke for a long time, until my tears dried up, and he even managed to make me laugh. I knew he was right. I would never forgive myself if I lost college credits. My hair would grow back, it wasn't such a big deal. Why did I get so stuck in my own way?

As we ended the conversation Alec told me that he'd just got notification that a package he had sent me weeks ago arrived that morning. "Don't open it, honey. It's just gonna make you sad. Had I known, I wouldn't have sent it."

I felt much better walking home, noting the fact that it was true, I always hid behind my hair. My hair was my protection, my shield; it was probably time for me to come out from behind it and face things head-on. Perhaps there *was* a silver lining to this catastrophe. There was nothing I could do about it now anyway; my hair was gone, I was staying in Italy, I would have to accept it.

When I got home Alec's package was sitting on my bed. I ripped it open: three large bottles of Flex hair conditioner, my favorite. With my new haircut it would last me a lifetime.

Once I resolved to stay in Florence I decided it was crucial that I come to terms with my new identity and stop complaining about what I didn't have. I bought a jar of hair gel and a brand-new bright red lipstick. Every day I slicked back my hair, slapped on my lipstick, and headed out to class feeling a bit like a warrior. *I will overcome this.* For a week after the incident I searched for the people who owed me the hundred dollars I'd been promised for the hair show, but they had skipped town without paying. I bumped into a few of the other girls from the show, and none of them had been paid either.

When Christmas break finally came I got to the airport in Rome three hours early. I was not going to miss this flight. When I landed at JFK I saw Alec waiting for me, a bouquet of red roses in his hand. I stood in front of him and at first he didn't recognize me. Finally, we threw our arms around each other and held on for a long, long time. I was home. And I was so grateful to be there. I could have kissed the ground.

The two weeks of Christmas break flew by, and before I knew it I was back at JFK headed to Italy. As I waited to board the plane, that nauseating feeling crept back into my stomach. I didn't want to go back. I called my mother from a phone booth.

"I don't want to go back there, Mom." I was on the verge of tears. "I hate it there, I want to stay in New York!"

She tried to comfort me, but as she spoke I began to get a clearer picture of what I needed to do. I decided in that moment that I was going to fly back just to collect my things. I had suffered enough, I had moved around enough, I knew what made me happy, and Florence wasn't it. I was miserable there, I wanted to be home, back in Bronxville, back at school with people I knew and trusted. I didn't want to be hanging on by a thread or have to power through something that made me sad. I couldn't do it anymore.

The first night back in my somber room I sat on the bed, looked around at the few items I had collected while I was there, and began to pack. Once I was done, I trudged to the post office to call my father and let him know I was coming home. School hadn't started yet back in the States. They still had a week to go, and I knew if I got back in time, I could figure out a place to live, talk to the dean, and get back to school without losing any credits.

When I finally got to a phone, my father's machine picked up. I left him a message and lumbered back to get my things. I didn't have a train schedule for Rome, or a plane ticket back to New York; what I did have was the credit card my father had given me my freshman year in case of emergencies. I had never used it. This was an emergency. I would scrub toilets if I had to and pay him back, but I wasn't staying in that place one more night.

I couldn't use the phone to call a taxi so I slipped out of the apartment as quietly as I could, not wanting the signora to see me. I walked with my two heavy bags to the train station, stopping every now and then to rest on the sidewalk. When I finally got to the station, the ticket booth was closed. I sat on the platform, using my suitcases as a leg rest, and waited until the train pulled in hours later. I don't remember the train ride to Rome, or how I got from the train station to the airport, or even purchasing my ticket home. I do remember vividly calling my father when I got to Alec and Bill's apartment to tell him I'd landed safely and he said, "Oh, Juli, I tried calling you back but you had left already. I really wanted you to stick this one out, it would have been good for you."

For the first time in my life I was so glad I'd missed his call.

# TEN
# out for
# justice

After I graduated from college, Alec and I moved to Carroll Gardens, Brooklyn. We found an affordable, charming floor-through apartment on Fourth Place, a few houses in from Court Street. It was the top floor of a brownstone, a three-floor walk-up. I was waitressing at a new "in" place called 150 Wooster in Soho and auditioning for acting jobs during the day.

I would take the F train to the restaurant, getting off at the Broadway-Lafayette stop, walking four blocks from the subway to Wooster Street. I would begin my shift by prepping the restaurant for the night: folding napkins, setting tables, memorizing the specials, learning the wines. I would giggle in the bathroom with the other waitresses as we applied our red lipstick, tying on our black aprons, making sure we had pens, corkscrews, and order pads in our front pockets. Then the onslaught of customers would begin, at first at a slow burn, but by 9:00 it was constant movement until midnight, running from one table to the next making sure everyone had what they needed. Firing the entrées with the kitchen, timing each one perfectly to be ready for when the appetizer was finished. Always trying to stay ahead of the demands: "I want half café with half decaf and steamed milk on the side!" "Just spinach, that's all I want!" Slinking into the kitchen afraid the chef would scream at me with orders of "just spinach"; he usually did. "Well, charge them for the fucking steak. This isn't a vegetable stand, Jesus!"

Tempers were frightening in that steamy, hot kitchen; food expediters, sous chefs, dishwashers, chugging down huge plastic containers of over-iced Cokes while sweat dripped down their backs. On the restaurant floor all of us tried to appear calm, shielding our customers from the mayhem behind the scenes. Prince, Julia Roberts, even Elizabeth Taylor came to dine. The place was buzzing with excitement every night. Celebrities galore, royalty. "That's the princess of Greece," Brian McNally would bark at me, "make sure she's taken care of."

I was usually given the VIP section, not that you could really tell the difference from one section to the other; everyone seemed to be *someone*. My section was chock-full of movie stars, famous authors, clothing designers, photographers, musicians. I was diligent about keeping a vigilant eye on everything at all times; learning the regulars' drink orders so I could have the drinks waiting at their table when they arrived. I liked people to feel taken care of; they were paying for my service, and I depended on my tips.

I doubt people were there for the food; they were mostly there to be seen. This was 1989–90; food wasn't the attraction. It was normal to see endless trips to the bathroom during the dinner service. I would meticulously write down where each person was sitting; all seats were numbered so when the food runner came out with the hot dishes, he knew exactly where to put them. Getting it right was essential to running a tight station, and I liked to have everything in place, all boxes checked. Nine times out of ten, the food runner would come rushing out of the kitchen holding five plates at once, then screech to an abrupt halt when he saw that no one was at their seat; some would be mingling with friends at a nearby table, others would be wiping their coke-rimmed noses as they walked back from the bathroom.

One night Russell Simmons came in with five guests, mostly young women, and they sat him at a corner booth in my station. I immediately went over to take their drink order, as was the rule of the house: *sell as many cocktails as you can before dinner.* I stood before them in my black 1940s flowy, wide-legged pants, a tight olive-green three-quarter-sleeve T-shirt, my hair swept back in a snood with a black velvet twisty tie at the top of my head, and my bright red lipstick accentuating my mouth. (There was an unspoken dress code, we abided.)

"Can I bring anyone a cocktail?" I asked as sweetly as possible, keeping one eye on the table next to them to make sure the food runner had placed everything correctly.

"We want wine and cocktails NOW!" Mr. Simmons snapped his fingers at me like I was a servant in his castle. I was taken aback. I had been working there for four months and no one had ever spoken to me in such a degrading manner. The snapping of his fingers was what did me in. I knew better, I should have just smiled and said, "Sure, what would you like?" The customer is always right, no matter how nasty, rude, or crude. That's the rule. You are never supposed to let it get to you, *just serve them with a smile and nod.*

I couldn't do it. I snapped right back, "Well, the wine is downstairs and the cocktails are at the bar, so what do you want first?"

He eyed me as he stood up, I'm sure wishing he could tower over me. But my fabulous black suede platform wedges made him shorter than me. He tried to stare me down. I stood there, unflinching.

"You will *not* be my waitress, I'm going to the manager." And with that he turned on his heel, went to the maître d', and told her he wanted someone else to serve His Majesty.

My friend Todd, one of the two male waiters on the floor, was designated to take over my table. I was mortified and also pissed off.

All night long Todd, who hailed from the South and had the sexiest gentle Southern accent, would walk by me and whisper: "The guy's a dick, honey, don't worry about it." He knew I was upset.

If you worked the late shift, you didn't have to be there until five, right when the dinner service began. But then you would have to stay until the last customer left. Some nights went on until three or four in the morning. I took a taxi home to Brooklyn at night; subways were too dangerous. About three months into this job, the same taxi driver started waiting outside for me every night; I don't remember his name, but he was always there, waiting for my shift to end so he could drive me home.

We were compadres, he and I. The first time I took his cab we started talking about the service industry and how much shit we had to eat to make our tips. There was never any sexual tone to our banter, he seemed to just enjoy our conversation and knew that I would tip him well after the fifteen-dollar cab ride over the Brooklyn Bridge, home to the little third-floor walk-up apartment I shared with Alec.

On a good night I could take home upward of $250, on a bad night maybe $125. This particular night was bad. After six months of our being the hottest spot in the city, the customers were on to the next shiny penny and the restaurant was starting to tank. I realized this as I counted out my tips that night. For the first time since the place opened I didn't even clear $100 after tipping out the busboys, the food runners, and the bartender. My driver was there at the end of my shift to take me home. This was before Waze and Google Maps, and he took our usual route over the Brooklyn Bridge back to Carroll Gardens. As we approached the bridge we could see that cars were backed up, sitting still while the traffic lights turned from green to red to green. Drivers were getting out of their cars to see what was causing the traffic jam. We were told that Bruce Willis was shooting a scene on the bridge, we would just have to wait. I stared at the meter as it ticked up every twenty seconds. Up, up, up it went. I watched in horror as every dime I'd made that night was going to be spent on the cab ride home all because of Bruce Willis, who was making millions of dollars and didn't care that the pileup he was causing would steamroll me. Sinking down in the backseat, I looked out the window silently crying, thinking how unfair the world was, how hard I had worked slinging hash to ungrateful customers for peanuts while Willis was rolling around in barrels of cash. I hated him.

By the time we rolled into Brooklyn the meter read fifty-four dollars. I began to count out my bills to pay the fare, swallowing the tears with my anger, when my driver said, "Oh no, you don't pay that much, that wouldn't be right, just the usual fifteen dollars will do. I know how tough it is out there; we don't treat each other like that." He smiled in the rearview mirror and gave me a salute with his hand.

"You're an angel," I said. "Thank you so much."

A lot of great things came out of that waitressing gig too. *Interview* magazine decided to do an article on what it was like to be a "Waitress at the World's Most Glamorous Restaurant," and they chose me as their subject. Patrick Demarchelier photographed me. They gave me an entire full-page spread. The night before the shoot I was so nervous I broke out in hives. I woke up in the morning and half of my face had red bumps all over. *Oh my God!* I was beside myself. I had no choice but to head into the studio for my first ever professional photo shoot with an ugly rash on my face, speeding down to my neck. The makeup artist was very kind, telling me not to worry, the photo was black and white. Patrick positioned me with my head tilted to one side, leaving the outbreak in shadow. The hairdresser arranged my hair as big as he could make it, partially covering that part of my face. I used that photo as my head shot for years. The only problem is that I look much more ethnic in it than I am in real life.

Sidney Lumet brought me in four times for a role but couldn't quite understand what was stopping him from hiring me.

"Ummm . . . are you Black at all?" he finally asked as kindly as he could.

"Well, no," I admitted. "Not Black, Jewish actually."

"Ahhhhh, that explains it."

I didn't get the part.

Spike Lee had me come in for *Jungle Fever;* once I got past the casting director they had me come back twice for him until at the last audition he cocked his head, staring at me quizzically, and finally said, "There's no Black in you at all, is there?"

"Nope, not a lick, but it's been such an honor getting to meet you," I said as I walked backward out of the room.

Helmut Newton came into the restaurant one night. I was wearing my black 1940s pants and a halter top, carrying two grapefruit mousses in martini glasses with two perfectly placed raspberries on top. I had one mousse in each hand balancing on a plate I was steadying with my thumb. He wasn't sitting in my station, but I had to walk by him to get to my table. He called out to me as I passed and said, "Stand right there, don't move, hold the glasses up a little higher, higher, yes, perfect." *Click.* In the photo I am somber, the mousses placed exactly in front of my chest, giving the raspberries a new meaning, a very German Weimar cabaret vibe.

*Condé Nast Traveler* published the photo on a full page. The caption read: GERMAN BAR MAID AT NEW YORK WATERING HOLE. Years later, when I was on *ER,* Helmut Newton passed away and I tried to buy the photo but was told it would cost me $80,000. I declined.

The good far outweighed the bad in that job. For all the nasty, snooty people, there were kind, lovely, generous ones. We felt privileged to work there; as exhausting as it was we knew how lucky we were to work in a place like that. We became a family; even on our days off we would go out to dinner, celebrate our birthdays together, hang out at one another's homes. Most of us were in our early twenties, some younger, some older. Many of us stayed in touch long after the place closed down.

———

Before I graduated from college I had sent my head shot and résumé to all the talent agencies in New York and as a result I found an agent, Mike Casey, at a small agency on Varick Street. I'm pretty sure I was his only client. He mostly represented models. He asked me to bring in a monologue, which I performed for him in a stairwell, the only quiet place in his office. I sat on the steps and recited a monologue from Lanford Wilson's play *Balm in Gilead* that I had performed in college. He took me on and began sending me out on auditions.

About six months later, just after the restaurant had closed, he sent me on an audition for the new Steven Seagal film, *Out for Justice*. I had never heard of Steven Seagal and had no idea that he was a big action star. I read the description of the character I was going in for: Rica, a hooker with a heart of gold. Not thrilled but desperate to get my SAG (Screen Actors Guild) card, I knew the only way to do that was to get a role in a film or on TV. After my first audition I got a callback. A day or two after the callback I was told that Steven Seagal had seen my audition tape and wanted me to come in to read with him. This would be the last and final audition. I was excited; I had never come this close to actually getting a part in a film.

I wanted to look my best, so the night before the audition I decided to put a mayonnaise mask on my hair. I heard that if you let mayonnaise sit in your hair for an hour or more, the next day you would have silky, shiny hair. Against my better judgment, I put the entire jar all over my head, wrapped it in cellophane as instructed, and went over my lines for the next day so I would know them by heart.

The phone rang at 10:00 P.M.; it was the casting director.

"Hi, Julianna, it's Pam. Steven wants you to come to his hotel suite and work on the scene for tomorrow. Can you be at the Pierre Hotel in an hour? Just go to the front desk. They have your name and will give you the suite number."

Feeling the heat permeating through the plastic wrap on my head as I touched it, I paused before answering.

"It's really late and I live in Brooklyn. I don't take subways after ten." I was stalling, a few things going through my mind. It was true, back then the subway stop in Carroll Gardens was dangerous after ten at night. Beyond that, I didn't feel comfortable being in a hotel room with a man I had never met. And I had mayonnaise in my hair. I would never make it there in an hour.

"Don't worry, take a car service; we will reimburse you when you get here and pay for your car home. This is a big deal, Julianna. I think you, out of all the girls up for this part, have the best chance of getting it."

*Oh my God!*

Alec was at work, so I had no one to bounce this off of. I didn't want to mess up my chances of getting the part, but something was telling me this wasn't a good idea. I was excited and perturbed at the same time. The casting director continued, "I will be here to run the scene with you. I think you would be making a big mistake if you passed up this opportunity."

That made me feel better. Okay, I could do this. Pam would be there. I just had to get the gunk out of my hair.

I jumped in the shower and washed my hair as fast as I could. What no one had told me about mayonnaise is that it takes a good four hundred washings before it comes out. I didn't have time for that, so I brushed the greasy mess on top of my head into a ponytail (my hair had thankfully grown back at this point!), threw on my clothes, and called a car service, noting with regret that my hair stank like rotten eggs.

When I got to the suite, an hour later, Seagal answered the door. I was taken aback by his height. He stood six feet four inches, towering over me in a black velour tracksuit with the jacket zipped to his sternum revealing a gold chain and what looked like a shaved chest. He had a Cheshire cat grin on his face and he spoke in a low whisper.

My father, Paul Eli Margulies, at Dartmouth College, age nineteen.

My mother, Janice Marylin Gardner, age eighteen.

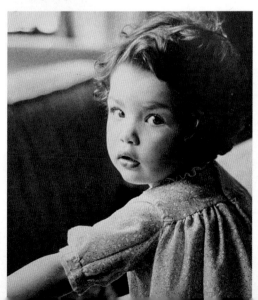

About two years old at our home in Spring Valley, New York.

My sister Rachel and I during our time living in Paris. My father bought me this bright red leather coat, which I wore every day until I finally grew out of it.

Four years old with my dad in London, still in the red leather coat.

My sisters, Rachel and Alexandra, with me asleep while we were on vacation in Majorca with our dad.

Five years old with my mother in England, outside Pock Hill Cottage.

Me, Rachel, and Alexandra at our father's house in London on Christmas morning, 1971.

I loved this T-shirt. Ten years old at my dad's apartment in NYC.

This was the passport they stamped TWO MONTHS when Rachel and I arrived at Gatwick Airport.

I loved competing in horse shows. This was my first riding jacket along with the hat my dad gave me for my ninth birthday.

Baronet, the pony I found on the marsh in England. Here we are standing in the backyard at Paige and Loraine's house.

My father, always the snappy dresser, Vicky, and I in NYC. I loved going out to dinner with them.

At Camp MacCready with Misty, one of my favorite horses.

My closest friend, Rowena, when we first reunited in sixth grade. I looked so much younger than she did. It drove me nuts!

Sophomore year in high school I starred in an original musical.

Age eighteen, outside the apartment I shared in London with Rowena and Gwendolyn.

This is right when I got back from Tenerife, overly tanned, looking orange from head to toe.

My first big waitressing gig, at Conscience Point Inn in Southampton, New York. I had just turned twenty.

Bill, me, and Alec in my dorm room on our way to a fancy dress party. Yes, I am actually wearing a small hat with black netting over my face.

With Rowena on her wedding day. I was her maid of honor.

A weekend getaway with my girlfriend Nancy during the first season of *ER*.

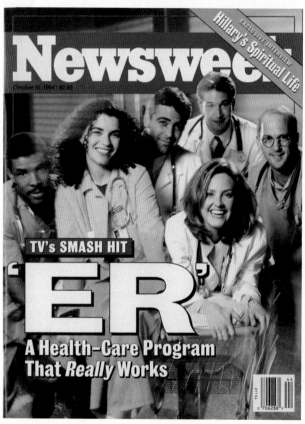

We made the cover of *Newsweek* after being on air for only two months.

Me, George, Noah Wyle, Anthony Edwards, and Sherry Stringfield taking the new bikes George gave us out for a spin on the Warner Bros. lot.

Heading in style to our first Emmy Awards. It was a fun idea, but the school bus broke down and there was no air-conditioning. We were sweating through our formal wear when we finally arrived.

This was taken during the episode I did with Ewan McGregor. We shot most of the episode in Chicago. I loved filming there as it was the closest I could get to a city like New York.

Every year we had to have new photos taken. I have no idea why I am looking so serious, probably because I was sick of the pink scrubs. I wanted to wear blue, but all the nurses had to wear pink or peach.

Working with George Clooney always felt seamless. We were both aware of how lucky we were to be a part of *ER*.

The Florricks. We had so much fun that day, filming a fancy party scene at a house on the Hudson River. Graham Phillips, Chris Noth, Makenzie Vega, and me. I loved those kids. When we started the first episode Graham was shorter than I was, and when we finished the last episode, he was towering over me. I miss them.

Josh Charles (Will) in the last episode of the first season, just before he and Alicia go to the hotel room. Josh and I had known each other for years before *The Good Wife;* when they were looking for a Will, I knew he would be perfect. Working with him was a dream.

The amazing Christine Baranski. This scene is right after Will's funeral. Diane and Alicia awaiting much needed martinis.

I could never do a scene with Alan Cumming and not crack up. He would act using his perfect American accent, and right after they yelled cut he would just switch back to his Scottish brogue and continue the conversation we were having before the scene. He always had me in stitches.

With Keith on our wedding day. The best day of my life. You can't see the huge baby belly I had going on in the front of that dress, but it was very prominent.

This was taken a few weeks after our wedding.

On a beach in Mexico during our two-week winter hiatus from *The Good Wife*. Our son, Kieran, was about to turn three.

If Kieran was napping, I was napping. I took any sleep I could get.

The first and only time the three of us stood together before
the cameras.

With my mom on her birthday. Cherished moments.

This picture was taken by my stepmother, Vicky, at her and my dad's house in Great Barrington, Massachusetts. It's always been one of my favorites.

He asked me to come in and directed me to the living room.

"Where's Pam?" I asked, assuming she must be somewhere getting the room set up for our reading.

Barely audible, he said, "She had to go home, it was getting late." He led me into the room and told me to take a seat on the couch. I sat down and then jumped up. Something under the cushion, hard and uncomfortable, propelled me back to standing.

"Whoops," he whispered with a slight laugh, "must have left my gun there."

He came over and lifted the cushion, revealing a handgun, quite large, black, and shiny.

"I need this, see; there are all sorts of crazies out there, so I need to protect myself." He held the gun in the air, looking at it affectionately. My head started to spin. *I'm in a hotel room with a huge man and he's holding a gun!* I had never seen a gun in real life. To me they were weapons of war, causing death and destruction. Gangsters had guns, police had guns, the military had guns. No one I knew owned a gun. I couldn't take my eyes off it; I wanted him to put it down, hide it away. I was scared just being in the same room with it. And now I began to understand that I had been duped, put into a situation beyond my control. I needed to keep my head on straight and figure a way to get out of there. No one knew where I was. I had to think fast. I tried to stay calm, at least in appearance. So far nothing threatening was unfolding; I just needed to keep my wits about me and steer this in another direction. Pretending that I wasn't shitting myself was the best course of action. *Just start talking, say something, deflect . . .*

I began rattling off things about the character, the audition, how much I liked Rica, how I felt she could go much deeper than written, blah, blah, blah. He smiled and said nothing, making me more uncomfortable. Finally he told me he had had a really long day and he needed to lie down. He asked me to come into the bedroom, saying we could talk on the bed. My stomach was lurching, and I could feel my skin getting clammy. He ushered me into the bedroom, which compelled me to talk faster. I was trying to buy time. I had to talk my way out, that much I knew. I had no chance of survival against a giant with a gun.

He asked me to sit on the bed and sat beside me; he put the gun down on the bedside table, took my hand in his, and in all seriousness said in his stage whisper, "Julianna, I am a healer. I can read your palm and tell you what kind of pain you're in. I can help you out of your pain."

I had no idea what pain he was referring to, but obviously this was his shtick.

He studied my palm for a long time, then looked me in the eyes and said, "I see you have very weak kidneys."

"Umm . . . I don't . . ." I was about to tell him I didn't think so, but the almighty healer jumped in. "I can heal them for you."

Then he took my other hand and studied the lines in that palm even longer than he had the first one. As he examined the state of my decaying kidneys he offered, "You are a very talented actress, that much I know, and I want you to make me a promise that one day, when you win your Academy Award, you won't thank me."

I was flummoxed. "Okay? I won't."

I glanced at the clock on the table and saw it read midnight. I had to get out of there. I stood up with pretend confidence and told him I needed to get home, I wanted to rest up before the audition and it was so nice meeting him, yada, yada, yada. As I said this I backed out of the room and then turned and headed for the door as fast as I could without breaking into a sprint. He followed me a few steps but seemed to find the whole scenario amusing as he leaned one arm on the doorjamb of the bedroom and watched me scurry.

When I got into the elevator, I breathed a sigh of relief and then realized I hadn't been reimbursed for the car there or given cash for the ride home. I was poor enough that without thinking I went back and knocked on the door. He answered with a huge smile on his face as if I had come to my senses and changed my mind. I stayed in the hallway and made sure to speak loudly so anyone in the next room would hear me.

"Pam said you would give me money for a cab home."

He laughed at me, put his hand in the pocket of his tracksuit without losing eye contact, and handed me some money. I gave him a polite thank-you and rushed back to the elevator.

On the way down to the lobby, my heart was pounding so hard I thought my head would explode. My sweat had activated the mayonnaise still left in my hair, and the smell was nauseating. I looked at the cash he had shoved in my hand and then looked again, sure I had seen the wrong amount. One hundred dollars. I did the math: if I had just survived being in a hotel room with an action star and his gun, I could probably manage a subway ride home this late at night. I took the train and used the money to pay off my credit card bill that month.

The next day I went to the audition. I was determined to get this part so I could join the union and call myself a "working actor." Seagal gave me a smarmy smile as I walked in and took my seat. I shrugged it off, acted my heart out, and got the gig.

They flew me to L.A. for a two-week shoot, paid for my hotel room, and gave me a per diem. I couldn't believe that there was an envelope full of cash left for me at the check-in counter. I was so elated, I ran to the nearest drugstore and bought Flex shampoo and conditioner.

When I got to the set for my first day of work, I asked the hair and makeup people to make sure one of them was always with me. I didn't want to be left alone in a room with Seagal, ever. When the director yelled cut and the crew piled off the set, I made sure I was with them. I wasn't about to make the same mistake again. Seagal gave me a hard time, making jokes at my expense when we were on set. I paid no attention. I wanted that card. I needed this job, and the truth is I was having a blast with the other actors. I loved being on a set, and getting paid to act was the dream I had been waiting for. I wasn't about to let him spoil that.

Even before the movie came out, just having it on my résumé made it easier to get a bigger agent, and the ball was rolling. I was now officially a working actor.

About three years later, halfway through shooting our second season of *ER*, I was walking on the Warner Bros. lot where we filmed the show on my way to lunch in my pink scrubs. I loved that lot; on any given day you would see famous actors driving in their golf carts, eating at the commissary, or walking to their bungalows, where their offices were. Clint Eastwood and Kevin Costner had offices right near stage 11, where we filmed *ER;* the cast of *Friends* was right next door to us; *Lois & Clark* filmed two stages down. Our first Christmas on the show, George Clooney gave the whole cast bicycles with our names engraved on them. It was so fun riding around the lot, swerving around these huge airplane-hangar-like buildings, seeing Dean Cain's Superman cape waving in the California breeze as he stepped out for a break. I couldn't believe I belonged here. This life was too surreal, this Hollywood world I had always heard about but never thought I could be a part of. Yet there I was with my very own parking space; I couldn't believe my luck.

As I walked to the commissary to get my lunch, I noticed an oversize movie star trailer a few hundred yards away from my own. As I got closer I realized it was Steven Seagal sitting out front with his posse. I steered my eyes to the ground, praying I wouldn't be noticed, desperate not to make eye contact with any of them, sure that he wouldn't remember me anyway. I had just won the Emmy for best supporting actress two weeks before, and as I walked past them Steven called out to me, "Hey, Margulies, you didn't thank me!"

I looked up, not sure how to respond, stunned that he knew anything about me.

"Well, it was an Emmy, not an Oscar." I smiled politely and moved on as fast as I could.

# grandma henrietta

Henrietta Greenspan Margulies, my paternal grandmother, was one of the earliest women to graduate from NYU Law School, in 1924. She was in the same class as Marley Margulies, my grandfather's sister. Irving, my grandfather, would say to me when I was a kid, "You never know what's going to happen. If you make a left instead of a right, you might bump into the man you're going to marry." That's how he met Henrietta, just by chance when he picked up his sister Marley at school. She walked out of the building with Henrietta and the rest is history.

When I was growing up, my relatives used to tell me how much I was like Henrietta. I didn't like hearing that. Grandma was described as "bossy," "forceful," "bullheaded," "determined." I thought these were negative traits. I inherited her round face and green eyes. I was sporty like her, willful like her, determined. My eldest sister, Alexandra, reminded people of my great-aunt Marley; long and lean with crystal blue eyes, an elegant beauty. No one ever said that about Henrietta. I wanted to resemble Marley.

As I have gotten older and learned more about my grandmother, who she was, especially what she accomplished as a woman coming of age in the 1920s, I can only hope that I have an ounce of her courage, her intellect, her savvy, her leadership.

I mention her now because I wonder what she would have done had she been in my position with Steven Seagal. How aghast she would be to hear that I went to his hotel room, that I escaped from this smarmy, gun-toting movie star and *still* went on the audition the next day. She was alive when all this happened. I didn't tell her. I didn't tell anyone but Alec, and that was after I got the part. Deep down I felt shame even though ultimately nothing physically happened to me. I didn't want anyone thinking I got the part based on anything but my talent.

My grandmother grew up in Liberty, New York, where her family ran a hotel. She was the eldest of five children; of all the siblings it was clear that Henrietta was the one with a sophisticated kind of intellect. All the children had to work in the hotel, but it was Henrietta who, at age thirteen, ran the place. Her nickname at the hotel became "Henrietta the Lawyika." She was born with business savvy; she knew how to navigate her way through the hotel books, keeping track of everything. She had a natural ease with customers, calming them down when they were unhappy, figuring out how to solve each problem that arose. She was masterful at it. She could mediate arguments among the staff and never forget her other duties when things became hectic. She ran that hotel with an iron fist, all her ducks in a row, nothing amiss, everything working, people happy, food ordered, linens sent to the laundry. She did all of this at thirteen!

Her maternal grandfather, Samuel Tieger, had a keen awareness of her talents. My grandmother's mother, Molly, grew up in a female culture, with eleven children in all, nine of whom were girls; the two brothers died at an early age. It was the women who were the dominant figures in Molly's household. When Molly and her sisters grew up and got married, each husband they chose knew exactly who wore the pants in the family.

Henrietta's family had very little money, only enough to give one child a formal education. Samuel insisted that Henrietta would be that recipient. They sent her to a prestigious high school in New York City to prepare her for law school. Back then you didn't go to college before graduate school; they sent you to prep school to prepare you for the profession you were going to study in college. New York City was where she discovered her love for the theater, literature, art, music, and culture. Sadly, soon after she left Liberty, the hotel that had been thriving under her watch went bankrupt, closing its doors. Her father, Willy, ended up moving the family to Brooklyn, where he became a butcher.

My grandmother was also an athlete. She played basketball on a women's team called the Blue Bloomers. She was only five feet four inches, but she could run and score with the best of them. This was 1921–22. Women had just won the right to vote. My grandmother had been acting with a conviction that women had the same rights as men since she was a child, because that's how she was raised. She was a pioneer, although I don't think she ever thought of herself that way. She did what she did because that's who she was and she was great at it. She didn't see herself as an early feminist, even though she was. She didn't march in the streets for equality, she just did what she felt was right and quietly got the job done. Perhaps that speaks louder than words; she walked the walk every day of her life.

When she graduated from law school in 1924, she took the New York State Bar exam and passed with flying colors. But when she went to sign up to join the New York Bar Association, she was denied because she was a woman. She didn't yell or scream or sulk. Instead, she turned around, rallied the few women that had been in her class, and formed the Bronx Women's Bar Association. It still exists today, with more than one hundred members.

A few years ago the association honored my grandmother for her commitment as a founding member. What struck me most that day was when my uncle Michael stood up to accept the award on my grandmother's behalf, in a female judge's courtroom in front of more than one hundred female lawyers, and said, "As a boy I remember my mother taking my brother and me to court with her one day. This was the first time we ever saw her at work. I was maybe eight years old, my brother ten, so this would have been in 1946–47, and I was completely dumbstruck when I looked at opposing counsel and saw that it was a man! I truly thought up until that moment that all lawyers were women!"

What astonishes me is that my grandmother never boasted about her accomplishments to her children; she never used the word "female" before "lawyer"; she was a lawyer, no gender attached, and her children knew no different. To do what she did at that time is remarkable. Like Ginger Rogers dancing with Fred Astaire: he got all the credit, but Ms. Rogers was dancing the same steps backward and in high heels.

After hearing about the impact my grandmother had on so many female lawyers and judges who came up to me after the ceremony to tell me about her legacy, I went home and sought out more information about these remarkable women. I came across an interesting letter from *The Washington Post* in response to an article that had been written about Ruth Bader Ginsburg.

### FIRST GENERATION FEMALE LAWYERS
July 4, 1993

I thoroughly enjoyed the biography of Ruth Bader Ginsburg (news story, June 15). But it was in error about the most outstanding women of the second half of the 20th century. The article describes the Supreme Court nominee as "mentor, role model and heroine—for the first generation of feminist lawyers." This is incorrect. Had it said the "second generation," it would be appropriate.

I must go back to the late 1920s and 1930s. When a group of young women lawyers, graduates of New York University Law School, friends and members of the same sorority, banded together and formed the Bronx Women's Bar Association as a result of having been ignored by the New York State Bar Association. The members who formed this group were Nettie Rosenblatt Reese, Clara Tepper, Rose Schnep (many years assistant corporation counsel in New York City), [Marley] Margulies Berk, Bertha Schwartz (later Judge Schwartz) and Henrietta Greenspan Margulies (politically active in the Bronx and later assistant to many New York City judges). I believe there were several others who also worked in the formation of the Bronx Women's Bar Association. This group helped set the stage for the wonderful role Ruth Bader Ginsburg played in later years in helping to open the door much wider for participation of women important in this field.

These women made footprints for the rest of us; we need to always remember that and honor them for paving the way.

I was fortunate enough to have PBS ask me to participate in an episode of *Finding Your Roots*. When they first asked, I was hesitant; the idea of opening myself up to my family history on camera made me uneasy. I didn't want to be vulnerable to the viewing public with such personal information. I changed my mind when my husband explained that this could be the biggest gift I could give my family and my son. He thought it was the chance of a lifetime, and he was right.

It is a remarkable thing to sit down with a book of your family history in front of you, not knowing what will be on the next page. I became emotional when a story about my great-grandmother Ida, from my mother's side, one that I had heard over and over as a little girl, came true right before my eyes. Ida used to tell me the story of her harrowing passage to America from Russia when she was thirteen. How her father and sister came first, and when they had worked hard enough and saved enough money, they sent for Ida and her mother. The ship they traveled in was as large as the *Titanic*, with seven hundred passengers on board. In the middle of the night it hit an iceberg and began to sink rapidly; within twenty minutes the whole length, from bow to stern, was submerged in water. Ida's mother, my great-great-grandmother Rebecca, was a large, strong woman. She picked Ida up in her arms and ran with her to the side of the ship. The lifeboat below was full; people were screaming, crying, dying. The captain of the lifeboat raised his hands in the air and said no more passengers, but Rebecca lifted Ida over her head and threw her to the boat below, throwing herself after her. Rebecca pleaded with the captain to take them; she told him they would sit at the very edge with their feet in the water so as not to take up any room. For six days, in their nightgowns, they sat, fingers clasping the side of the boat, feet numb to the icy water. The only sustenance they had were drops of water doled out from an almost empty wooden barrel. Ida used to tell me in her thick Russian accent, "Then one day I woke up and thought maybe I died. I was in a warm bed, my feet were wrapped in bandages, and a nice Englishman helped me lift my head as he gave me warm milk. I thought maybe this was heaven. I looked over and there was my mother. They gave her hot rum."

I told this story to Henry Louis Gates, Jr., when he asked me if there were any stories from my family that usually were blown out of proportion, as stories passed down through family histories often can be. I gave him my rendition of Grandma Ida's story, feeling so lucky to have had her in my life until I was twelve and knowing the story well. His eyes widened as he told me to turn the page in my *Finding Your Roots* family history book. There was that story. A few things were different, and there were more details. It was a Scottish ship that found them and brought them on board, ultimately saving their lives. Out of the seven hundred passengers, only one hundred survived. The ship went down so fast the rest were killed. It took three weeks for the Scottish ship to bring my great-grandmother to America. Hundreds of Russian immigrants were waiting for the arrival, not knowing if their loved ones had drowned, not knowing who would be getting off the boat. I try to envision my great-great-grandfather, waiting every day at the dock to see if his wife and daughter were among the living. I can't imagine that kind of anxiety. I can't imagine a life that difficult. They fled an anti-Semitic regime to find a better life in America; they survived a colossal accident and lived to tell the story, grateful to be alive in a country that accepted them. They settled in Harlem when they first came to New York. Ida could barely walk and always had a limp, her feet having dangled in the cold sea for almost a week with no relief. PBS found a letter my great-great-grandfather had written to the shipping company, demanding that they pay the medical expenses to help his wife and daughter walk again. And still, they were so grateful to be able to work in a sewing factory where they could sit and make enough money to provide food and shelter for their family.

After we'd spent several hours uncovering the history from both sides of my family, hearing about how hard life was back then, my great-great-grandparents having to start over from nothing in a new country and managing to make a life for themselves, Professor Gates asked me what I would be taking away from this part of my family story.

"The footprint," I said. "They worked so hard to make a footprint for me and my generation, so we might follow with less hardship, like the mama bear who walks ahead of her cubs in the snow so their journey is made a little easier."

We have to pay attention to that and remember it with honor and dignity.

When I was younger I truly thought I would be a lawyer like Henrietta. Before college, when I was asked what I wanted to do with my life, I would say I wanted to be a lawyer. But I found out pretty early on that I didn't have what it took to be a lawyer. I hated reading the fine print.

To this day I find completing any kind of form laborious. Filling out my son's camp form is a chore I try to pass off to my husband. I freeze at the doctor's office when they hand me medical forms to fill out; I am never finished when they call my name. I think it is money well spent to have a professional handle all my business affairs, by and large because I panic at the sight of long contracts or detailed financial planning documents. I don't have the stamina for it. I thank God every day I married a *recovering lawyer* (his words) who seems to breeze through the fine print, understanding every word, and translates it to me with patience and clarity.

I have accepted that I did not inherit my grandmother's lawyerly brain, but I see now that I did inherit her determination, her strong will, and her sense of responsibility. Many times I have regretted that I didn't try just a little bit harder and force myself to pay better attention and learn to read what repelled me. Maybe I could have been a lawyer. That's why I loved the character I played on *The Good Wife* so much. I loved how her brain worked, what she said, how she said it, and how cleverly she chose when not to speak. I loved pretending to know what I was talking about, even though most nights when I was learning difficult dialogue I would turn to my husband and ask him to explain what I was saying.

Playing a smart lawyer for seven years was my way, inadvertently, of giving back to my grandmother for creating the path so characters like Alicia Florrick could exist in a meaningful way and inspire other women to become lawyers. Nothing thrills me more than when young women come up to me on the street and tell me that they went to law school because of me. I want to tell them I had nothing to do with it, I am just an actor, but then I realize that even though I hate reading the fine print, maybe in my own way I am making a footprint for someone else.

# TWELVE
## ER

By age twenty-five I had been steadily working as an actress for a couple of years: off-Broadway plays, regional theater, a few guest-starring roles on *Law & Order, Homicide: Life on the Street,* and a pilot. I had a commercial agent and was kept afloat by a few national commercials. I wasn't going on spending sprees at Bergdorf's by any means, but I could call myself a working actor. Right after college I had written in my journal: *If I can support myself as an actor by the time I'm 25 I will keep pursuing this dream, if I can't then I will go back to school and become something else, a lawyer maybe? A psychologist? I will not be living on a futon forever.*

Alec and I still lived in Carroll Gardens, but I was becoming restless. We had no sex life. We loved each other very much and the comfort he brought me for a long time far outweighed my desire for a more intimate relationship. I think I must have shelved any sexual desire because I didn't want to leave what felt so comfortable and safe. But as the years wore on it became harder and harder not to suspect that he was gay. Yet we never talked about it, I was afraid to. I didn't want to embarrass him, or make him feel unworthy of my love. In truth I simply didn't know how to handle it so we just kept on going as we were and never spoke of it. I don't know what I was waiting for. I suppose I was scared of change, afraid also that I would hurt him. He meant the world to me. Confronting him about his sexuality was out of my league; I simply didn't have the tools.

I went to see an off-Broadway play that one of the students in my acting class was in. I had never given him a second glance in class. I thought he was talented, but my eyes didn't stray until I saw him onstage, and even then I had no plans to be unfaithful to Alec. He was mesmerizing, playing a down-on-his-luck white rapper, all muscle and brute male energy. I couldn't take my eyes off him. After the play I went backstage with a bouquet of flowers, as I always do when seeing someone I know perform in the theater. I couldn't get over the depth with which he played this character.

The next week in class he asked me out to lunch. I innocently thought he was going to ask me to rehearse a scene with him for class. Instead, he let me know that my gesture of giving him flowers meant more to him than I realized, and before I knew it, we were bumping knees under the table. One hand grazing the other, a touch that set my skin on fire. I had no idea how much I was craving pheromonal connection until it happened. There was no going back; as though I were unleashed from constraints, once out of the bottle I couldn't help myself, I had to have more.

To make ends meet I was checking coats at a restaurant downtown. He would wait till my shift was over, letting me see him through the window as he walked back and forth on the sidewalk. When the last customer left I would run to him, and we would stand in doorways making out till dawn. I was wildly attracted to his masculinity, like a dog in heat; his big arms and strong back threw me into a tailspin. I couldn't eat, couldn't sleep, I was living on fumes, daydreaming about having him all to myself. I hadn't felt that way about a man since Kuel. The craving was so intense I couldn't wait another minute.

I foolishly assumed Alec would be relieved I had found someone else. That he would understand, that this would set him free to explore his own sexuality. Instead he was devastated, angry, and hurt beyond repair. He let me know that if I did this, left him for someone else, he and I could no longer see each other. Our beautiful home, our communal friends, our life together as we knew it was over. And just like that, it ended. I couldn't see past my desire, my needs. I only wanted what was in front of me. And so I left.

I moved into a one-bedroom apartment on Fifty-third Street and Second Avenue. My aunt owned the building and let me pay minimal rent, five hundred dollars a month. For the first time in my life I was living on my own. I was so excited for this new life, this new relationship; nothing deterred me. My career was going pretty well, I was feverishly in love with this incredible actor, and I had my own place. That first month I felt like I won the lottery.

Then, a few weeks later, the cracks started to show. Every relationship red flag that was waved directly in front of me I chose to ignore. Absurd things I had never experienced before: one day hot, the next ice cold. Rules he announced out of the blue: "I need two weeks with no contact." In those two weeks I was a wreck, wondering where he was, what I had done to make him leave. *Wait . . . he said he needed two weeks, does that mean he'll be back?* I found myself off-balance, not knowing where I stood with him, always second-guessing myself.

I was lonely. The network of friends Alec and I had that were always there for me had understandably chosen Alec; all except for Bill, but he lived in California. He remained neutral in our breakup with the caveat that neither Alec nor I could ask him questions about the other. I missed Alec, my best friend, whom I told everything to. I missed our home that we'd so lovingly furnished together, Alec making everything more beautiful with his designer eye and creative brain. Turning an old dusty radiator in our bedroom into a beautiful vanity for me. Alec, who was always happy to see me. Cooking dinner together, inviting friends over, stretching every last penny to make a gourmet meal. Now I was with someone who had rules about food: no white flour, no sugar, no alcohol. I was so wrapped up in my physical attraction to him I didn't care. I didn't need alcohol, I didn't give a shit about sugar or flour, I just wanted him. I signed on and didn't think twice.

Then came the responsibilities he bestowed on me. He lived in Queens with his dog in an unfurnished, barely lived-in apartment with a bed, a couch, a few forks and plates, not a rug on the floor or a cozy corner to fall into; stark and bare, cold and unloved. He would ask me to take the train out to his place to walk the dog. Or go get his car, put the dog in it, and come pick him up after his play got out. I spent more time on the F train riding back and forth, walking the fifteen minutes from the train to his apartment, getting the dog, driving in traffic all the way back to Manhattan, where I would wait for him only to drive all the way back to Queens. I was in transit for the first six months of that relationship. Everything was on his terms. I could have said no, but I didn't. I did everything he asked of me without batting an eye.

After the two weeks of no contact he had demanded, he showed up at my door as if nothing had happened, charmed his way inside, and in a minute flat I forgot about the fourteen days I'd spent crying, wondering if he was ever coming back. He dominated my existence.

He had no interest in integrating himself into my life, meeting any of my friends or family. We got into a fight when I asked him if he would like to have lunch with my father, who was working in New York at the time. There were always excuses: *Not today, maybe next week . . . I'm in the middle of a play. I need to concentrate. I don't have time . . . Why do you want me to meet him right now anyway?*

Not for a moment did I wonder if I should leave this man who didn't seem all that interested in my own life. I was in love and so I stayed.

The way he introduced me to his one and only friend had been staged, a joke at my expense. We were eating in a restaurant and a man at the table next to us interrupted our dinner by claiming to have seen me in *Out for Justice*. "Hey, I know you, you were Rica, right?" He went on and on; at one point he began to recite a passage from *Raging Bull,* mimicking Robert De Niro. I was extremely uncomfortable, wondering why my boyfriend didn't stop him. This must have gone on for over fifteen minutes, until finally they both broke out laughing, leaving me completely stumped and then mortified when I found out this was his friend Joe, whom he had been telling me about. I was so embarrassed I ran to the bathroom and cried. *Who does that to someone? Why would he want to humiliate me like that?* When I told him later that I didn't think it was funny, he got angry at me, raising his voice and making me feel like an idiot for not finding the humor in it, for not appreciating all the planning it took to come up with that scene.

And still I stayed.

When he was cast in a TV show in L.A., he asked me to take care of his dog and two cats until he found an apartment there and then I could ship them out to him. I was left with a huge dog that had never been trained on a leash. When I walked him in the morning the garbagemen used to yell out, "Hey, looks like your dog is taking you for a walk!" The dog was so high-strung and nervous he shat all over my apartment the first night, while the cats left their markings on every surface they could find, scratching at the one nice rug I had, pulling out all the threads one by one, each day creating new holes.

I didn't want to take care of his dog or his cats. I lived in a fourth-floor walk-up on the noisiest street in Manhattan. It was hard enough for me to find peace and quiet in that apartment with Second Avenue below me, cars coming off the FDR and from the Fifty-ninth Street Bridge, blowing horns every two seconds. But I didn't know how to say no to him. As I write this I know how ridiculous it sounds, but at the time I felt like he was all I had. My insecurity around him was absurd. I didn't recognize myself, I couldn't speak up, I lost my voice. I try to imagine how or why I behaved like such a victim. I had never been like this in my previous relationships.

All I can come up with is the fear I had that if I said how I really felt he would leave me and then what? Wouldn't I be just like my mother? When I was a teenager, I had made a vow to myself that I would never be like her, with that revolving door of men coming and going. I was determined to make this relationship work.

I wanted to be the person who could show him how wonderful life could be. He came from a tough childhood. I heralded him as a survivor, as he made his way to New York because of his gift for acting. I was so impressed that he beat the odds because of his talent. I was on a mission to show him that he could let his guard down and trust that there could be love in his life without a price to pay. I thought I could be the one to push him out of his past and into a loving, hopeful, exciting future.

I realize now how ridiculously naïve I was to imagine I had such power, to think that if I loved him enough I could change a pattern in his life that was so much bigger than me. I was ill-equipped for such a monumental task.

When he was settled in his apartment in Los Angeles, he invited me to come and stay with him for a while. I packed my bags and hopped on the first plane I could. I had it all worked out:

1. I could audition in L.A. My agents had been asking me for a year to go out there, and this was the perfect opportunity.
2. Once he realized how wonderful it was to live with me, he would want me to stay forever.

I was excited for this new chapter in my life. I needed a break from New York, which held too many reminders of my life with Alec. I missed him much more than I had thought I would. I tried getting back in touch with him, but he wouldn't return my calls. I called him every year on his birthday for ten years; he never answered.

I was heartened to know that Bill and my sister Alexandra were both in L.A. I was looking forward to that old familiar feeling of friendship and history I shared with them.

When I got to L.A. things seemed to go fairly smoothly. We were in love and living together in his large, fancy, unfurnished apartment in Santa Monica. I wanted to help him turn it into a home, hang paintings on the walls, buy furniture. When I arrived the only things he had in the apartment were a bed and a large TV on the floor. He was making good money from his TV show. I figured this job was what every actor dreamed of. I thought his hard exterior would soften now that he was making a good living. I assumed our relationship would reap the benefits of his new job. I knew if the shoe were on the other foot, and it was me that got such a lucrative gig, I would want to share in the victory of being an employed actor. I would want to be celebrating my success. But this job seemed to have the opposite effect on him. Some days he seemed so withdrawn and depressed that I didn't know how to respond to him.

I told him I would help him shop for furniture. Surely this would make him see how valuable it was having me around. Picking out colors for him, showing him how pretty this would look with that. Instead, my attempts at decorating his space drove him crazy. He couldn't make up his mind about anything. I discovered that shopping, or even suggesting we furnish his home, put him in a foul mood.

"Well, you need at least a couch to sit on and a table and chairs so we can eat on something," I reasoned. "Fine," he said, looking miserable. He ended up committing to that, but he wouldn't budge on anything else. He hated the idea of putting a nail in the wall to hang up a picture, too permanent for him; when I pushed too hard we would end up in a fight. I gave up trying; it was his apartment, his money. I couldn't afford anything as I was paying rent for my place in New York and hadn't worked in a while. I was counting on my residual checks from commercials to get me to the next month.

After a few months he told me that I should look for a place of my own. In fairness he had told me all along that he wasn't ready to live with someone, this was temporary. But in my eyes I had failed. I never thought he would ask me to leave. I really believed once he had me around all the time he would come to his senses and want me to stay. Not the case. He didn't kick me out, he just asked me to start looking, telling me it would be better for our relationship. *So he's not breaking up with me, he just doesn't want to live with me . . .* I couldn't feel anything but rejection.

Again I found myself on uneven territory with him; he called all the shots. I had been dependent on him for a place to live in L.A.; he didn't make me pay rent when I lived in his apartment, and I was grateful for the break, but now I would have to figure out how to pay two rents with no full-time job.

I found a room to rent in Laurel Canyon, in a lovely house with two other women I didn't know. My room was small but warm and cozy. I had two windows, one looking out onto the street from the second floor and the other off to the side of the house, into the neighbors' bedroom, a leggy pine tree obscuring the view. The carpeting was a thick wall-to-wall emerald green, a color I never would have chosen but for some reason found very calming. I loved the feel of the plush pile under my toes. I had a full-size bed with a white cotton duvet, white sheets and pillows. A small stool as my bedside table held the only things I bought: a phone with an answering machine and a small reading lamp.

There was a serenity in my simple dwelling, coupled with the extraordinary stillness of Laurel Canyon, apart from the occasional howling of coyotes at night. I quite enjoyed being there. I was closer to my sister, who lived in Sherman Oaks, and Bill, who lived in West Hollywood. Because my commute to Santa Monica was at least forty-five minutes, I stayed with my boyfriend on weekends and sometimes during the week. But I discovered I was always happy to return to my cozy room in the Canyon. I felt safe there, strangely unattached but safe.

If I was going to stay in L.A. I needed a job. My agents told me I had to find something to showcase my talent. Casting directors didn't know me in L.A. the way they did in New York.

I scoured the pages of *Backstage* (a magazine listing all the projects that were open for auditions) and saw an original play being produced, a two-hander. They were looking for one man and one woman. I auditioned and got the part. I don't really remember what the play was about except that my character was complicated, layered, and dramatic. I invited my agents and dropped off flyers with casting directors . . . No one showed up. When I called my agents to ask why no one had come, they told me that imagining they would drive all the way to the Valley to see a no-name actor in a small black-box theater was wishful thinking. No one had that kind of time.

My financial status was not looking hopeful. I soon realized that I needed to go back to New York, where I had a reputation as a theater actress. I had secured my Equity card two years prior at Yale Rep in a colorful production of *Fefu and Her Friends* by María Irene Fornés that received mostly positive reviews. I needed to get out of L.A. I was nervous to leave my boyfriend, sure that I would be replaced, but I had no choice. I was running out of money.

A few days after my decision to go home, my agent called; they wanted me to audition for a new television pilot written by Michael Crichton and produced by Steven Spielberg.

The role wasn't big; it was a recurring part that had potential to grow if the chemistry was right with one of the leading men, George Clooney. This was huge. Steven Spielberg and Michael Crichton were names I knew, admired, and respected. When I read the script, I could see that this show was going to be something special, and I wanted to be a part of it. Even if it was just a small role, I wanted to make a big impression. Just knowing I would be auditioning with them in the room made me nervous. I got to work preparing. I liked to know the dialogue inside and out. I had learned from experience that when you're nervous, you forget lines even if you think you know them, so I overprepared for everything.

This was February, which is, or used to be before streaming platforms, pilot season. As it happened, I had three auditions that day. *ER* was the first. I drove out to Burbank much too early in my little four-door gold Mazda rental car. In general, I'm too early for every appointment; I would rather sit and wait outside than panic thinking I am going to be late. I know this stems from my experience as a kid because of my mother's inability to show up on time. I can't break the pattern; even when I try to be right on time, I am always early. I have accepted this about myself.

I took a seat in the waiting room full of hopeful actors and waited. One hour turned into two hours; by the end of the second hour I was indignant. *This is bullshit, I should just leave, I'm going to be late for my other auditions if I don't leave now.* I stood up to go just as John Levey, the casting director, came out of the office and called my name. I tried to hide my anger as I walked in, steam coming out of my ears. I stood in front of the director, Rod Holcomb; Michael Crichton; and the producers, John Wells and Steven Spielberg. John Levey read the scene with me; it was meant to be flirtatious and lighthearted. But I read the scene with a terse, snide energy I couldn't keep from coming out of my mouth. I found this whole process demeaning. Auditions often ran late, twenty minutes, a half hour maybe, but two hours late without at least an apology was just rude, I didn't care how important the people in the room were.

After I read the scene, knowing I had blown it but not really caring after the way I felt I had been treated, John Levey walked me outside and said, "You're not quite right for that part, but there's another part we would like you to read, Carol Hathaway. She's the head nurse who dies at the end of the pilot." He handed me new pages of dialogue, to which I responded, "I don't do cold readings. I actually prepare for my auditions." John smiled at me, his reading glasses perched on the end of his nose. "Take as much time as you need, just knock when you feel you're ready."

I studied the scene over and over until I felt I was ready, thinking, *Just do it and get it over with, you will never see these people again.* I couldn't wait to leave. I read the scene and hightailed it out of there to my next auditions, where I knew I did poorly because I couldn't shake off my mood.

When I got home there was a message from my agent telling me to call her immediately. I thought she was going to scold me for having such a bad attitude. *They probably called her to tell her never to send me in for anything again. I can't wait to get out of L.A.* I called her back.

"You got the part!" She was shrieking on the other end.

"What part?" I was completely dumbfounded.

"Nurse Hathaway! On *ER*!" It sounded like she was jumping up and down.

"I . . . WHAT?"

She told me that it was only a guest-starring role for the pilot, but it was a big deal. This was Crichton and Spielberg, this was one of the biggest pilots of the season, and I was going to be in it.

Still, I wasn't that excited. My character died. I would be jobless at the end of the pilot.

"What are they paying anyway?" I asked.

"Twenty thousand dollars." I dropped the phone. Then *I* started jumping up and down. I picked the phone up off the floor. "Can you say that again? How much?"

I had never made that much money in my life. I couldn't believe it; I was about to make as much money in three weeks as my mother made in a year of teaching.

We shot the pilot of *ER* in an abandoned hospital in a seedy part of L.A. I loved everything about it. I loved waking up at 5:00 A.M. I loved having a place to go every day where I was making my living acting. The cast was warm and welcoming; the set was so much fun to be on. When they yelled "Wrap" at the end of the day, I was always a little sad to leave.

My boyfriend's show had just been canceled, and in the middle of my new job he decided to go on a retreat in Arizona to recharge. He was happy for me when I first got the job on *ER;* he seemed genuinely enthusiastic. He had always been supportive of me as an actor. But the moment his show was canceled and I was too busy working to come to him when he called, his behavior toward me became passive-aggressive. He never said it out loud, but it was as if he was angry at me for having a job at all.

Once again he asked me to take care of his pets while he was gone. "You can stay in my apartment and keep an eye on things, walk the dog and feed the cats."

I was having so much fun with my castmates, sometimes going out for dinner with them after work, I didn't want the responsibility or the hassle of driving all the way to Santa Monica. I didn't like staying in his cavernous, empty place anymore. I liked my simple, cozy room in the Canyon. I was creating my own space, and I wanted to stay there. But I was petrified to say no to him.

Nancy was one of the few close friends I had made since coming to L.A. We met by chance when an old friend of mine from New York was subletting her apartment. I had gone to pick him up and take him out to dinner. When I got there, Nancy answered the door. She had a Louise Brooks black bob with bangs and was smoking a cigarette, wearing a black turtleneck sweater and red lipstick. She was the closest thing I had seen resembling New York in the two months I had been there. I immediately loved her.

"Hi, I'm here to pick up Andrew. Are you staying here too?" I asked, a little confused, because I thought Andrew was living there alone.

"Yeah, I'm *staying* here too 'cause it's *my* apartment and Andrew doesn't seem to take a hint that his sublet is over," she said with the straightest face as she exhaled the blue smoke from her lungs. I didn't know if she was joking or being serious, I couldn't get a read on her, but I was mesmerized and wanted more. She invited me in, and the three of us sat at her kitchen table for what I thought would be a few minutes before Andrew and I headed out to dinner.

As we sat there she started asking me questions about myself. How was I liking L.A.? Did I have an agent? What kind of acting experience did I have? Et cetera . . .

"L.A. is okay I guess, but I miss New York. I'm having a hard time understanding why all the women here wear Uggs with mini-skirts," I said, trying to convey to her that I was one of her kind. "And the amount of fake boobs I see makes me dizzy. I'm always amazed by them; you just don't see that in New York."

"Mine are fake," she stated bluntly, arching her back a little so I could get a better look at her stacked chest. *Shit*. I had her all wrong and now I had insulted her. How was I going to rectify this situation? I sat there motionless, unable to muster a response, knowing that whatever I said would be the wrong thing.

I don't know how long she let me sit in that uncomfortable silence thinking what an idiot I was, but it felt like a very long time and then she started laughing.

"I'm kidding! These are all mine, honey. I'm from Toronto. Oh, and this isn't mine either," she said as she removed her black bob. The wig came off in her hand, and underneath was a head of brown curly hair. She couldn't stop laughing, and then she sweetly said, "Oh my stars, I wasn't sure you would buy any of it. But I couldn't stop; it was so much fun. Sorry if I was being rude, I had just put this wig on when I was rehearsing a scene for my acting class and you knocked on the door."

Without asking if Andrew would mind, I invited her to dinner and from that moment on we became friends. Nancy was the one who helped me find my room to rent in Laurel Canyon and I don't think a day went by when we didn't see each other after I moved there. We spent nights on her bed in her apartment in Hollywood, eating Chinese food out of the container, watching TV, talking about anything and everything; no one I knew could top her sense of humor, and she was my go-to when I needed advice.

So now I called to ask what she would do about staying at my boyfriend's apartment if she were in my shoes.

"Well, you don't want to do it, right?" she asked.

"No! I'm having such a good time, I don't want to schlep out to that morbid apartment and clean up after his dog."

"What's the worst that can happen?"

"He's going to be furious if I say no."

"And then what?"

"Ummm, I don't know, break up with me?"

"If he breaks up with you because you don't want to take care of his shit, then I say good riddance."

She had a point. I was finally feeling confident. I had a job I loved and worked with people I wanted to hang out with. I lived in a house I enjoyed going home to at the end of the day. Why was it so hard for me to say no to him? Plenty of people had said no to me and I still loved them. She was right. I was being ridiculous. I plucked up some courage and told him no, then braced myself for his response. Just as I thought, he blew up.

"Well, what the fuck am I supposed to do then?" he yelled into the phone.

"Sorry, but you'll have to find someone else. I can't worry about running all the way to Santa Monica to walk your dog if I'm working late." I was so glad this was happening over the phone so he couldn't see my flushed cheeks and red hot ears.

"There isn't anyone else. You can't do me this one fucking favor?"

"No, I'm sorry, I really can't. I don't want to."

"Why?"

"I just don't want to. I'm working and I don't want that responsibility."

"Fucking great. Thanks a lot. Jesus." *Click*. He hung up on me.

———

His temper always unnerved me. He never laid a hand on me, I think he was well aware that if he raised a hand to me I would be gone in a flash. That was the one virtue my mother had instilled in me regarding men: *"If a man so much as touches a hair on your head in a threatening way, you walk!"* But when he got angry he would yell with such force it always shocked me into silence.

Looking back I am acutely aware of my part in all this. I allowed it from day one. He cast a spell over me from the moment I first saw him in that play. I made excuses for his behavior that make me blush in embarrassment now. I wish I could say I didn't know any better. From a distance I can see I wasn't happy. I knew how much power I handed over to him, letting him dictate whether we would have a good day or a bad day. His highs were so high, only confirming that his lows would be too low for me to handle, yet I couldn't pull myself away from him. The payoff was too intoxicating—his apology so sincere, I couldn't see anything but the love we had for each other.

We weathered that storm. He found someone else to take care of his animals, and he didn't break up with me. But I noticed the power begin to shift in our relationship. I wasn't as needy of him in our second year together. I still found it hard to say no to him, though, and even after realizing the world didn't end as a result, I still rarely refused him.

After the *ER* pilot filmed, I said goodbye to the cast, wishing them luck with the show, packed my bags, and flew back to New York. After one week home, I was offered a job as a series regular for a show I had guest-starred on the year before called *Homicide: Life on the Street,* which filmed in Baltimore. Tom Fontana, the showrunner, to whom I owe my career in many ways, called to say that they wanted me to join the cast.

He and I had met when he cast me in a pilot the year before in a small recurring role. That show was about firefighters, and the part was for a character named Linda, a nurse at a Philadelphia hospital and the almost ex-wife of the main character. Tom was the first person who fought for me. The network felt that I was too ethnic looking for the part; they wanted an all-American girl. Tom was set on casting me and took them to task, eventually winning that fight. I heard that a lot during my auditioning years: What is she? Black? Hispanic? Black Irish? I never heard Jewish, but the feedback was, more often than not, that I looked un-American.

My first day of the shoot was fairly simple. I had one tiny scene, where I run to peer through the window in the door to a hospital room where my husband is lying in bed. He's been in a ravaging fire that injured him badly and killed his captain, a man he looked up to as a father. He is weeping, inconsolable, and alone. That was all I had to do, just look.

I was waiting in my trailer, the size of a postage stamp (the bench I sat on doubled as the toilet when you lifted up the seat), but I didn't care, I was just so happy to be there. Being paid to sit and wait was a new experience for me, one that I found quite luxurious.

The wait for my scene became longer and longer; production assistants popped their heads in from time to time to apologize and ask me if I needed anything. After about six hours, Tom and the director came to my door, apologizing profusely for the long wait, and told me they were having a difficult time filming the scene. The actor playing my husband couldn't get there emotionally and they really needed that emotion to hook the audience, to make them care for the main character. Tom announced that he'd rewritten the scene and was wondering if I could do him a favor.

"I would love it if you could run to the door, look at him lying there, and break down crying. I think that will show the audience how well you know him, that even though your marriage is on the rocks, you know he is weeping *inside* after what happened. You cry for *him,* for the pain he's in that he can't express. That way the audience will understand just how devastating losing his captain is to him."

"So . . . you want me to look in, cry, and walk away?" I asked, trying to picture the scenario in my head.

"Yes! I know it's not in the script, but we need to be creative here, we're losing this location in an hour and we need the emotional aspect of this scene. Otherwise it just won't work."

My brain started ticking, trying to figure out how to get there emotionally in such a short time with no dialogue.

"Okay . . . Do you think I could have five minutes somewhere quiet on set to figure this out before you film?"

"Whatever you need," Tom said with a small smile spreading across his face.

While they set up the shot, I was ushered into a fire exit stairwell next to the room they were shooting in. I began to recite the only thing I could think of to bring me to tears, the last monologue in the play *Uncle Vanya,* where Sonya tells her uncle that one day they shall rest:

What can we do? We must live our lives. Yes, we shall live, Uncle Vanya. We shall live through the long procession of days before us, and through the long evenings; we shall patiently bear the trials that fate imposes on us; we shall work for others without rest, both now and when we are old; and when our last hour comes we shall meet it humbly, and there, beyond the grave, we shall say that we have suffered and wept, that our life was bitter, and God will have pity on us. Ah, then dear, dear Uncle, we shall see that bright and beautiful life; we shall rejoice and look back upon our sorrow here; a tender smile, and we shall rest. I have faith, Uncle, fervent, passionate faith. We shall rest. We shall rest. We shall hear the angels. We shall see heaven shining like a jewel. We shall see all evil and all our pain sink away in the great compassion that shall enfold the world. Our life will be as peaceful and tender and sweet as a caress. I have faith; I have faith. My poor, poor Uncle Vanya, you are crying! You have never known what happiness was, but wait, Uncle Vanya, wait! We shall rest. We shall rest. We shall rest.

That monologue brings me to tears every time I read it. The words are enough to carry you, they transport you on their own. There's no need to act; just say the words, that's all you need.

Someone popped their head in to say they were ready for me. The director yelled, "Action!" I ran up to the window, looked inside the room, and silently wept for Sonya and Uncle Vanya. One take. Done. Wrap. Go home.

Tom never forgot that. The pilot didn't get picked up. But Tom remembered me and cast me as a guest star on *Homicide,* which I filmed a few weeks before I headed out to L.A. to visit my boyfriend. (On a funny side note, years later ABC aired the pilot episode and critics chastised Tom for being so unoriginal by casting me as the nurse. Just for the record, Tom Fontana was the first person to cast me as a nurse.)

So there I was, back in my walk-up apartment on Fifty-third Street and Second Avenue, having just returned from shooting the *ER* pilot. I could never hear myself think in that apartment, with all the traffic barreling down Second Avenue. How quickly I had forgotten about this noise when I was in my Laurel Canyon hideaway.

The restaurant that occupied the corner storefront of my building was called the Royal Canadian Pancake House. Their gimmick was that their pancakes were the largest ever served and what you couldn't eat went to the homeless. On Sunday mornings there were lines all the way down Fifty-third Street to First Avenue. If only those people knew about the little rodents that squeaked through my kitchen radiators, fat and content from these doughy, large discs of sweetness. I bought Brillo pads, cut them up, and stuffed them into any hole I could find, hoping to redirect the mice's journey away from my kitchen.

I was standing in my apartment, excited about the *Homicide* offer and nervous at the same time. I would have to move to Baltimore if I took this job, but Tom Fontana and Barry Levinson were at the helm of this heralded show filled with great actors, and it would be a full-time job! I wouldn't have to worry about money for a long time; maybe I could even move to a quiet, mouse-free apartment. I decided to go for a run in the park to clear my head before calling Tom back. Moving to Baltimore was a huge decision for me. I needed a minute to adjust to the idea of it. But to tell the truth, I knew I would take it; this was a great opportunity and I was in no position to turn down work.

When I got back to my apartment, there was a message on my answering machine. It was George Clooney:

Hey, it's George, I heard through the grapevine that your character tested really well. I can't say for sure, but if you are thinking about taking another job you might want to hold off. I think they are going to offer you something on *ER*.

I was shocked. How on earth could they offer me anything? My character overdosed in the pilot, I came in brain dead on a gurney.

I called George and asked him specifically what he knew. He said he had been to a screening and overheard Steven Spielberg tell John Wells that they should keep me on, the character was too interesting to lose. Plus he knew from John Levey that when they tested the pilot, audience members were unhappy that my character died.

In that moment I felt like I was playing Russian roulette. How could I walk away from *Homicide,* a firm gig, without a direct offer from *ER.* And even if I did walk away and I got the job on *ER,* a first-time TV show was a crapshoot; you never knew if it would actually make it to a second season. *Homicide* was a seasoned show, already going strong. Who was I to walk away from that? I needed job security.

I called Tom to tell him of my dilemma. In two minutes he set me straight.

"I think you should wait and see if they offer you *ER*."

"Really? But what if they don't? Then I've walked away from *Homicide* and I'm back to being unemployed."

There was a gentle silence on the other end of the phone, and then Tom said, "Sometimes in life you have to take the risk of losing something in order to gain something. But I can promise you if the *ER* gig doesn't work out, I'll find you a role on *Homicide*."

A few days later I was offered the role of Nurse Hathaway on *ER*.

That decision changed my life. Till the day I die I will be thankful to Tom and George.

# THIRTEEN
## my decision

I moved back to L.A. This time NBC paid for my flight and gave me money to relocate. I couldn't believe my luck; this was really happening to me. I set myself up in an apartment in Venice, a two-bedroom by the ocean in a modern building Nancy and I jokingly named "The Ugly Clown Building." It had a grotesque clown, larger than life, stuck smack on the front of the building.

I liked Venice because it was close to the airport and I could walk to stores and rollerblade on the beach. Also, the air was always ten degrees cooler than in the rest of L.A.

For the first couple of years I would tell myself, *I work in L.A. but I live in New York.* L.A. wasn't the best fit for me, as much as I loved my job. I desperately missed the change of seasons, which had always made me feel like I was moving forward. I needed the struggle of winter to feel the relief of spring. This is not to say that I wasn't having the time of my life in L.A. I think I was still in shock that everything had happened so fast. I went from zero to a hundred in such a short amount of time it caught me off guard. And it took a long time for me to redirect my self-image from the struggling actress, which I kept having to remind myself I no longer was. I was so accustomed to "just getting by" and saving every penny that it never occurred to me that I could go out and buy a new dress if I wanted one. I remember walking down Robertson Boulevard with Nancy and gazing into shop windows. There was a mannequin wearing a beautiful taupe chiffon dress that hung just to the knees with short puffy sleeves. "Oh that's pretty," I mused to Nancy. "Get it!" she said. I was confused. Did she mean I should just walk in there and buy it for myself? I didn't think that way; if I needed to buy myself something, it had to be practical, something I would use every day, all the time. A pretty dress that might just hang in my closet for most of the year was never on my radar.

"Oh my stars! Julianna, you are on a TV show now; you can afford a new dress. Get it!" Nancy quipped. "If I had just gotten your job, I would walk in there right now and buy it if I loved it." She made it sound so simple and perfectly sane, but for me this seemed strangely naughty, like I was breaking the rules. If Nancy hadn't been there, I would have walked right by without purchasing the dress. Instead, I walked into the store feeling slightly giddy, tried on the dress, and bought it. It took a long time for me to get used to the idea that money was no longer a problem. Many actors will tell you that they always think the job they are on could be their last, so they don't spend frivolously. That was how I felt, so much so that at twenty-six, unmarried and childless, I started putting money away for my future child's college education.

Who knows why some shows are hits and others fail even when they are brilliant? Sometimes it's how the stars align. I had no idea what ratings meant at the time. When our first episode of *ER* aired, we garnered 44 million viewers, Super Bowl numbers I was told.

This was all before cable or streaming networks. Those kinds of numbers don't exist today. *Game of Thrones* in its seventh-season finale would be the equivalent in today's market.

*ER* was an instant hit. I lived in a bubble, not realizing what a big deal this was. I knew only what people were telling me. I didn't feel the enormity of the show at first because I was always at work. I was in my car at 5:00 A.M. driving an hour to Burbank, worked all day on the Warner Bros. lot, and pulled my car into the garage at night, only to start all over again the next day.

They put the cast on the cover of *Newsweek* two months after the show first aired, and I still wasn't quite understanding what that meant. I didn't have anything to compare it to. I was overwhelmed and exhausted from the grueling hours; we sometimes clocked in at eighteen hours a day in that first season. I wasn't complaining; I loved everything about my job. I just didn't exist outside the studio or my Venice rental for that first year.

I began to acknowledge that people recognized me when I would go out to dinner or stand on line to get my coffee in the morning, but it wasn't until I went to visit Rowena in England while on my summer hiatus that I truly understood how my life had changed. When I disembarked at Gatwick and walked to passport control, I prepared myself for the usual probing questions, the austere faces informing me that I didn't belong there and my days were numbered. This time, the year after *ER* aired worldwide, the customs officer did a double take when he saw me, jaw dropping with excitement as he exclaimed in amazement, "Oh my goodness, it's Carol Hathaway. Welcome to Sussex!" I couldn't help but think to myself in that moment how different this scenario had played out when I was eleven, ushered to a fluorescent-lit room with Rachel, thinking we were going to prison. How funny that the one thing I was not allowed to have as a child, TV, was the catalyst for changing my life.

———

I received a lot of flak when my six-year contract was over and I chose not to stay on the show. This is a story I am loath to discuss ever again, but it is something that seems to have defined me in the entertainment industry, so I feel it's important to mention. Many other people talked about my decision, all with judgments and opinions of their own, but the first time I spoke about it publicly was during the commencement speech I gave at Sarah Lawrence College in 2010. The reason I brought this up in my speech was that I wanted to impress upon the students that life decisions should be made for only yourself. I wanted them to understand how important it is to make choices based on your own needs and beliefs, not someone else's.

In 2000, my contract was up on *ER* and I was ready to move back to New York. Jon Robin Baitz had written a part for me in his new play to be performed at Lincoln Center with Jason Robards and Ethan Hawke. My very first regional play had been Baitz's *The Substance of Fire* at the Asolo Theatre in Sarasota, Florida. I had admired his work since I first saw Sarah Jessica Parker perform the part at Playwrights Horizons.

During my hiatus from *ER* one summer, I chose to workshop a play at New York Stage and Film at Vassar College. Robbie had seen me in the play, and after the performance he gave me a manuscript of a new play he had written called *Ten Unknowns*. As he handed me the script he told me he had written the part with me in mind and he would love for me to do it. This is every actor's dream, to have such a well-respected playwright, someone you have admired for years, tell you they were thinking of you as they wrote their next play. It is the biggest compliment any actor can receive. I was dizzy with excitement, bowled over that somehow he entrusted my talent with his words. I let him know before I even read the play that I had one more year on my contract and if they produced the play the following year I would be able to do it.

What I didn't know at the time was that I would be offered $27 million to stay on the show for an additional two years. I am well aware that this is a staggering amount of money. My decision to leave was not an easy one; it was perhaps the hardest one I've ever had to make.

My boyfriend, who seemed to have a love-hate relationship with my success, told me I would be foolish not to take the money. He had a tough time navigating my career because he always compared it to his own. I would tell him that there was no part on this earth I could ever take away from him, trying to console him into understanding that it wasn't a competition between us. The easiest way for us to live together was to make distinctions between TV and film and theater. He was the theater-film actor, I was the TV actor. Somehow that made him feel better about himself; at least that's how I interpreted it. I was always heralding his talent, letting him know how much I admired him as an actor. Which was the truth. But I think in doing so I also talked down my own achievements on a daily basis to make him feel better about himself. I know now that I did not possess that power, to make him feel better about himself, but at the time it was easier for me to shrink myself down to "just an actress on a TV show," thinking it would somehow make him stop comparing his career to mine. The one time he did take a TV job that was offered to him years after his first television show, our relationship weathered the worst storm in our history. He came home angry every night, furious at the writers, or upset at the schedule, declaring the stupidity of everything to do with TV and how he had to get out of his contract. He would stew in his bad mood, sitting on the couch watching sports on TV, and wouldn't speak to me. It got so bad that when his show was finally canceled I told him if he ever did another TV show I would leave him. I couldn't live through that again. So when *ER* offered me all that money to stay, I actually thought he would tell me to leave. Instead he made his argument: "If you take the money you will never have to work again." I didn't trust his opinion. I was never sure where he was coming from. Did he want me to stay on the show so I wouldn't be a threat to him in the film or theater world? Was he being genuine and really thought this was the right thing to do? Did he want me to make all that money so he didn't have to work and I could support him? There were too many variables with him, and our relationship was already on a downward spiral.

I went about asking everyone I knew for their advice—friends, my agents, anyone I could think of whose opinion mattered to me. Almost unanimously their conclusions mirrored my boyfriend's: I would be nuts to turn down that amount of money. No one made money like that. I was thirty-two, and if I took the money I would, indeed, never need to work again. (That was a strange argument to me. I loved working and I hope I'm working when I'm ninety, if I get to live that long.) One argument for staying was that I would never be offered a deal like this again; it was a once-in-a-lifetime opportunity.

Every argument had the word "money" woven through it. I would leave these conversations thinking, *Not one person said, "Because you love what you're doing."* I had worked hard and enjoyed my time on the show for six years. And because of that work I was being given the opportunity to work with Jason Robards in a play by Jon Robin Baitz. When would *that* opportunity ever arise again? I was left increasingly uneasy after each discussion. So I called the only person I knew who would think beyond a monetary reason: my father.

My father had moved back to the States and settled down in Great Barrington, Massachusetts. He was finally where he had always dreamed of being, in a picturesque New England town, surrounded by his many books.

I called him from my home in Santa Monica. (I had bought a charming Spanish house in the Santa Monica Flats, close enough to Montana Avenue that I could walk to get the paper and my coffee in the morning.)

I told him of my dilemma, and there was a long pause before he spoke.

"Here's how I see it, Juli. When is enough, enough? Don't you have money in the bank? The question you need to ask yourself is this: Do you want to spend two years of your life wishing for it to be over so you can live the life you really want? What if you get hit by a bus tomorrow and your last thought as you are leaving your body is . . . *I only wish I had done such and such.* The question isn't anything more than *What makes you happy?* Money isn't everything. I know a lot of rich people who are very unhappy. Did you ever, in your wildest dreams, think you would have the money you already have? You need to go with your heart, never your bank account."

I ruminated on what he said, picturing that bus hitting me, my mangled body on the hard pavement bleeding out, my last breaths slowly coming to an end. What would I say to myself in that instant? Was I living my fullest life?

I needed more answers. I went to the Bodhi Tree bookstore in West Hollywood. I honestly don't know what led me there; something beyond my comprehension was urging me to go. I ran my fingers down an aisle of books, walking slowly, touching each one, and saw a book titled *Awakening the Buddha Within* by Lama Surya Das. I bought the book based on the title. I had been practicing yoga for a few years at that time, trying to learn to breathe through moments of discomfort, searching for how to traverse the constant ups and downs with my boyfriend without abandoning ship. Practicing yoga was very helpful. The classes I had been taking were based in Buddhism. I was learning how to stay calm and think clearly when he couldn't. This had a tremendous effect, on both of us. When he would flare up in anger, I would breathe in deep and remain calm, watching him. My breathing allowed me to take a beat before reacting. It stopped me from tensing up and saying something out of anger instead of being rational. When I reacted to him in this way it stopped him in his tracks. He realized he wasn't getting the response he was used to, I wasn't going in for the fight, and this would render him weaponless.

I brought the book home and walked directly to my bedroom,

closed the door, and sat down with the book on my lap. I closed my eyes and opened the book to a random page, ran my finger down the page, and stopped halfway. I opened my eyes and what was written before me was this:

I decided to learn more, not earn more.

The author of the book had been an investment banker on Wall Street, earning millions of dollars a year. He woke up one morning and realized he wasn't happy. He gave up everything he had and found his happiness through Buddhism, living a simple life that felt true to who he was.

I am not, nor have I ever been, a religious person. I am a big believer in giving back to the world, being kind to people, helping those in need, but religion has never played a part in my life. In that moment, reading those words, I had a glimmer of what it must be like to believe in Divine Intervention. There it was, my answer—and coupled with my father's wise words, I felt confident in my choice; this was my decision, no one else's. After months of harrowing soul-searching, I decided the right choice for me was to go with my heart. The next day, with supreme clarity, I politely turned down the offer from *ER*, called Robbie, and signed on to do the play.

What I hadn't anticipated was the backlash. I'm sure there was plenty of whispering going on in the halls of my agency, people in the business thinking I was crazy. No one ever said it to my face, everyone who represented me stood by me, but my decision became fodder for gossip. One day I was at the gym, the TV was tuned in to the daily talk show *The View,* and I was mortified to find that I was their topic of conversation. Barbara Walters held up the cover of the *New York Post,* or the *Daily News,* I forget which one, with the headline ER ACTRESS TURNS DOWN $27,000,000!!

"Who does she think she is?" Barbara exclaimed to the other hosts, perching on their stools, drooling to get in on the discussion.

"I mean, this girl is already thirty-two years old, not some spring chicken. Does she think she's going to be a big movie star?" Barbara said in disbelief.

Joy Behar sharpened her knives and dug in. "I'll be waving to her on my way to work in the morning cause the only job she's gonna get will be as my doorman!" Cackle, cackle.

I was stunned. I stood still on the treadmill and stared at the TV set. I watched in horror as they discussed all the reasons they thought I had left, none of them true, yet all of them believed without ever asking me. They labeled me "delusional" and left me on the floor, Joy giving me a few solid kicks in the ribs before they slammed the door in my face.

I called my father.

"Dad"—my voice was quivering, on the verge of tears—"they're making fun of me, saying I'm an idiot for walking away from so much money. I want to crawl into a cave and hide. I feel sick!"

My father gave me a gentle laugh. "Well, honey, you turned down the American dream. What upsets them is that you made a decision they would never have made and that makes people angry; it throws your choice back on them. How dare you not think that money is all that matters, how dare you choose differently? This is just their own baggage, it actually has nothing to do with you."

I knew he was right, but it didn't make it any easier. Eventually I grew thicker skin. In time I learned not to care what others thought. This was my life, my decision, and I know for certain had I stayed those two extra years, I wouldn't have the life I have now, and there is no place else I would rather be.

# waking up

I don't mind getting older. Not because I delight in seeing laugh lines, or needing reading glasses now when I once had perfect vision. All of that is a drag. But with age comes the realization that we have the freedom to change. I was trapped in an idea of how I was supposed to live my life, something I imposed on myself. My childhood dictated much of my adult life until my mid-thirties because I had made a vow as a teenager to *never* be like my mother. The one thing I planned out with great detail through all the years I lived with her was my adult agenda:

> I would not flit about from man to man. If I got married, I would never, ever get divorced.
>
> I would not live my life in chaos, never knowing what things were in which drawer, unable to find a hammer when I needed one. My home would be organized. My closets would make sense.

If I had children they would always have the right clothes to wear to school and I would never be late to pick them up.

My adolescent lists went on and on. I would never depend on a husband for my income. I would make my own money and depend on myself.

If something broke in my home, I would fix it right away. My mother tended to let things go without repair, sometimes due to the fact that she didn't have the money, but often because she just didn't think they were that important. Instead, she made do with what she had, even if that meant living in dysfunction and disrepair. I never wanted that life. I would cross my t's and dot my i's.

During my years with my mother in New Hampshire, when I was old enough to envision what kind of life I wanted for myself, I made my future story the opposite of hers.

And so I weathered the storm of my ten-year relationship because leaving seemed so much worse in my mind than staying. Leaving was what my mother would have done. Plus I was sickened by the thought of hurting him, being the bad guy. Causing him pain. Subconsciously, I think I was always trying to live up to my given title as a child: Sunshine Girl. That title which was bestowed upon me out of love, ultimately was my handicap when it came to making hard decisions.

The drama in this relationship, the inconsistency, never knowing if I would wake up to a good day or a bad day, had nothing to do with him and everything to do with me. I see that clearly now. I was more worried about hurting him and repeating my mother's mistakes than I was about my own happiness. Here I was having the most amazing career, every opportunity dangled before me, but I chose to hold myself back, staying in a relationship that crippled me.

I would complain about him to my parents. My father told me after a Christmas we had spent with him, "Juli, he swallows all the oxygen in the room. There's nothing left for anyone else." I heard him, but I chose not to listen.

We were apart a lot, which meant that I could put the impending breakup on the back burner. The easiest, happiest time for me in that relationship was when he was away on a job. I loved being alone, I favored being loved from afar. Many romantic reunions, just as I had when I was a child, living across the ocean from my father. Being loved by a man from afar was what I knew, my comfort zone. But when he was in the house I tiptoed around him, not knowing what might trigger a bad mood, grateful for the good days and devastated by the bad days. What was I doing?

The obvious reasons smacked me in the head the minute I was on my own: We are often drawn to what we know. I knew how to survive these ups and downs. I was good at it. When I was a child, my mother had constantly thrown curve balls my way. But as I got older I realized I wasn't interested in that anymore. I did drama for a living, I didn't want to come home to drama in my real life. I didn't have the stamina for it anymore, and even though it took me years to finally come to terms with this, I began to realize how spent I was trying to keep it going.

I have logged many hours on a therapist's couch trying to figure out why I didn't leave sooner. I never intended to write about this relationship. Honestly it's the last thing I wanted to write about, but it has shaped who I am today, how I live my life now. Without that experience I wouldn't have been able to envision the life I truly wanted. The only way through the shame I felt for staying so long was to study my own behavior and take responsibility. I could have walked away numerous times—no one had a gun to my head, I wasn't in captivity. I chose to stay.

I kept trying to change myself in order to make it work: going to yoga classes, practicing breathing techniques, learning to remain calm when he was being irrational. These things all helped me, but they didn't change *him*. Ultimately I was up against the same recurring theme: I was with someone who had his own, very heavy load of baggage, which I took on as *my* burden, mixing my own childhood grievances in with his, all entwined into one big knot.

After years of trying to make it work, I began to recognize my own thoughts apart from his. I began to listen to myself, letting him know what worked for me, what was not acceptable. I didn't care if this caused an argument or displeased him. I was learning to respect my own needs for the first time. I was finally drawing my own boundaries.

At thirty-five I woke up. Finally admitting to myself that I could not keep living in this state of joylessness, realizing that I would rather be alone than in a relationship that ultimately made me more lonely.

Nancy said the best thing to instigate my final departure: "When you're happy twenty-five percent of the time and miserable seventy-five percent of the time, it's time to go. If it were the other way around it would be worth fighting for."

I understand why my mother was so shocked when I finally ended things with him and told her about some of the behavior that I had accepted for so long, things I had never divulged to her because I was ashamed to. Now that I had finally left him I told her everything.

"But, Julianna," she said, "you're so strong! I don't see you that way at all. Why would you put up with that?"

In every other aspect of my life I *was* strong. I didn't let people walk all over me, I didn't put up with bad behavior from anyone else. I was vocal, outspoken, driven. Why then did I hide that side of myself with him?

When I finally gathered enough courage to end the relationship, he tried to scare me into staying. "You're going to regret this. A year from now we'll bump into each other on the street and I'll be with my pregnant wife. You'll realize that could have been you, but now you're throwing ten years away and it'll be too late by then."

He was referencing my age. He was letting me know that I was probably too old to ever get married or have children. I would be lying if I said I was fine with that, I wasn't. I felt a wave of anxiety wash over me when I heard him say it. I second-guessed myself one more time, but by then the one thing I was certain of was that I would rather be alone than with him and in misery.

I think it was the late Andy Rooney from *60 Minutes* who said, and I'm paraphrasing here: *Never date a woman under thirty-five. You never have to ask a woman over thirty-five what she's thinking, she'll tell you. A woman over thirty-five will never ask you what you're thinking, she doesn't care.*

When I heard him say that I laughed out loud. What a relief to know that getting older was a good thing. Once I walked away, I knew that whatever relationship I ended up in I would take that with me.

After I left him, my friendships grew. I had spent so much energy treading water in our relationship that I didn't have anything left for anyone else.

Years later, when I was married and had a baby, I read a book someone gave us called *Zen Shorts,* by Jon J Muth. In it is a story titled "Heavy Load." I read this story many times to my son, and now that he has outgrown the book, I still read it to myself:

Two traveling monks reached a town where there was a young woman waiting to step out of her sedan chair. The rains had made deep puddles and she couldn't step across without spoiling her silken robes. She stood there, looking very cross and impatient. She was scolding her attendants. They had nowhere to place the packages they held for her, so they couldn't help her across the puddle.

The younger monk noticed the woman, said nothing and walked by. The older monk quickly picked her up and put her on his back, transported her across the water, and put her down on the other side. She didn't thank the monk, she just shoved him out of the way and departed.

As they continued on their way, the young monk was brooding, preoccupied. After several hours, unable to hold his silence, he spoke out. "That woman back there was very selfish and rude, but you picked her up on your back and carried her! Then she didn't even thank you!"

"I set the woman down hours ago," the older monk replied. "Why are you still carrying her?"

That story reminds me to stop carrying all the baggage from my past, to stop blaming my mother for every choice I make, and every choice she made, to know I can make my own decisions without the judgment of others. I wish I had read that story a long time ago, but then I probably wouldn't have learned from it; I wasn't there yet.

When I was finally on my own and over my fear of being alone, enjoying rich friendships, making up for years of hiding away in a relationship that had no room for anyone else, I flourished. As corny as it sounds, and I know it does, I felt free to fly anywhere the wind would take me. I was open to possibility, excited for new adventure. I set the tone for my own life, and I loved every minute of it. There were moments of dread, the fear of my age, which society injects into women who have not yet had children. Those thoughts would pin me down now and then. But I had tools now from therapy and life experience. I understood how to manage my moments of doubt. *Maybe I'm not meant to have children? Maybe that isn't my journey? Maybe I will never experience marriage. All of that is okay. I am happy right now, that is enough.*

The underlying theme in my life had always been the search for home, a permanent sense of belonging. I had that in my work life, I felt at home on a set. I loved the routine of work, the challenge of creating a character, living in that person's shoes. My challenge was being at home in my own shoes. When I was with my boyfriend and we would go out to a restaurant, I used to watch other couples, and I found myself wanting to be at their tables; they seemed happy. I was always comparing my life to those of people I didn't even know. *Why don't I feel the way she looks . . . so at ease and happy?* Once I was on my own, I didn't pine for other tables, I liked sitting at my own table, I was content with that. I remember my yoga teacher telling the class to stop comparing ourselves to the person on the mat next to ours. "Maybe they have short legs and that's why they can touch their toes," he would say, just when I was judging myself for not being able to wrap my wrists around my ankles.

"Maybe that's as far as you can go," he said, "and that's okay." I had never thought that way. I always thought I had to be able to do what everyone else was doing, otherwise I was failing. The time I finally managed to put my heavy load down, and ultimately to rest, is the time when I finally felt comfortable in my own shoes.

My father's favorite philosopher was Socrates. He connected to the ancient Greek's way of thinking: *An unexamined life is not worth living.* It turns out, I hadn't been examining my life enough. I grew up thinking that both my parents examined their lives too much, which stopped them from seeing the needs of others, namely their children. My reaction to their self-examination was to run in the other direction.

I had always had a boyfriend, from the age of fifteen to thirty-five, so I hadn't yet discovered who I was on my own. My plate was always full of each partner's interpretation of me.

Now, without a partner for the first time, I felt somewhat unmoored. The silence overwhelmed me as much as it comforted me. I was caught in between loving my freedom and thinking, *Do I really exist if no one is here to see me?*

Mornings were the toughest. I couldn't sleep past five; a tremor in my stomach would start to flutter, waking me up. I had no work to distract me, only time and myself, two things I wasn't used to.

As I tried to figure out what I needed to do to work through this angst, I remembered that no matter how chaotic my life was growing up, the one consistent thing that my mother insisted on was sitting down for dinner together (at least up until her boyfriend Charlie moved in). As preoccupied as she was with her own life, dinner was the one time we could catch up on the day, share our experiences. My mother was at her happiest singing in the kitchen as she prepared dinner. When we sat down together, she would marvel: *Look at the broccoli. Can you believe anything can be such a rich green! Oh, those beets! I want curtains in that color! So beautiful, can you see that? Nature is remarkable!* My mother could see the beauty in an asparagus spear the way most people look at the *Mona Lisa*. We teased her endlessly, but as I get older I understand it. Now I catch myself commenting on how remarkable nature is whenever I'm in the kitchen.

Thinking back on this idea of dinner, I knew that I needed to do something creative, work with my hands, feel something other than the pounding of my heart.

The moment my inner alarm clock went off, I padded down to the kitchen, made a pot of coffee, and began to read cookbooks, deciding what to make that day. Cookies seemed to be the most fun to make, so I began there. I learned quickly that baking is an exact science, and at first I wasn't very good, adding a little too much of this, not adding enough of that. But whatever the outcome, even if the cookies splayed out like flat little pancakes to be thrown into the trash, the smell wafting from the oven was intoxicating, and enough to make me want to try again. I bought a range of books on baking and took on this latest project like I was researching a character I was about to play.

I organized my kitchen to accommodate my new vocation: large white canister for flour, another one for sugar, a smaller one for brown sugar. I bought the right kind of cookie sheets, a double boiler for melting chocolate, Silpat to line my cookie trays to prevent burning. I made sure I always had room-temperature unsalted butter at the ready. All of a sudden I couldn't wait to get up in the morning, the earlier the better. With each day there came the discovery of what other cookies I could master. I made every kind under the sun—chocolate-dipped macaroons, black-and-white cookies, shortbread, white-chocolate-chip-cranberry-macadamia-nut cookies, almond cookies, sugar cookies, marbled cookies—setting my dough in the fridge to cool, running to the kitchen in the morning to preheat the oven while I sliced into the dough, which had hardened overnight. This became a bit of an obsession. But there was something about baking that calmed me, brought me happiness, and, as it turned out, a houseful of friends.

Real estate agents tell owners the trick to selling a house is to bake a batch of cookies so when people come to see it they are drawn to the sweet aroma filling the house. I discovered my friends would make excuses to stop by to see me, knowing there would be a plate of cookies waiting for them. Before I knew it, by 6:00 P.M., my home became their destination, full of laughter and conversation, moving from cookies to opening up a bottle of wine, figuring out what to have for dinner.

Bill was still in L.A. then, and we decided to venture out and take cooking classes at the Epicurean Center. We took weekend workshops together, learning how to wrap sea bass in brown paper infused with vanilla bean, serving it over a bed of basmati rice. We threw dinner parties with all the dishes we learned, testing them out on our friends. I never knew how much I loved to cook. I had been with someone for ten years who had so many rules about food that I never bothered to cook, as it would always be the source of an argument. *What's in it? How did you prepare it? Is there a lot of butter? It's sweet, did you put sugar in this* . . . I gave up. Easier to go to the local health food restaurant, order what he knew he could have. I found food boring and too restrictive when I was with him. What was the point?

And while cooking brought me closer to my friends and warmed my home, it also gave me confidence in myself that I hadn't felt in a long time. Nothing made me happier than a table full of people I loved, eating the food I had prepared for them.

As my first New Year's Eve being single was approaching, I decided to tackle paella, a labor-intensive dish infused with many flavors and ingredients. This seemed like the perfect meal for a party of fifteen. I was excited to try something new and challenging. I went to the grocery store with my thoughtfully written out list, crossing off each item as I threw it into my cart. When I got home I lined the ingredients up on the counter, figuring out which one went in first, when to my horror I realized I didn't have a paella pan and not one of my frying pans would suffice for this dish. I ran back out to buy a larger pan. The place was packed to the gills with last-minute shoppers; it was late in the afternoon on New Year's Eve and the clock was ticking, people were coming at 7:00, I had a lot to do before then. I ran to the section that sold pans and found the last paella pan they had, a huge, round copper vessel that looked incredibly intimidating. I grabbed it and jumped into the long checkout line.

I had been off *ER* for about three years at this time, and managed to go about my days mostly unnoticed. But as I was standing with the throng of restless shoppers, a woman recognized me and loudly announced how much she missed me on the show. I said thank you and went back to my mental list of all the things I still needed to get done before dinner. She kept talking. "I mean, you and George were my favorite couple. I loved the ending when you go to him in Seattle." I smiled, quietly nodded, painfully aware that other people were now starting to look at me.

Another woman ahead of me turned around to take a gander. "Oh, man, Thursday nights with you and George, that was it for me. No one in my house was allowed to talk until the show was over!" Again I smiled, clutching my pan, praying for the line to move before more people chimed in. The wait was endless, more people began to share their opinions, often talking to each other about me as if I wasn't present. I kept nodding politely, wishing I could somehow disappear until finally it was my turn at the cash register. I handed the cashier my pan, took out my wallet, and heard her say, "That will be three hundred and fifty dollars please. Cash or credit?" *What?* In my haste I hadn't bothered to look at the price tag. Please remember I am the girl who walked away from $27 million. I wasn't poor, but who pays that kind of money for a pan? I wanted to tell her to forget it, put the pan back, and run out of there.

But when I turned around, I could see the whole line staring at me with blank smiles. I hesitantly handed over my credit card with my tail between my legs, bought the ridiculously expensive pan, and cursed the whole way home.

The paella turned out great. I've never made one since.


Through Bill I found out that Alec had been living in L.A. for a while. He still refused my annual birthday calls, and I still missed him terribly.

He and I remember the moment when we finally reconnected differently. I thought I called him for the tenth year in a row on his birthday, and I remember he finally answered. He says he heard me on his machine leaving a message in tears and he couldn't bear to hear me so upset, so he picked up the phone; I have no recollection of that. Whatever way it unfolded, in that tenth year, the year I finally broke free from the man I had left him for, he picked up the phone and allowed me back in his life.

He was living with his boyfriend in Los Feliz. We fell back into each other with such ease. Alec had always felt like home to me, like stepping into my coziest slippers and never wanting to take them off. This time we could be what we were meant to be all along, the dearest of friends, no elephant in the room; we came to the table exactly as we were without trying to be anything else. Heaven.

Eventually, when he and his boyfriend broke up, Alec moved in with me. I had plenty of room and was so happy to have him there. He made every room brighter just by walking into it. The kitchen became our epicenter. We cooked together, for each other, talking long into the night, licking our wounds, and healing our scars from past relationships. Catching up on the ten years we had been apart.

# new
# life

I moved back to New York permanently in 2005, rented out my house in L.A., and relocated to Soho. Alec was doing the same; together we were venturing into the next chapter of our lives. I flew to New York; he decided to take an adventurous drive cross country, by himself, a scary thought at first, but as he says, one of the best experiences he has ever had.

A few months after I had settled into my new place, my agent, whom I had been with for over twelve years, decided to quit the business. I tried to take the high road, telling him I understood, but I was upset. When you work with someone for that long there is a naturally easy rapport: he knew what I liked, what I hated; we worked seamlessly together. Now I would have to start all over again. I found the whole process daunting. I inhaled deeply and began my search, interviewing the agents that had been recommended to me.

At the same time I was having a blast in New York. I had never lived there as a single person. Every night there was something exciting to do, friends I hadn't seen in years, plays I had been yearning to see. The nightlife was illuminating, never a dull moment. My world was opening up to me in ways I had never imagined.

I had narrowed down my choices of agents to three. One of them, Tony Lipp, had asked to meet with me over dinner around the corner from my apartment at Raoul's, a neighborhood bistro that has been there for decades. The restaurant is old-school New York with red leather banquettes, a crowded bar to wade through before finding your table, waiters who have been there since its opening, romantic lighting, and my favorite thing in the world, steamed artichoke vinaigrette.

Tony was waiting for me when I got there. As I am always early, I liked him instantly. We sat down at 7:00 P.M. and didn't leave until midnight. Our conversation flowed easily. He had gone to Dartmouth and had been a philosophy major—*oh, my dad will love this guy*. We spoke about religion, authors, plays we loved, our childhoods, our birthdays, everything under the sun, and with every sentence I liked him more and more. Before we finally said good night we had gone through two bottles of wine. As we bid farewell we exchanged phone numbers and promised that, whatever choice I made, we would see each other again. "You're not going to be one of those Hollywood actresses that says that then never shows up, are you?" he said with a cheeky grin. "Dear Lord, no!" I relented. "I would never do that, I mean what I say."

In the end I didn't hire him as my agent, not because I didn't think he was good enough—he was that in spades—but because the agency he was with felt too big to me. I didn't want to be a small fish in a big pond. I sent him flowers explaining my decision and told him that if he were with any other agency I wouldn't have thought twice about hiring him. We parted ways very amicably. Three months later I remembered his birthday; we had talked about birth dates at dinner; his was the same as that of my maternal grandfather, Michael.

I texted Tony to wish him a happy birthday. He responded right away, inviting me to his birthday dinner at Raoul's. He said it would be a fun group of friends, mostly theater actors; he had a big table and would love for me to join.

At the time I was working on the last season of *The Sopranos* and starting my first Broadway play the next day, so I politely declined his invitation, telling him I needed to learn lines and prepare for my first day of rehearsals. He texted back: "Ohhhh, so you *are* like all the other actresses." That did it. I told him I absolutely was *not* like them and would come for a pre-dinner drink but then I really needed to get back and work.

I showed up at 7:00 on the dot, hoping to have one quick drink, then scuttle off to my apartment and hunker down for the evening with my script. A few of his friends were already hanging out at the bar. I gave Tony a big hug and said hello to most of his friends. Standing a little off to the side of the bar was a tall, dark, and extremely handsome man with piercing blue eyes. He made his way over to me and introduced himself:

"Hi, I'm Keith."

"Julianna, nice to meet you."

"So how do you know Tony?"

"We met a couple months ago. I was interviewing agents."

"Oh, you're an actress?"

"Yup, sad but true."

We started talking. He was calm and confident and being a bit flirtatious. I needed to stop him before I fell into his eyes.

"Listen, before you get any more tempting, I just want you to know, I don't date actors."

I had sworn to myself that I would never get romantically involved with another actor. I love *working* with actors, but I knew from past experience that actors were only trouble. I had dated a few of them after my big breakup but ultimately decided it would be wiser to stay away from them. I was in such a good place in my life and was very protective of myself when it came to dating. I wasn't looking anyway, I was too busy.

"Great, I'm not an actor."

"You're not?"

"Nope, lawyer."

"Really? You're a lawyer?"

"Sad, but true." He said with a mesmerizing smile. *Shit*.

He brought me a glass of champagne and we continued our conversation. He was smart *and* funny, charming to boot. He knew Tony from Dartmouth, he too had been a philosophy major. *Shit, shit*.

He told me he had just quit the law firm where he worked. He had been on the fast track to partner but realized after some soul-searching that he actually didn't enjoy what he was doing. When I met him he had just come back from an eleven-day silent retreat in the Berkshires, trying to figure out the next steps in his life.

Needless to say I stayed for dinner, the cake after dinner, the after-dinner drinks, and then, when the party was finally over, Tony, Keith, and I crawled to Fanelli's Café for a nightcap. Keith walked me home. We have been together ever since.

I can't count the number of times I have said out loud to myself or anyone willing to listen, "What if I hadn't gone to Tony's dinner?" Keith and I didn't run in the same circles; we never would have met. How fortunate that I remembered Tony's birthday. If Keith hadn't quit his law firm, he never would have been out on a Sunday night. This confluence of events led me to the person I now can't imagine my life without.

We married on November 10, 2007. I was seven months pregnant. We had been together over a year when Keith proposed to me in Paris, along the banks of the Seine on the Île Saint-Louis. I was forty years old. Throughout our relationship I had let him know that it might not be a good idea for us to get too attached to each other. I wanted to give him a chance to find someone younger, as I knew from our time together how important family was to him. He came from a solid background, parents who were happily married and had given their boys, Keith and his brother, Geoff, a wonderful childhood with a strong familial foundation. He grew up in Michigan, where he lived for most of his life, and had good midwestern values, which were completely foreign to me. When I pressed the issue further, Keith responded simply, "I think it's more important to find the person you want to spend your life with, the rest will follow."

Keith embodies a kind of equanimity and a calming stillness that draws people to him. I had never met anyone like that. On our second date the waiter led us to our table, Keith pulled out the chair and stood behind it; I walked around the table to the other side and sat down. He stood there, holding the chair, finally sat down, looked sweetly into my eyes, and offered, "I think you might want to raise the bar a little. I was pulling the chair out for you."

I didn't even notice; I was so unused to chivalry, I assumed it was dead. Not with Keith. I had never felt more alive than when I was with him. I knew at the six-month point in our relationship that if he asked me to marry him I would say yes. But I needed to be sure that he really was who he appeared to be. I had doubts in the beginning: *How can someone be this lovely? Surely there is something going on I don't know about . . .*

About three months in, we were on the Lower East Side having dinner. He was most likely sensing my hesitation when he said, "Julianna, this is who I am. The other shoe isn't going to drop, this is it. I can tell you're waiting for something bad to happen."

I was, I was holding myself back, not fully, a bit. I didn't want to invite heartbreak into my life. I was stepping cautiously. I never dropped my plans with friends to come running to him when he called. I would always invite him to join us, but I never disappeared into *his* world the way I had always done with other men I had dated.

When he proposed after a year together, there was not an iota of doubt in my mind. I had never, ever felt more sure of anything in my life. I wasn't thinking of the what-ifs, I was only thinking how lucky I was to be feeling so high on life, love, and possibility. This was the man I wanted to share my life with. Never in a million years had I thought I would ever feel that way about anyone.

When we got back to New York, after four days of bliss in Paris, I discovered I was pregnant.

We were elated. This little being came into our lives purely out of love.

"I guess we wait till the baby's born and then get married?" I said, thinking he would agree.

"I really want to be married before the baby comes," Keith replied. For him it was important; I didn't feel one way or the other, I was just happy these were my choices.

We got married at the Wheatleigh Hotel in Lenox, Massachusetts, not far from Great Barrington, where both my parents now resided, a mere seven minutes away from each other. After all the years I'd spent traversing the Atlantic Ocean to see each of them, the irony was not lost on me and my sisters now that they were practically neighbors.

I remember standing at the top of the stairs in my wedding dress, my friend Narciso, who made my beautiful dress, there next to me. I was holding my big belly in my gloved hands, and I looked at Narciso and said, "I couldn't picture this day any other way." I was so grateful to feel this little being inside me, for him to be there on the happiest day of my life.

As I walked into the garden, my mother and father on each side of me, I couldn't stop smiling, my cheeks ached. There was Keith waiting for me under the chuppah, a wide smile spread across his face, lighting up his eyes. Alec and Bill stood beside him, each holding one pole of the chuppah, Mario and Adam, two of Keith's best friends, holding the other two. Nancy and Geoff stood in wait as our maid of honor and best man. My sisters and nieces, uncles and aunts, cousins, all our friends holding candles to light the ceremony. *This is magic!* I thought as I held on to Keith's hand and took my vows. *This is exactly where I want to be.*

# the whole elephant

After finding out I was pregnant, I had unexpectedly become the person I never thought I would be: a doting mother-to-be. I had never felt so complete, housing this pea-size baby in my belly. I was in my office, finally going through all my papers, getting things organized and rearranging items from "important" to "can wait." I was so at peace, thinking about the stories I'd heard over the years of a mother's strength when it comes to her children, how women could lift cars off their trapped kids because of their fierce, warrior-like instincts when it came to their children. Sitting there among the "to keep" and "to throw out" piles, cross-legged on my carpeted floor, I understood where these women found their strength. I hadn't even met this baby and I knew if he were ever in harm's way I would instinctively know how to protect him.

Those first few months of pregnancy, when only you and your partner know, before you tell friends and family, felt sacred to me.

That this miraculous being had found his way to us despite my age, all on his own, wandering in from wherever he had been to share his life with us made me emotional just thinking about it. And, yes, I know I was hormonal, but I was going with the feeling, the excitement. Despite the occasional waves of nausea, I had never felt so strong or more sure of anything in my life.

Among the piles, I discovered a box that my father had given me six months before as a Christmas gift. Inside was a bundle of letters I had written to him when I lived in England, when I was eleven and twelve and he had been living in New York. He had saved every single one, tied them in a big red ribbon, and given them to me, telling me how wonderful they were. To read them, he said, was to understand the love of a child.

I must have stashed the collection away for a rainy day. I opened the box, untied the ribbon, and dove in. Perhaps if I had read these letters before I was pregnant I would have reacted differently and taken from them what my father saw in them. But this wasn't the case, and as I read each letter my shoulders began to slump and I felt the heat rising off my face as it reddened in anger. Word after word my body sank deeper into the carpet, picturing my father receiving these letters from his young child, these sad cries for help, these SOS signals he didn't see, or chose not to notice. Why didn't these letters trigger him to jump on a plane and come to our rescue?

Sept 6, 1977

Dear Daddy,

I miss you VERY MUCH I have never in my life missed you so much I wish I never left Spring Valley. Whenever I start to think of you I start to cry because I miss you so much. When I come back to America I will never leave.

Do you think we should come home for Christmas or do you think it's best we stay here for the year. I would like very much to come home but I know it's expensive. Well anyway, it will soon be over and before I know it I will be in your arms.

I love you and always will I miss you ever so much.

Love love love love love love love xoxoxoxoxoxoxoxoxoxoxoxoxooxo
love you so much.

LOVE LOVE LOVE

Julianna xoxoxoxoxoxoxoxo

[Not Dated]

Dear Dad you sweet Loving Father,

I just put your letter down and I am going to hang those lovely
Angel women and flowers up on my wall. I was very daddy-sick
yesterday, I just cannot wait until I see you. I have had a bit of the
flu but it's gone now except for a little cough. I love you with all my
heart and I always will love you.

Julianna

They went on and on, two years of letters. There are some that
aren't as homesick. A few where I ask him how his new job is, how
he is, how Vicky is, if he could describe his day to me so I could picture him walking to work and what he had for dinner.

As I read these letters I began to seethe with rage. Why hadn't he
stopped my mother from taking us away from him? Why didn't he
put his foot down and say, "No, this is unacceptable, they are my
kids too and I want them here"? Why didn't he stand up to her and
fight for us? And why was I sending his letters to such a posh address when we were living in a home for mentally challenged kids
and sleeping on horsehair cots? Why did we live so close to the bone
while he seemed to live a life of luxury? He lived on the Upper East
Side, Vicky wore Chanel suits, they dined out at Elaine's with all
their marvelous friends, while I was wearing my mother's skirt
hiked up with a belt so it wouldn't drag on the ground. He never
once met my teachers in England, he knew nothing of my life there
except what was in those letters. How could he not have cared? Yes,
he sent me beautiful letters and always with such love in them, but
he never showed up, not once in two years, to make sure we were

doing okay. To see where we were living, what our life was like. As I read these letters it dawned on me how much of my childhood he missed, how absent he really was.

I called him.

He wasn't aware that I was pregnant; the last conversation we'd had was about the wedding and where we were thinking of getting married. My father loved Keith, two Dartmouth men at ease with each other. When I told him we were getting married, my father was elated. "You're living a fairy-tale life, Julianna, I'm so happy for you."

We were on great terms; my year in London before college had brought us closer, and since then we'd had an easy rhythm together.

He answered the phone, happy to hear my voice until he caught my tone.

"Why did you give me those letters from when I was a kid, Dad?" I spoke slowly, my words measured, trying to hide my emotion.

"Because they were so beautiful, I thought you would want to read them to see what a sweet kid you were."

"Did you ever once think how messed up it was that I was writing to you, completely miserable, living in practical squalor while you and Vicky were living on East Eighty-ninth Street? What could you possibly have been thinking? How could you be okay with that situation? Why didn't you try to stop Mom from taking us from you? Weren't we important enough to fight for? Can't you see how crazy it is to me that you were living the high life while we were suffering? What part of that is sweet and cute or good?"

I was crying. Vocalizing what had been brewing brought the pain to the surface, and I couldn't stop the flood of tears. "It's unconscionable to me that you didn't do anything to help us. Rachel and I were so miserable and you just went about your life as though we didn't matter! How? How could you stand by and not lift a finger to help us?" Now I was wailing, snot dripping onto my upper lip.

My father dreaded conflict of any kind. He wanted all of us to just get along and love each other. Any kind of familial conflict rendered him mute. There was an achingly long, strained pause. This certainly wasn't the phone call he was expecting.

"Juli, my back was up against the wall when it came to your mother. I couldn't fight her on anything. She always did exactly what she wanted. I did the best I could under the circumstances. I'm sorry you feel this way, I didn't mean for those letters to bring you so much pain. I thought they would bring you joy. I'm really sorry."

A few days later I received a long letter, handwritten, from my father, yellow legal pad, blue ink.

July 2nd, 2007

Sweet Julianna,

You and your sisters are the most precious beings in the world to me and you always have been. So I was crushed by our conversation last week. That period in our lives was also the most stressful for me, and I never realized how extremely dire it was for you also. Had I known, believe me I would have done something.

Truthfully, I missed you as much as you missed me . . . and I simply wasn't perceptive enough to read between the lines the depths of your anguish. For that I am deeply sorry. Please forgive me. We are all limited by our standpoints. You know the story of the blind men and the elephant. "It's thin and flexible like a serpent," says the one holding the tail. "You're wrong, it is like a thick vine," says the one holding its trunk. "No, it is like a tree in the forest," says the one with his arms wrapped around a leg . . . etc.

So there I was, the one on the ladder holding its ear and thinking it was a banana leaf. I left you and Rachel in a comfortable house in Spring Valley. I went every day to a job I didn't really like to keep paying the bills. You may not know this but I was struggling financially. I was salaried. One third went to the government. One third went to alimony and child support. One third was left for my expenses. Vicky was working freelance and helped pay the bills. I never missed an alimony check/child support. I always made up for the school bills, etc., that your mother failed to pay. I made sure I got to see you, no matter what, every summer, every Christmas, and every time I could get away, or bring you to me, no matter what the cost.

I had to clean up the mess your mother left in Spring Valley . . . twice. I had to borrow money to pay for the apartment on 89th street, and if Vicky didn't work we couldn't have afforded it.

I felt trapped in my job. For every campaign that got produced, twenty were rejected. You always felt insecure in your job if you were a creative person in advertising. You were always at the mercy of someone's ego, or someone's fear. You were only as good as your last campaign. When I finally had enough good campaigns that were produced, I finally achieved some security . . . but I never felt I was doing anything worthwhile. I couldn't wait until you were out of college so that I wouldn't have to work in advertising any longer . . . enough.

You and Rachel and Alexandra are still the most precious beings in the world to me. I am working very hard to get down off the ladder and see the whole elephant. I am now able to appreciate my years in advertising and see them as an opportunity to see how the world works . . . and to appreciate the friendships I've made and to be grateful for the salary which enabled me to put my three children through Waldorf Schools, and two colleges, and the school of American Ballet. I did all I thought I could do. Now I see I should have done more. I'm sorry.

I love you,
Dad

I had no idea. I never knew Vicky contributed to the household in New York City. I never realized how paralyzed he was with a job he didn't like. That letter, which I cherish and hold up to my nose on the off chance I may encounter his aftershave and be able to inhale a small part of him, will remain a treasure. I am so grateful I was hormonal enough to have the balls to confront him. I am so grateful that he was open enough to hear me, that he was not defensive and could explain his side of that story, yet also understand my pain.

He told me he did the best he could and saw now that that wasn't enough.

For me, that letter was enough. His acknowledgment was enough. His remorse for my sadness, his inability to pick up on my struggles as a kid, yet his ability to see it now, rather than hide from it, was enough.

I read his letter several times over before I called him. When I did I thanked him for being so open and honest. I told him I knew how hard that must have been for him. I explained to him that as children it's hard to fathom that your parents are simply people too, with flaws and hiccups and struggles of their own. Children don't realize we are all just human beings, trying to find our way. All I needed was "I'm sorry, I should have done more."

This was not the first time I had confronted a parent in my adult life. At twenty-three I had challenged my mother and demanded an apology for the trauma she had put me through in high school with her twenty-one-year-old boyfriend. The anger I had filed away from that time in my life hit me in the face out of the blue when I was living in Brooklyn with Alec. I woke up one morning and felt paralyzed by my feelings toward her. I called her and vented my rage at her that she had never put my needs first, never considered my feelings or my well-being. She always assumed I could handle what was thrown at me. I wanted a meaningful apology and I would take nothing less. We ended up in a fight and didn't speak for almost a year until one Sunday morning she called me and in her dramatic way assured me that "I would rather die than not have you in my life!" We worked through it; she wept to me that she felt so ashamed by her behavior, so embarrassed. She confessed that it was easier to pretend it never happened than to acknowledge it. And she apologized over and over through her tears, wishing she could redo that time in our life together, how differently she would have done things. My heart has always been wide open to her, and in the year that we didn't communicate I had missed her. Now that I could hear how truly sorry she was, I chose to believe her. I wanted us to have a relationship. "Please forgive me!" she kept repeating. And I did.

As self-centered as my mother was, as debilitated as my father seemed, I was able to question both of them at different times in my adult life and heard the words "I'm sorry, forgive me." And I forgave the moment I heard "I'm sorry," because having relationships with them far outweighed not having them in my life. I am reminded every day how lucky I am that I had tremendous love from both my parents, though perhaps not in the conventional way. Neither of them stopped their lives for me and my sisters. As I've gotten older and have become a mother myself, I wonder if I would have wanted them to. We do the best we can, and sometimes that has to be good enough. No one is perfect. Both my parents, separately, told me all they wanted for me was a happy, fulfilled life. That is the most I want for my child, to be happy, to feel fulfilled.

I know I was born with a leg up in this world. Maybe the wind wasn't always at my back, many times I had to fight hard to stay on track, but without the fight perhaps I wouldn't have learned how to navigate my way, how to make my own decisions, how to fend for myself. Their inattention gave me courage to forge the life I now appreciate. I yearned for so many things when I was a child, mostly a family that was together, or at least in the same country; maybe that's why I waited so long to get married. I knew I didn't want to make the same mistakes my parents made.

I never would want for my own child to be burdened with the anxiety I felt when I was younger, that responsibility I carried on my shoulders thinking somehow I could make things better for everyone else if I just tried a little harder. That's not an easy walk, but at the same time I don't want to stand in the way of his struggle. I don't want to smother him in a coddled life, crippling him, leaving him not knowing how to fend for himself, think for himself, tie his own shoes.

I write "tie his own shoes" with embarrassment. My son is twelve now, and, yes, he knows how to tie his shoes, but when I was working fourteen hours a day, for the first seven years of his life, I overcompensated when I was with him because of the guilt I had about my long hours away from him. Every day I would lovingly dress him; this was my way of showing him I cared, I was there, he could count on me. It became a joke between us; he would lay back on his bed, arms folded behind his head as though he were sunbathing. I would put every single article of clothing on him, even his underwear. He would watch me as I struggled to pull up his pants, and then I would tie his shoes. By the age of seven he refused to wear lace-up sneakers and insisted on Velcro straps. It dawned on me then: he didn't know how to tie his own shoes because I was doing it for him.

I try now to get out of his way and let him figure things out on his own. Some days I succeed, some days I fail. Maybe that will be his complaint when he grows up, that I did too much for him? I hope that's not true. I'm sure I will find out soon enough. My hope is to guide him as best I can to steer his own ship with confidence. My parents guided me as best they could, I have to do the rest, as will my son. The biggest message I took from both my parents is that I am responsible for my own life.

# *the good wife*

*T*he *Good Wife* pilot was shot in Vancouver, in March 2009. Kieran was thirteen months old. Keith and I had discussed at length how we could make this work. I had never been away from Kieran for more than two days at a time, and I was panicked; for me, for Kieran, for all of us. Keith was calm, always my steady hand in times of stress; he reminded me of the wise words our babysitter once told me when she couldn't come and I had to work over a weekend, leaving Kieran under Keith's watch for forty-eight hours when he was six months old.

*He might not do it your way but he'll get it done.*

She was right; when I came home, the house may not have been as I would have left it, but Kieran was giggling, well fed and dry, happy with his daddy. I had worried for nothing.

A month, however, is a different situation. We knew that visiting would be impossible. In order to get all the filming done in under a month, we worked six days a week. There was no point in trying to come home only to leave again; I would have been clocking more hours of travel time than Kieran time.

The first week in Vancouver was brutal. Being without my husband and son for the very first time threw me into a kind of shell-shocked state, as if my limbs were cut off from my body, the first day an arm, the next a leg. I forgot how to move in their absence. By the second week I was grateful we'd decided I'd be there on my own; the days were unbearably long and the dialogue excruciating to learn. I needed any spare time I had to learn lines and sleep.

When I got home after that long month, we fell into a natural rhythm again in no time. While I thought Kieran would suffer the brunt of my time away, he was fine, too little really to understand exactly how long I had been gone. I was the one who suffered the most, feeling guilty for leaving him. Missing him the way I did was new to me, a different kind of longing and a constant tug at my heart, torn between wanting the job and being a mother.

After the show was picked up and fortunately moved to New York, I still struggled with trying to find balance. I wanted more than anything to let Keith and Kieran know I was there for them, that they were my first priority. But weekends were the only time I could demonstrate this. I would plan dinners, shop and cook for them, hoping that if I created a warm, homey retreat on the weekends, it would spill over until the next weekend. All the while I was trying to recover from the sixty-plus hours of work I had just put in and prepare for the next week coming up. Like a revolving door, I just kept going round and round.

On a television show we call Fridays "Fraturdays" because the production can film all night long, well into Saturday morning. This would mean (especially in the first season), that we would shoot until five in the morning on Saturday. When I came home I would tiptoe past Kieran's bedroom, praying he wasn't awake yet so I could fall into bed and get a few hours of sleep before our day began. If he was awake, how could I ignore him? I couldn't walk by his room without going to him. I needed to hold him, play with him, fix him breakfast. He was my baby, he needed his mother. This is how I rationalized my ceaseless state of exhaustion. Keith would tell me to just wake him up so he could take care of Kieran and I could get some sleep, but I could never do that. Even when I tried, the guilt would worm its way into my dreams, waking me up.

During the workweek, if my pickup time was an hour later than usual, I would make every effort to show Kieran how much I loved him by making art out of his breakfast. Oatmeal was never *just* oatmeal. Instead I would carve, shape, mold fresh fruit, berries, anything nutritious I could find and create pictures for him in his bowl. I needed to make up for the time I wouldn't be spending with him that day, thinking that through my laborious creations he would somehow understand how much I loved him. If Keith left early and Kieran was still sleeping, I would clean out Keith's closet, organizing his shirts the way I used to at the shop on South Molton Street in London, putting them in color order, placing each sleeve in the vee of my fingers and putting them down so his closet resembled a store rack.

I took pleasure in doing these things when I had a spare minute. I needed them both to know that I was there as a mother, as a wife. I was so afraid they would feel abandoned, not realizing that the only person I was abandoning was myself.

Time was a luxury I dreamed about. Sleep was something I craved every day. Looking back, I have no idea how I managed any of it. I threw myself into my work with such force sometimes I didn't recognize myself. My plates were always spinning, torn between work, baby, husband, parents, friends. I was climbing a mountain every day and never reached the top; I was always behind. I am a person who likes to stay ahead, write lists, check the boxes, be organized, so life is calmer and easier for me and everyone around me. There was no room for error. Ever. Yet I couldn't complain. I was living the dream, even though all the while I was so busy spinning plates I was barely present for any of it, always thinking about the next thing I needed to do.

Kieran's first sentence was "Mama work." His next one, "Mama tired."

When the marketing campaign for *The Good Wife* launched, my image was suddenly on buses all over Manhattan. Kieran would be out in his stroller and he would point at them. "Mama bus!" he would exclaim with a mixed look of confusion and delight. I was plastered all over the city, on billboards, sides of buildings, subways, wherever you looked there was his mama in a red dress staring straight at him. He saw me more during the week on posters than he did at home. In a strange way I was somehow present for him even though I wasn't there.

When we began to do publicity for *The Good Wife,* often with the whole cast sitting in chairs in front of the journalists, Chris Noth and I both had boys the same age, and at every press junket a journalist would ask me how I juggled motherhood with my workload. I instantly felt a stab in my heart. I answered as honestly as I could, explaining that I tried my best but was always worried it was never enough. I told them I struggled with the guilt I carried because I wasn't home as much as I would like to be, that I struggled to find time to sleep, letting them know that there is no such thing as "balance" when you are working fourteen to fifteen hours a day. Not once, in the seven years of that show, did Chris ever get the same question. Granted, his role on the show was less demanding than mine, but it always struck me as odd, and a bit irritating, that men are never asked that question.

I walked away from those press junkets feeling more anxious than I had when I walked in. And I was already wearing a heavy weight of guilt around my neck.

My mother recently told me that her friends who were stay-at-home moms are chastised by their adult children for not having a career. My mother, on the other hand, was criticized by all three of her daughters for putting her work and herself before us. "You can never win," she says, laughing off the irony.

I am wired to think I am never doing enough. If I am not on a set working, my free time never feels carefree. Writing this book has tortured me because any spare minute I have I think I *should* be writing. If I'm not scolding myself about not writing, I am harping at myself to clean out closets, get rid of things, organize: *I should be more organized*. This goes on all day. When I am able to get things done I feel accomplished, and only then can I relax until the next day dawns and the lists are written down as I sip my morning coffee. I'm sure I drive my husband nuts when I blurt out in a panic, "Oh God! I need to call so-and-so." He will wisely exclaim, "Well, honey, they haven't called you either." Which amazes me. I never think in those terms. I'm trying, as I get older, I am really trying now to allow for idleness.

I hear my girlfriend Nancy saying to me so many years ago, *If I treated you the way you treat yourself, you wouldn't be my friend*. She's right, I would never be so hard on anyone else as I am on myself.

As a child, I craved boundaries. I wanted someone to check my homework, make sure I was home at a decent hour. I didn't have that, so I made up my own rules, and they were absurdly rigid. Both my parents would argue that maybe that's the best way to raise children, let them fend for themselves, guide them with love but let them figure out what rules work for them. I'm not so convinced. Perhaps if my parents had expected more of me I wouldn't expect so much of myself? And then again, is that a good thing?

Both my mother and my father leaned in the opposite direction of their own upbringings. My father ran as far away as he could from his controlling mother. My mother chose to never be in a loveless relationship like her mother, thus flitting from one man to the next. I, in turn, never wanted to be like them, divorced and living a life in chaos.

When I was on *The Good Wife* I had to learn some tough lessons. You can't have it all *all* of the time, you can have it all *some* of the time. I was lucky to have seven years to figure it out and a supportive partner who is levelheaded and rational in helping me understand when to fight for something and when to just let it be. In time I learned to accept that I couldn't be everywhere at once, that I wouldn't be doing a good job if I was always feeling torn.

Our winter break was coming up, and Nancy was coming to New York to see some theater with me. I was excited to do normal things I never had time for: seeing friends, having dinner out, going to a play. But halfway through act one my mouth began to fill with saliva, the kind that you feel right before you're going to throw up. My stomach was cramping, and I broke out into a cold, clammy sweat. I had to get out of the theater before I threw up in the aisle. Nancy, thank God, happened to have a barf bag from the plane ride in her purse and she handed it to me. I made it through the first act without retching, then ran out of the theater as fast as I could, jumped into a cab for the bumpy ride downtown, barf bag at the ready. Of all the taxi drivers in New York City, I got the one guy who wanted to have a conversation. He had a thick Eastern European accent. The second the door closed and we were headed down Ninth Avenue he began asking me questions. I was hunched over in the backseat, my cramps getting worse. All I wanted was my bed and a cold washcloth over my face.

"So, where are you from?" he asked, glancing in his rearview mirror.

"Here," I said, trying to sound like I didn't have a dirty sock shoved down my throat.

"You like it here?"

"I do." *Please stop talking to me.*

"I come to this country twenty years ago, I love this country."

"I'm so glad." *He's not going to stop.*

"You married?"

"I am."

"And your husband, he's good man?"

"He is." *Oy, it won't end.*

"You have kids?"

"Yup, one boy."

"You work?"

"I do."

"You like your work?"

"Yes, very much."

"You are living the American dream!"

As we made our way across Bleecker Street, clutching my stomach, sweating through my coat, I looked out the window at the twinkling lights, New York City at Christmastime, magical. I laughed.

"Yes, I am. I am living the American dream. I am very lucky."

My *Good Wife* life left no room for error. I didn't have time to get sick. If I had a cold I ate Sudafed and DayQuil till they were coming out my ears. Every minute of every day was put to use when I worked those long hours. I needed to get as much done at work as I could so I would have time with my family when I got home. When a ten-minute break was called for lighting a scene, I ran to my dressing room to learn lines for the next day, or take a power nap. I became an expert napper, lying down on my couch and making sure not to crease my fancy suits or muss my hair and makeup. I lay on my back, arms crossed over my chest like a mummy, closed my eyes, and the next thing I knew they were knocking on my door to come back to set. Even a ten-minute nap revived me. Minutes . . . I was always counting minutes: *I have ten minutes to close my eyes, three minutes to run to the bathroom, five minutes to scarf something down . . .*

Minutes became my mantra. I became adept at figuring out my timing, and I knew that in order to stay on top of things I had to eat healthy foods that sustained my energy and kept my brain sharp. I kept fresh fruits and vegetables in the minifridge in my dressing room: raw almonds, energy bars, anything that I could eat in five minutes to feel sated. One particularly hectic day, I ran to my room on a ten-minute break and munched on some carrot sticks while I prepared for the next scene. Reading my lines without thinking, I chomped down hard on a carrot and felt a strange tingling sensation way up in my gum line where I had lost my tooth all those years ago. *Hmmm . . . weird, probably nothing.* I went back to the set when I was called and finished the day's work.

Two months went by; every now and then I would feel something out of the ordinary when I ate. I wasn't in terrible pain, but I knew something was off-kilter. But I kept ignoring the warning signs because I didn't have time. I waited for all my personal medical needs to be dealt with during my two-month hiatus. Every doctor, dentist, mammogram, eye exam, you name it, my hiatus months were packed with appointments.

Trying to fit a workout into my schedule was next to impossible, but once Kieran was in school, I managed to work out in the morning if I had a later call time. When I did get an hour to myself in the morning, I liked to be outside as much as possible, because most days I was cooped up in the studio without any fresh air. One sunny morning, after getting my kid off to school and bidding my husband farewell on his way to work, I decided to go for a run along the river. It was a gorgeous day, clear blue sky, gentle breezes, perfect temperature—I felt lucky to be alive. As I ran I recited the five-page summation I was to deliver to the jury that day. About halfway through my run I felt a pain shoot up through the roof of my mouth and into my skull. Thinking that I was probably overdoing it, I slowed down a little until the pain subsided and then picked up my pace again. By the time my five-mile run had ended, the throbbing in my head had escalated to a full-blown migraine. I didn't have time for headaches, so I popped some Advil and headed off to work, willing the pain to go away.

We rehearsed the scene, and I went to my dressing room to eat some breakfast. The second I began to chew a sharp pain charged from my mouth up to my head, stabbing the back of my eye with sharp jabs. It became so unbearable I doubled over, clasping my head with both hands. I called Marc, my dentist from the yellow pages.

"Something is definitely wrong with my fake tooth," I said, trying to remain as calm as I could, though panic was rising.

"Are you in pain?"

"Uh-huh, it's shooting up to my head every time I bite down. I went for a run this morning and I feel like my head is going to explode."

"You need to get in here right away."

"I can't, I'm in court all day."

"Then come after work, I'll wait till you get here."

I managed to get through work, popping Advil like M&M's. I finally got to Marc's office late that night.

Because I had waited so long to deal with my tooth, Marc discovered that the metal post holding my porcelain tooth had broken off from the root, and due to the break my gum was receding to the point where I needed a gum graft immediately. The X-rays showed him there was no other way to fix the problem.

I went to work the next day propped up on painkillers and broke the news to our line producer, Kristin Bernstein.

"So. . . . it looks like I have to have a gum graft. I can do it tomorrow after work and I should be fine by Monday." I was trying to sound confident.

She looked at me like I was an alien.

"Ummmm . . . Jules, I think that's kind of a major surgery, no? We need to change the schedule. You won't be able to speak, let alone act, with stitches in your mouth."

"I'll be fine, how bad can it be?"

Somehow Kristin knew more than I did about gum grafts and rearranged the schedule so I could have Monday off. She insisted, I gratefully accepted. I knew what went into producing our show, how many moving parts there were to make it work. I was irritated that I would be causing any delays and embarrassed that this tooth, which sat right in the front of my mouth for all to see, was still causing me problems.

I have a built-in habit of assuming that everything is my fault. I liked my production team knowing that I was the dependable workaholic, the reliable actress who came in every day on time, knowing my lines. I needed to set an example; if I could do it with the long hours I logged in and a small baby at home, how could anyone else complain? There were days when my exhaustion got the better of me, when I wanted to scream, cry, beg someone, anyone to let me sleep for a week, but I powered through, entertaining myself with little fantasies: when an actor would swagger into the makeup room yawning an hour after I had gotten there, complaining about how tired they were, I would picture myself squeezing their head off their neck. The head would fall to the floor and I would watch it roll before giving it a good kick in the teeth, screaming with each thud from my boot—*You haven't been here in three days! How can you be tired, you don't even have a kid, how dare you come in here and complain?*—whack, whack, whack . . . Fantasies, they got me through some of the toughest moments on that show.

Christine Baranski understood the pressure of being on a show and having a small child. She was my rock during my moments of doubt and feelings of failure. She could tell from the moment I walked into the makeup room in the morning just by the look of exhaustion on my face that I had been up all night with a baby. "Don't you worry, darling. He will be fine, you will be fine, it all will get done, and you'll both survive. I promise you," she would tell me in the most soothing voice. Her words and compassion, the fact that she had been through this with her own children always made me feel better.

———

What I hadn't anticipated with my tooth was the actual procedure. When you need a gum graft, they have to slice the perfectly healthy tissue from the roof of your mouth and adhere it to the receding gumline with stitches, which leaves a gaping hole in the roof of your mouth that they then close with more stitches. Six hours of surgery later, I was in a drug-induced haze, propped up in my bed at home. *This is a piece of cake, I barely feel a thing.*

And then the drugs wore off. The pain without the drugs was torture. I was taking Percocet to function. Here's what they don't tell you about Percocet: *You can't remember a thing!* Three days later I was back in court, cross-examining a witness. I had spent the weekend high on painkillers, memorizing my lines. The teamster assigned to me was Joe, the person I miss most from that show, the first person I would see in the morning and the last person I would see at night. We had an unspoken rule: "Whatever is said in the car, stays in the car." He picked me up on Tuesday morning. As I settled into the front seat he asked me how I was doing.

"I'm great!" I stated with a frozen smile on my face. "Peachy, yup, all good."

"Oh boy," Joe muttered, shaking his head as he pulled away from the curb and headed to Greenpoint.

My face was still swollen from the surgery, so we decided that Alicia had changed her hairstyle that day. I wore it dramatically to the side, covering one half of my face. Baby steps, but it worked. I walked onto the set, head held high—*you can do this*—then I tried to speak. This was more difficult. I was having trouble remembering my lines. I knew them in my head, at least that's what I thought, but when I opened my mouth to speak, my brain couldn't connect to my tongue. As I struggled with the dialogue, I could feel the stitches dangling from the roof of my mouth, dancing on my tongue. I was disoriented and struggling desperately to look on top of the scene, but the stitches kept getting in my way. Absent any thought,

I tried to move them out of the way so I could speak properly. In my attempt to gain control of the situation I pulled on the dangly threads midsentence. In that idiotic moment, I reasoned with myself that they had told me the stitches were the kind that disintegrated, so if they were coming loose, they must be ready to come out. Made sense.

Important to remember that I was high on Percocet. I pulled on the tiny threads and, in doing so, ripped all of them out as I delivered my garbled cross-examination.

Six hours of surgery down the toilet, just like that. Out popped the gum, the hole in my mouth opened up, sending trickles of blood down my throat. I had to redo the entire surgery.

The whole ordeal took six months, which I could have avoided if I hadn't ignored the signs. During that time I lost too much weight, missed too much sleep, and spiked up my already loaded anxiety meter. I felt defeated at every turn. Where I had once managed to keep my plates spinning, now they were all broken, lying at my feet in splintered pieces. I hadn't paid attention to myself, I didn't heed the warning signs, I just kept moving through the revolving door, checking my boxes without checking myself. A hard lesson to learn.

# this is where
# i belong

One of my favorite things to do is go to a farmers' market in upstate New York, first thing on Saturday mornings. My husband and I bought a house near there when Kieran was eight months old. We came to the conclusion that if we didn't take a breath and smell the pine trees, see the circling hawks and the vast sunsets, experience the aroma of sweet blooming lavender, witness the majestic white owl that lives in the woods along our dirt driveway, we may very well end our days holed up in concrete.

As a parent and an adult, I felt the most important thing was creating a peaceful home, a place where our son could grow up in familiar surroundings. I wanted for him to have what I dreamt about as a child; a solid foundation, a place to come home to. I wanted to create traditions for him to look forward to, to feel held by at all times. I wanted the word "family" to bring a smile to his lips with warm memories of relatives and friends, sitting around the kitchen table. I'd had glimpses of these moments when I was a child, but they were fleeting; as an adult I needed to change that narrative for myself.

Keith and I were looking in and around the Hudson River Valley for a place to rent when we came across an interesting piece of property that was way overpriced.

"Well, that's ridiculous," I told him. "I mean, if it were for sale I may consider buying, but renting at that price is silly."

He agreed, and we didn't spend much time there. We told our realtor to keep looking.

A few days later we got a call asking if we were interested in buying the house. The owner, who had built the place in 2000, by moving a 1790s saltbox house from Connecticut and then adding on a new structure, keeping in style with the old house but raising the ceilings to ten feet to fit his six-foot-five frame, was getting divorced. He and his wife were giving us an opportunity to make an offer before they put the house on the market. We put our baby in the car and drove back up to take a better look.

The house sits at the end of a shabby dirt driveway about a quarter of a mile long, up on a hill. The dusty, unfinished screened-in porch, with weathered wrought-iron outdoor furniture so cranky I could see the cobwebs from a distance, showed off a panoramic view of the Catskill Mountains on the other side of the Hudson River. Rolling up to the mountains were green hills with flecks of grain silos surrounded by lush patches of trees. The instant I witnessed that view, I knew I was home.

The rest of the house needed loving care. There were so many conflicting colors swirling around, from the canary yellow living room to the bright blue dining room, the soft peach family room, all with a wilted gray wainscoting. The large kitchen floor resembled a dilapidated hacienda, worn-out orange terra-cotta tiles clashing with the red granite countertops, veins of disco silver running through the surface. This would be a huge project.

Kieran was happily bouncing on the dining room floor while

Keith and I walked through each room, over and over. The master bedroom had a bizarre closet with a tiny sink shoved in the corner. "Do I shave in here?" Keith asked, as confused as I was.

The property itself was struggling: the house had been built on rocky soil making it impossible to sustain anything green.

As I walked around I took in all the flaws, thought of all the work that would be needed to bring this home to life. But whenever I glanced at the view of the mountains I felt a calmness wash over me, hypnotic.

*Do not buy this house. Too much work, move on, walk away.*

We bought the house.

The moment those keys were in my hand I went to work figuring out how to make it livable within a budget, as I was between jobs. I am a creative person, so if I am not working as an actor I need another outlet for that creativity. I love figuring out how to be thrifty when I need to, how to cut corners, create corners, fill corners.

Over the last ten years and thanks to my income from *The Good Wife,* the house has been cared for, tended to, loved. Step by step, I was able to make it the home I always envisioned. Slowly our dried-out, patchy lawn took on a lush green hue. The cobwebbed plywood porch has become our outdoor dining room, where we celebrate with friends and family, cooking farm-to-table food fresh from the outdoor market. Every morning, no matter the weather, Keith and I snuggle under blankets, sipping our coffee, taking in the one thing that hasn't changed since we bought the place: the view. I have never felt more at home and content, knowing this is where I belong.

Every year at Thanksgiving our house is buzzing with family staying for the four-day weekend, no fewer than twenty people around our dinner table, fires roaring in the hearths. I am happiest when I am cooking and can hear everyone enjoying themselves, playing games, discussing the day's events, coming in after a long constitutional.

I can't get over the dramatic deep red sunsets in the summer, cooling to a gentle pink in the winter. I am amazed every time I look at those mountains, bursting with a cacophony of ocher, burnt orange, and deep red velvet leaves in the autumn. Each season brings with it new colors, sounds, smells. The deafening orchestra of crickets in the summer, the blanketed stillness from snow in the winter. On any given morning you may see families of wild turkeys waddling across the lawn, deer grazing, rabbits hopping, squirrels hoarding their acorns. This is the magic of nature, and I am always surprised by it. Sheer heaven is watching my son running around on the lawn with his friends, playing soccer, touch football, or bocce. *This is where I belong.*

Oftentimes as I drive up to our house, I marvel at where I am in my life. My waitressing days are never far from my mind. There have been many instances in my acting career when I have said to myself, *At least you know you can always waitress if you have to.* There's something to that, knowing that all of this that I have right in front of me could go away at any minute but I would be able to survive. I never expected my life to feel this content, so peaceful and at ease.

I never take for granted the simple luxury of buying delicious food without worrying about the cost. Every night when I get into bed I thank the stars that Keith is there beside me. *Gratitude* by Oliver Sacks sits on my bedside table. I've read it many times but I keep it there next to me and will reread a chapter now and then to remind myself how much richer life is when gratitude is practiced.

None of my successes would amount to anything if I didn't have friends and family to share them with. That's probably why I love cooking so much, it's my way of being close and taking care of those I love. When we sit down to dinner on our screened-in porch, I always scan the table, grateful for the connection I have with each and every person there. I make a point to be present, to not take one drop of it for granted. And then I look out at the view, taking in the majestic beauty of the mountains in the distance, the deep pink sky cradling the setting sun as it slowly makes its way to the other side of the world. Extraordinary.

I am still amazed that this is my life. I am still dumbfounded that Keith and I found each other, that we have a child. I laugh to myself when I think of all the drama it took for me to finally get here. I hear my mother say, *You're exactly where you are supposed to be.* I hear my father: *You're living a fairy-tale life, Julianna.* They are right. I think of the hard road my ancestors took to pave the way for the rest of us, and I am forever grateful to them. And while I have known hardships in my own life, without them, I would have always been looking for something more. I would never have seen what was right in front of me. Instead, I am so grateful to be exactly where I am.

# acknowledgments

The events in this book have been written as I remember them. Other peoples' memories may differ.

Before I thank the people I know personally who have helped me with this book, I need to first acknowledge the writers whose words inspired me and kept me afloat, especially in those darkest of moments when I was sick with doubt, staring at the blank page in front of me. Mary Karr, *The Art of Memoir,* how many times I have underlined your words. Your book freed me to just write it down and let the rest come later. Stephen King, *On Writing,* I can't tell you how many times I referred back to your book. When I felt like a complete failure your words kept me writing. Stephen Fry, on a day when I thought the worst of myself and this book would never see the light of day, I heard you on a podcast telling the host that writing a book is like sculpture: you start with a big slab of stone and you keep chiseling away until you finally see a form. You have no idea how much hearing your words saved me.

Jennifer Rudolph Walsh, thank you for not throwing away the nine chapters I originally submitted to you. Instead, you enthusiastically said, "I think you have a book here!" And Suzanne Gluck for continuing the crusade after Jennifer. You were always encouraging and kind, two things that kept me writing.

Pamela Cannon, my wonderful, no-nonsense, brilliant editor. How you held my hand through this process without ever making me feel less than or unworthy of your time. Your encouragement and dedication to your craft are remarkable. My wish for any first-time writer is for them to have you by their side. And Lexi Batsides, thank you for being so helpful with everything and for never laughing in my face when my ineptness in technological capability reared its ugly head. To the entire team at Ballantine Books, thank you for your hard work and enthusiasm throughout this journey, it has truly been a pleasure being in your stable.

Tom Fontana, you are a beacon of light in my life. Your encouragement and generosity with your time were monumental in making this book come to life.

Bryan Cranston, I don't think you realize the effect you had on me when we were sitting on the set of *The Upside* and you said, "Of course you can write. We're actors, we're storytellers. Go tell your story."

Ali Wentworth, thank you for letting me take you to lunch so I could pick your brain about the book-writing process. Your help was my lifeboat when I thought I was drowning.

Thank you to my aunt Judy and uncle Michael for allowing me to take up so much of your time interviewing you both about Grandma Henrietta. Your support and love means the world to me.

Thank you to both my sisters, who protected me when I was little and smothered me with love. What would I have done without you?

Even though my father is no longer on this planet, he is with me every day. As I wrote these pages I could hear his voice: "Write what you know, Juli, and if you can't take a breath while reading out loud, it's a run-on sentence." I felt his guidance every step of the way.

Thank you to my mother, who gave me her blessing to write this book, and for all the times you picked up the phone and answered my many thousands of questions, never once telling me "Please don't write that." You gave me permission and freedom to tell my story and for that I am forever grateful. Reading each chapter to you as it unfolded, sitting on your porch with our cups of tea, laughing and crying together has been the highlight of this entire experience.

Alec Holland, thank you from the bottom of my heart for giving me your blessing and for the time you put into reading some of these chapters before they were finished. Your honesty and encouragement kept me going. You are forever my angel.

Alex Nhancale, if not for you I would still be wondering if I should write a book at all. You came with me on this long and arduous journey and were the voice of reason, the steady hand that I always could reach out to. Any task I set before you was meticulously done, always with a smile and excitement for the next challenge. Your dedication and work ethic are to be admired and heralded. I would be lost without you. Thank you.

Kieran, you were nine years old when I began this journey and by the time this book is published you will be a teenager! I overheard you once tell a friend, "My mom is writing a book!" I know to you that may have seemed trivial, but I heard the excitement in your voice and without you knowing this, those words inspired me more than anything. Every time I wanted to throw in the towel because writing felt too difficult, your sweet voice echoed in my ear. Your light shines so brightly, Kieran. I am so lucky that I get to be your mama.

And to my husband, Keith Lieberthal. You are beautiful inside and out. Writing about you was the easiest part. There has never been a moment since I met you that I haven't felt loved and supported by you. You championed me to write from the start and never once believed me when I told you I couldn't do it. I don't know how I got so lucky.

# photo credits

## ABOUT THE AUTHOR

As AN Emmy, Golden Globe, and Screen Actors Guild award winner, JULIANNA MARGULIES has achieved success in television, theater, and film. Margulies starred as Alicia Florrick on the long-running hit CBS show *The Good Wife,* which she also produced, and is well known for her role as one of the original cast members of *ER.* More recently, Margulies has starred on critically acclaimed series including *The Morning Show, Billions,* and *The Hot Zone.* She has been involved with Project ALS and Erin's Law and is also a board member of the New York City–based MCC Theater company. She resides in New York City with her husband and son.

Facebook.com/juliannamargulies
Instagram: @juliannamargulies

ABOUT THE TYPE

This book was set in Granjon, a modern recutting of a typeface produced under the direction of George W. Jones (1860–1942), who based Granjon's design upon the letterforms of Claude Garamond (1480–1561). The name was given to the typeface as a tribute to the typographic designer Robert Granjon (1513–89).